D1774295

Southern Victories
First Bull Run and Second Manassas

American History Archives™

Southern Victories
First Bull Run and Second Manassas

1 2 3 4 5 /10 09 08 07
ISBN: 978 1 84603 312 4

The History Channel Club
c/o North American Membership Group
12301 Whitewater Drive
Minnetonka, MN 55343
www.thehistorychannelclub.com

Published by North American Membership Group under license from Osprey Publishing, Ltd.

Previously published as Campaign 10: *First Bull Run 1861 The South's First Victory* and Campaign 95: *Second Manassas 1862 Robert E. Lee's Greatest Victory* by Osprey Publishing, Midland House, West Way, Botley, Oxford OX2 0PH, United Kingdom

© 2007 Osprey Publishing Ltd.

All rights reserved. Apart from any fair dealing for the purpose of private study, research criticism or review, as permitted under the Copyright, Designs and Patents Act, 1988, no part of this publication may be reproduced, stored in a retrieval system, or transmitted in any form or by any means, electronic, electrical, chemical, mechanical, optical, photocopying, recording or otherwise, without the prior written permission of the copyright owner. Enquiries should be addressed to the Publishers.

Editor: Lee Johnson
Page layout by DAG Publications Ltd and The Black Spot
Index by Glyn Sutcliffe
Cartography by Micromap and The Map Studio
3D bird's eye views by Cilla Eurich and The Black Spot
Battlescene artwork by Mike Adams
Originated by M&E Reproductions and Grasmere Digital Imaging
Printed in China through World Print Ltd.

The History Channel, "The History Channel Club" and the "H" logo are trademarks of A&E Television Networks and are used under license.
All rights reserved.

Author ALAN HANKINSON has completed two volumes for Osprey on the American Civil War. Highly respected in his field, Alan's authoritative text clearly displays his passion for, and knowledge of, the subject.

Author JOHN P. LANGELLIER received his Bachelor's and Master's degrees in History from the University of San Diego and his Ph.D. in Military History from Kansas State University. He is the author of numerous books and monographs, and has worked as a historical curator for several years. He has a particular passion for the people and events of the American Civil War.

Illustrator MIKE ADAMS has been a freelance illustrator for 25 years and has worked on a wide variety of subjects. He has a keen interest in history and has illustrated subjects as varied as the Anglo-Saxons and modern nuclear submarines, as well as numerous novels, children's books and sports prints. He has a degree in Art History and has taught in several London schools for a number of years. This is his first book for Osprey.

Dedication

To Brian C. Pohanka, exceptional Civil War historian and generous colleague

Acknowledgements and abbreviations

The author wishes to thank James M. Burgess, Jr., curator of the Manassas National Battlefield Park; Robert Krick chief historian Fredericksburg and Spotsylvania National Military Park, George S. Hobart, former curator of documentary photographs at the Library of Congress; C. Paul Loane (CPL); Dr Vincent A. Transano; Richard E. Weeks; Michael Winey and Randy Hackenberg of the U.S. Army Military History Institute (USAMHI), along with James Enos of Carlisle, PA; as well as staff members of the photographic divisions of the National Archives (NA) at College Park, MD, and the Library of Congress (LC) in Washington, DC.

Artist's note

Readers may care to note that the original paintings from which the color plates in this book were prepared are available for private sale. All reproduction copyright whatsoever is retained by the Publishers. All enquiries should be addressed to:

Mike Adams, 93 Hereford Road, Shrewsbury, SY3 7QZ, UK

The Publishers regret that they can enter into no correspondence upon this matter.

KEY TO MILITARY SYMBOLS

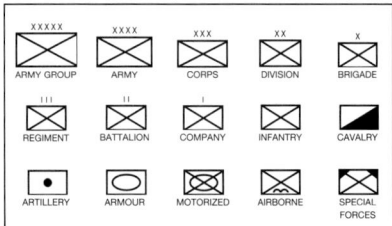

FRONT COVER
On the evening of 27 August Pope ordered Irvin McDowell and Franz Sigel to relocate their corps to Manassas, thereby leaving the road open for Longstreet to unite with Jackson. Among the troops who participated in this ill-advised move were the foot soldiers of Sigel's, 41st New York Infantry, who like their corps commander had been born in Germany. LC

TITLE PAGE © Anne S. K. Brown Military Collection, Brown University Library

SOUTHERN VICTORIES
First Bull Run and Second Manassas

CONTENTS

Introduction   4
Chronology   5

Part 1: First Bull Run 1861   9

Background	10
The Way to Civil War	11
The Opposing Leaders	16
The Opposing Armies	23
The Road to Bull Run	37
The Affair at Blackburn's Ford	42
The Battle Plans	49
The Battle Begins	55
The Fight for Henry Hill	66
Retreat and Rout	83
The 'Might-Have-Beens'	91
The Battlefield Today	94
A Guide to Further Reading	96

Part 2: Second Manassas 1862   99

Background	100
Origins of the Campaign	101
Opposing Commanders	103
Opposing Plans	112
Opposing Armies	114
Cedar Mountain, 9 August 1862	117
Brawner's Farm and Thoroughfare Gap, 28 August 1862	134
The Battle of Manassas	147
Aftermath	172
The Battlefield Today	175
Orders of Battle	178
Further Reading	186

Index   *187*

INTRODUCTION

In the early years of the American Civil War, two battles were fought almost a year apart under two different names at one location in Virginia. Both engagements were victories for the South – the first one more by luck and ineffective Union generalship than skill, the second one an overwhelming victory due to superior Southern leadership and fighting.

The Union had a tendency to name battles after the nearest river or creek. In this case, it was the stream known as Bull Run. The South leaned toward naming engagements after the nearest town – in this case, it was Manassas. In deference to the honor of the soldiers from both sides who died in these Virginia fields and woods, today we split the difference and call them First Bull Run and Second Manassas. But by any measure, they were savage battles that set the tone for the rest of the war.

In Part 1, First Bull Run 1861, you'll learn all the details behind the first major land battle of the Civil War. Under pressure from impatient politicians, Union General Irvin McDowell marched his Army of Northeastern Virginia toward Confederate General P.T.G. Beauregard's Army of the Potomac, which was encamped near Manassas Junction, Virginia. Only 25 miles from the capital itself, onlookers buggied out for the day to watch the show and observe a Union victory and a quick end to the war.

The show they got was a different story – revealing the horrors of war, and portending the longevity of the division of the nation, which lasted long after the fighting.

About a year later, under brilliant leadership that guided some of the best and hardest-fighting soldiers the world has ever seen, General Robert E. Lee's Army of Virginia was waging an effective offensive campaign. Union armies under both General John Pope and General George B. McClellan were on the run and trying to link up. If they did, Lee knew that their combined 180,000 men could overwhelm his force of 60,000.

By fate, the Union and Confederate armies came together again on familiar ground, and that's the story told in Part 2, Second Manassas 1862. The South won decisively. Their only mistake was not aggressively pursuing the Union forces they had defeated.

Of course, the North would outlast the South for final victory in the overall war. Improved leadership, superior industrial power and more soldiers was an equation the South could not ultimately overcome.

But here are the stories of some of the Confederacy's finest hours – two *Southern Victories*.

CHRONOLOGY

1776	The American colonies declare themselves independent of Britain
1783	Britain recognizes the independence of the United States
1812–14	War with Britain
1846–8	The Mexican War
1852	Uncle Tom's Cabin published
1859	John Brown raids Harpers Ferry, is tried and hanged

1860

November	Abraham Lincoln elected President
December	South Carolina votes to secede from the Union

1861

January	Six more Southern states vote to secede
8 February	The break-away states unite to form a new country, the Confederate states of America
9 February	Jefferson Davis elected President of the CSA
4 March	Lincoln sworn in as President of the USA
6 March	Davis calls for 100,000 volunteer soldiers
12 April	Beauregard's guns open fire on the Union garrison at Fort Sumter; within two days the fort surrenders

TO FIRST BULL RUN, 1861

15 April	Union President Abraham Lincoln calls upon the loyal states to furnish 75,000 volunteers
23 May	Virginia votes to secede; North Carolina, Tennessee and Arkansas also secede at this time
27 May	McDowell is given command of the army that is to invade Virginia
29 June	Lincoln's Cabinet agrees to McDowell's plan of attack
16 July	McDowell's march to Bull Run begins
17 July	Johnston receives Beauregard's call to hurry to Manassas
18 July	Johnston's army begins to move. Action at Blackburn's Ford
19 July	Jackson's brigade arrives at Manassas
19–20 July	McDowell reconnoitres a route for his flanking movement, then gives his battle orders. Johnston joins Beauregard and agrees to his battle plan

The battle, 21 July (times often approximate only)

2am	Tyler's division begins to move off
6am	First cannon shots fired across Bull Run
9am	Evans moves to Mathews Hill
9.15am	Evans opens fire on Burnside's brigade
10am	Bee and Bartow arrive to support Evans
11am	Sherman crosses Bull Run and marches toward Mathews Hill. The Southerners pull back to Henry Hill
11.30am	Jackson takes up his position on the top of Henry Hill
12 noon	Johnston and Beauregard decide to move to Henry Hill
11.30am to 5pm	The battle for Henry Hill
4.30pm	Elzey charges Howard's brigade
4.45pm	Early charges Howard's brigade
5pm	Beauregard orders a general advance. The Northerners retreat, then run. This is the Union's first major defeat in the field

TO SECOND MANASSAS, 1862

28 February–8 April	Relative inactivity in the eastern theater of operations contrasts with fighting further west along the Mississippi River where the Battle of New Madrid and the fall of Island No.10 brings recognition to Union Major General John Pope
April–May	Peninsula Campaign planned and led by Lincoln's new choice for a Union commander, 35-year-old George B. McClellan. The move to encircle Richmond's defenses does not succeed
23 March–9 June	In an effort to weaken the Union field force and thereby decrease the threat to Richmond, Confederate authorities dispatch Thomas "Stonewall" Jackson to the Shenandoah Valley, thereby drawing away the equivalent of three Federal divisions. Jackson succeeds in neutralizing or defeating a series of separate Northern commands and also prevents McDowell from sending reinforcements to McClellan
31 May–1 June	Battle of Seven Pines (Fair Oaks) Confederate General Joseph E. Johnston sustains a severe wound prompting Confederate President Jefferson Davis to replace the stricken commander with Robert E. Lee
26 June	President Lincoln appoints Major General John Pope as the commander of the newly created Army of Virginia, unifying the previously three separate corps commanded by Generals Banks, McDowell, and Sigel
26 June–2 July	Seven Days' Battles are waged as Robert E. Lee's Army of Northern Virginia pushes McClellan's Army of the Potomac back from the gates of Richmond
11 July	Searching for a commander who can bring victory to the North, Lincoln names Major General Henry Halleck as Union General-in-Chief
9 August	The Second Manassas campaign opens with its first major engagement at the Battle of Cedar Mountain (Cedar Run/Slaughter Mountain), fought as Jackson's Wing attempts to cripple an isolated portion of Pope's Army of Virginia

22 August	"Jeb" Stuart's raid on Catlett Station fails to destroy the Cedar Run railroad bridge, which will not burn because rain has soaked its timbers, but he captures General Pope's dispatch book, providing General Lee with information on Union troop dispositions
23 August	Clashes at Beverly's, Freeman's, and Kelly's Fords as the Confederates test Pope's defenses along the Rappahannock River
25 August, 3.00am	Jackson's Wing marches for Sulphur Springs to begin a wide flanking movement around the Union right flank. That night it camps near Salem
26 August	Jackson's men capture Bristoe Station and the huge Federal depot at Manassas Junction
27 August	As Union forces attempt to trap him, Jackson withdraws from Manassas in three columns. He redeploys his men north-west of Groveton
28 August	With Pope having failed to locate his forces, Jackson's Wing emerges to attack King's Federal Division on the march at Brawner's Farm (Groveton). Brigadier General John Gibbon's Brigade bears the brunt of the fighting. Late in the afternoon Longstreet's Wing captures Thoroughfare Gap in the Bull Run Mountains. The route to Manassas is now clear
29 August	General Pope opens the Battle of Second Manassas with a series of piecemeal attacks against Jackson's troops, who are defending the line of an unfinished railroad north of Groveton. The Confederates repulse the disjointed attacks
30 August	Unknown to Pope, Longstreet has joined Jackson and launches an attack against the Federal left flank, while Pope continues to hammer Jackson's line. Eventually the Federals are flanked. Determined rearguard fighting as Pope's men withdraw saves his army from annihilation
31 August	Skirmish at Germantown as Pope reorganizes his chaotic army at Centreville. Jackson's Wing begins a flank march to Fairfax
1 September	Battle of Chantilly (Ox Hill) as Stevens' and Kearny's divisions block Jackson's flank march. Both Stevens and Kearny are killed
4 September	The Army of Northern Virginia crosses the Potomac on march to Maryland
12–15 September	Harper's Ferry, Virginia, under attack by Jackson
17–18 September	Lee's Army of Northern Virginia and McClellan's Army of the Potomac clash at the Battle of Antietam (Sharpsburg) in the bloodiest single day of the war
22 September	Lincoln issues the Emancipation Proclamation

PART ONE
First Bull Run 1861

BACKGROUND

Bull Run is a pleasant, gently flowing river in northern Virginia, which runs through rolling green farmland on its way to join the Potomac. By American standards it is not much of a river, but it is wide and deep enough to present problems to an army on the move. The United States capital, Washington, is some 25 miles away to the northeast. The city of Richmond, Virginia, which became the capital of the break-away Confederate states in 1861, lies 80 miles or so to the south. The fact that it lay between these opposing capitals, abetted by the fact that it was close to the railway junction of Manassas, meant that a few acres of this peaceful countryside formed the stage for two fierce battles within the first fourteen months of the American Civil War.

The First Battle of Bull Run is significant for several reasons. It was the first major encounter of the war, and it is possible that had victory gone to the North, as it very nearly did, then the war – which was to go on for nearly four more years and to claim the lives of more than 600,000 men – might have ended then. It was the first battle ever fought in which the movement of men by railway played an influential part. And it taught both sides that they were in for a long struggle, which would not be won merely by dash and gallantry.

From the military point of view, the lessons it taught were negative. Neither army was ready for battle; the men were untrained, the commanders inexperienced. There was no inspired generalship. The issue was decided more by luck than by anybody's good management. It was a demonstration, more than anything else, of all-round military incompetence.

◀ *Scene of the battle's turning-point: the slopes leading up to Henry House and the summit plateau. The slight depression in the ground, where the trees stand, afforded the attacking Northern regiments a little cover, but once they were over the crest they came under withering fire from Jackson's line.*

THE WAY TO CIVIL WAR

Hollywood films have conditioned the world to see the United States of America in the first half of the nineteenth century as a land of violence – bitter feuds and banditry, shoot-outs and lynch mobs, and incessant Indian wars. English visitors at the time, such as Frances Trollope, Harriet Martineau and Charles Dickens, portrayed it as a crude and mannerless society, full of tobacco-chewers and spitoons, loud with drunks and their public brawling. In fact, though, to most of those who lived there then, and especially the hundreds of thousands who had recently escaped from the persecutions and deprivations of Europe, it was a land of boundless opportunity and optimism. The United States was a young country, still united, comparatively peaceful and, by world standards at the time, highly democratic. It was also prosperous and expanding. The population was growing rapidly. Vast new territories were constantly being added to the Union, with broad rivers and fertile plains and hills that were rich in minerals. A complex network of railways sprang up to make transport easier and faster. In the North, towns were growing into cities and many new industries were appearing. Every ship that arrived from across the Atlantic brought hundreds more immigrants from the 'old world', most of them young, many of them with specialist skills, all of them ambitious to make their fortunes in this 'brave new world'. The society they joined was tough and competitive. The rewards went to those who were strong and resourceful and ready to work hard. But the prizes were worth the winning and, compared with the countries they had left behind, there was remarkable freedom to pursue them.

But the very speed with which the country was growing and changing created strains. In a sense, three different countries were emerging. The West, where new territories were continuously opening up, was the place for pioneers; life there was primitive; families and communities had to be tough and self-reliant. The North-East was much more settled and it was here that towns were growing into cities and new industries were springing up. All was change and bustle in this region as descendants of the original colonists, mostly English, were joined by a heady ethnic mix of Italians and Irish, Scots and Germans, Slavs and Scandinavians and others. And the South was another world entirely, a near-tropical land of great plantations where white land-owners enjoyed a privileged and leisurely way of life. Unlike the other two regions, society here was static, rigidly based on conventions, fixed and hierarchical.

There were not only wide differences in character and climate; there were conflicts of interest too. The North, for example, wanted high tariff barriers against imports from abroad to protect nascent industries from European competition. But the South, heavily dependent on exports of cotton and tobacco to Europe, wanted free trade. Many Southerners feared, with good reason, that it was only a matter of time before the population disparity would be such that their interests would be over-ridden by the other parts of the Union. As early as the 1820s there had been talk, among the more extreme elements in the South, of secession, breaking away from the Union to go it alone.

The Slavery Issue

Even so, the majority of Americans cherished the notion of their country's 'manifest destiny', the idea that the push westwards would be maintained until they had built a vast and powerful nation 'from sea to shining sea'. The power of this vision, and the regard many held for the founding fathers and the unique democratic republic they had created, would almost certainly have held the country together had it not been for one further factor: the institution of chattel slavery.

By 1860 there were well over three million negro slaves in the southern states, most of them labouring on the plantations. The invention of the cotton gin, making the short-staple cotton that grew so abundantly there suitable for processing in the textile mills of Europe, paved the way for a lucrative export industry. In 1860 cotton represented 57 per cent of the value of all America's exports. The business was based on the labour of the slaves, descendants of West African tribespeople who had been shipped across the Atlantic in colonial times. The slaves were property – bought and sold at the markets, owned and entirely controlled by their white masters.

Slavery had died out in the northern states, for economic rather than for moral reasons. But, as the years passed, an increasing and increasingly vocal body of opinion grew up, demanding that slavery be abolished throughout the Union. By the middle of the nineteenth century, however, this was still a minority feeling. Most moderate opinion in the North, however much it disapproved of slavery in principle, was prepared to accept its existence in the South as a fact that had to be recognized. And most reasonable men in the South were happy enough to stay in the Union so long as there were no direct attempts to end the system by which they lived.

Unfortunately, there was a further complication. What should be the rule about the new states that were constantly joining the union? Should they be slave states or not? Should the question be determined simply by latitude, their geographical position? Or by some kind of plebiscite? Or imposed by Congress in Washington?

The issue arose over Missouri in the 1820s and there was long and heated argument. It surfaced again in the late 1840s when the defeat of Mexico brought extensive new territories into the Union. Feelings grew stronger and the language used more intemperate. Various solutions were devised and tried, found wanting and replaced by ever more complex compromises. By this time the fiercer opponents of slavery were organizing an 'underground railroad' to help disaffected slaves escape to the North. Southern landowners saw this as a direct assault on their livelihoods. The debate intensified and it grew ever harder to hold to a middle view. When *Uncle Tom's Cabin* was published in book form in 1852, its portrayal of plantation life was deeply resented in the South – but it sold 300,000 copies, mostly in the North, in the first year.

In the 1850s the accession of another new state, Kansas, brought a further intensification of the dispute. There was ballot-rigging and mass-intimidation. Gun-fights took place in the townships and armed gangs from neighbouring states, of both persuasions, raided across the border. In May 1856 a member of the national legislature, a senator from Massachusetts who had made a bitter anti-slavery speech, was attacked on the floor of the House, beaten to the ground with a heavy stick and badly injured by an irate congressman from South Carolina. Two days later a fanatical Ohio farmer, John Brown, led four of his sons and three other zealots on a night raid into Kansas and hacked to death with swords and daggers the first five men they found, assuming them to be slavers. More and more people in the South were beginning to say they would never enjoy peace until they broke away from the Union.

In October 1859, John Brown struck again, gaining himself immortality in song. With a handful of supporters he seized the Federal arsenal at Harpers Ferry in West Virginia. They planned to use the arms to stimulate a general insurrection of the slaves in the South. But their inept attempt was smartly dealt with by a detachment of US Marines led by a colonel called Robert E. Lee. Brown was tried, convicted of treason and hanged. From this moment on, the pace of events quickened ominously.

The next year, 1860, was presidential election year. The former political parties were in flux. The old Whig party had been replaced by a new force, the Republicans, representing Northern interests and opinion. Initially the Democrats, who spoke for the Southern whites, seemed in better shape, but when their delegates gathered at Charleston in April to choose their party's candidate, the meeting collapsed into a ferocious row between extremists and moderates, and in the end they split asunder, each group putting up a presidential candidate.

The Republicans, at their convention in Chicago, were also divided; but, aware that the disarray of their opponents gave their candidate an excellent chance, they finally reached an agreed choice. It was a momentous one. Their candidate was a big, strong, gangling, odd-mannered frontiersman, with little in the way of formal education but a formidable natural intelligence, a man of high integrity and astonishing powers of persuasion – Abraham Lincoln.

During his campaign for the presidency, Lincoln did everything he could to reassure the Southerners that if he won he would do nothing to threaten the institution of slavery where it already existed. Personally, he did not approve of slavery, but he prized the continued union of the United States above all else and knew that the one sure way of breaking the country up was to make the Southern system feel endangered.

The Confederacy

The South was not, however, reassured. Lincoln won the race for the White House, through the divisions among his rivals. The result was known in November 1860. Next month South Carolina, always the most extreme of the Southern states, voted to secede from the United States. Before the end of January 1861, six more states had left the Union: Mississippi, Alabama, Georgia, Florida, Louisiana and Texas. Their delegates met at Montgomery, Alabama, on 8 February and agreed to join together to form a new country to be called the Confederate States of America. They drafted a constitution and next day elected their own president, Jefferson Davis of Mississippi. There were Federal forts and arsenals within their territories and most of these were promptly taken over, without bloodshed.

Lincoln went to Washington and was sworn in as president on 4 March. In his Inaugural Address he tried to woo back the seven break-away states. 'We are not enemies, but friends,' he told them. 'We must not be enemies. Though passion may have strained, it must not break our bonds of affection.' He went on to say that his forces would never start the shooting. If civil war were to come, they, the Southerners, would have to launch it.

▲ *Abraham Lincoln, regarded by many as one of the greatest men who ever lived, had only just become President of the Union when it began to break up. He was not, at first, an outright opponent of the slave system – he thought each state should be allowed to choose for itself – but he put the preservation of the Union above all other considerations. He had virtually no military experience but became a formidable leader in war. He saw it through to final victory, and was beginning to work for the healing of the wounds of Civil War when he was assassinated by John Wilkes Booth in April 1865. (Anne S. K. Brown Mil. Coll., BUL)*

The response was unpromising. On 6 March, Jefferson Davis asked his confederate states to provide him with 100,000 volunteers for one year's military service. Five weeks later Southern guns opened fire on Fort Sumter, on an island near the mouth of Charleston harbour in South Carolina. This was one of the Federal army forts that had not been taken; it still flew the Union flag, and this was seen as an insult to the South. On 8 April, Lincoln sent a message to Jefferson Davis, saying that he planned to send a supply ship to Fort Sumter and promising that it would only deliver food to the garrison. Davis told his commander in

THE WAY TO CIVIL WAR

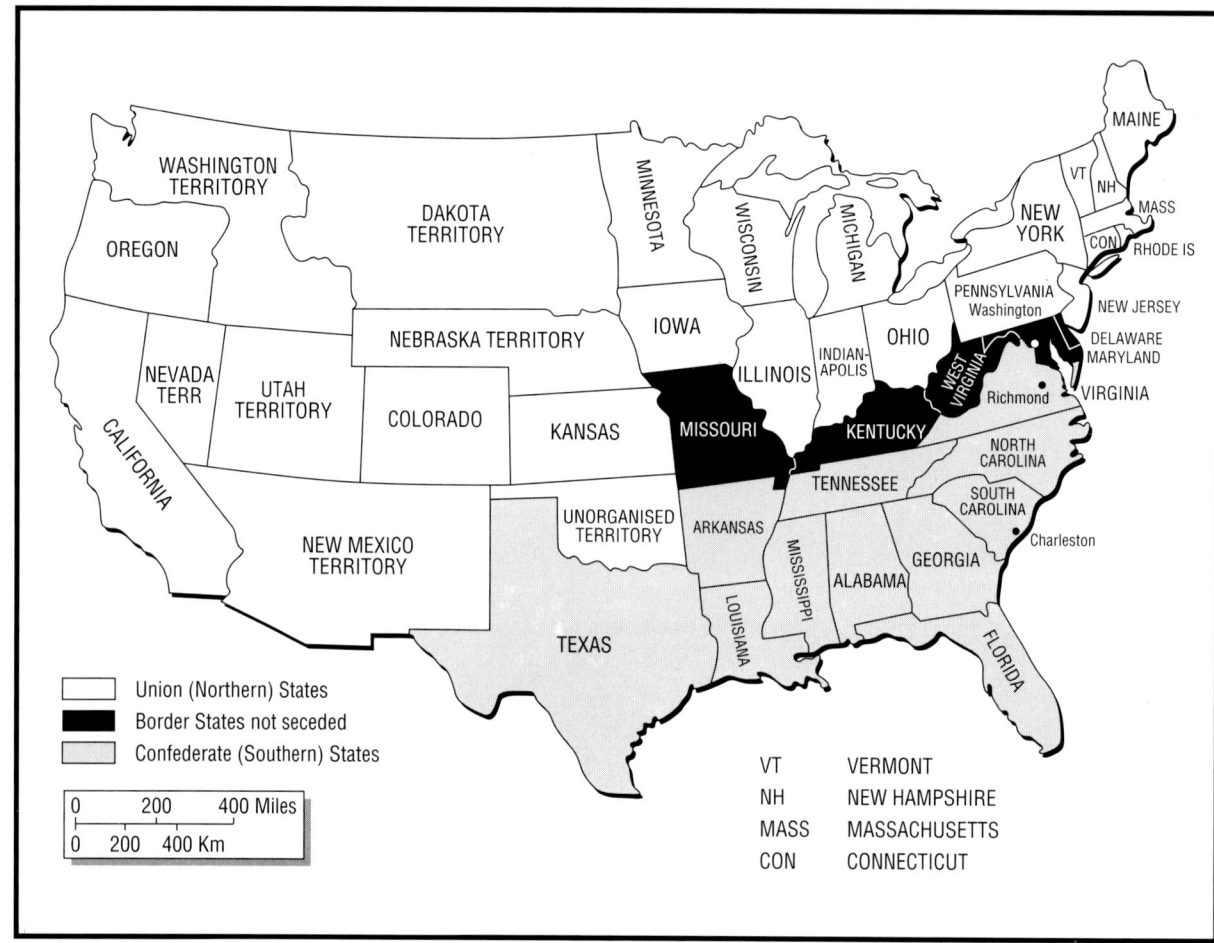

Union and Confederate: opposing states, July 1861

- Union (Northern) States
- Border States not seceded
- Confederate (Southern) States

VT — VERMONT
NH — NEW HAMPSHIRE
MASS — MASSACHUSETTS
CON — CONNECTICUT

the region, General P.G.T. Beauregard, to demand the immediate surrender of the garrison and, if this were not promptly forthcoming, to open fire. On 12 April, Beauregard's guns opened up; 34 hours later the garrison hauled down the 'Stars and Stripes' and surrendered. Not a man had been killed in the brief action, but everyone knew that this was the start of civil war.

To most people on both sides the outbreak of hostilities brought a welcome sense of relief. The long years of abuse, recrimination and threats were over. The matter would now be settled by combat. There was much public celebration, North and South, and a common conviction that the war would not last long and that they would be the victors.

Lincoln himself must have shared this optimistic view because he now asked the states loyal to the Union to raise 75,000 volunteers to serve for a period of only three months – an underestimate that was to influence the outcome of the First Battle of Bull Run.

Two days after the President issued that call, the key state of Virginia opted to join the breakaway – then three more states that had been neutral so far, North Carolina, Tennessee and Arkansas, brought the total number of confederate states to eleven.

So the battle lines were drawn. The statistics favoured the North: they had a total population of more than eighteen million, twice the number in the South, of which more than a third were slaves who could hardly be expected to fight for their continued subjugation. The great bulk of manufacturing power lay in the Northern states; most of the useful minerals; two-thirds of the railways; and virtually all the naval power. If it were to be a long war, there could be little doubt who would prevail.

The Southerners began the war convinced that their moral (and *morale*) advantages outweighed the material advantages of the enemy. Northerners, they believed, had been softened by their more urban and industrialized lives. It was a widely-stated claim that any Southern man 'could lick five Yankees'. And although it was their guns that had opened the firing, Southerners saw themselves as the victims of aggression. All they wanted was to go their separate way in peace. The North was seeking to conquer them. Most of the fighting would be done on Southern soil – they were defending their homeland. When this happens (as the Americans were to find in Vietnam; the Russians in Afghanistan, a century later) the key factor is not firepower but will power. Many Southerners also thought that Europe's dependence on their cotton would ultimately bring Britain, and possibly France as well, into the war on their side.

Soon after Virginia joined the Confederacy, Jefferson Davis moved his headquarters from Montgomery to the Virginia state capital, Richmond, within a hundred miles of Washington. In his *History of the English-speaking Peoples*, Winston Churchill commented: 'Thus the two capitals stood like queens at chess upon adjoining squares, and, sustained by their combinations of covering pieces, they endured four years of grim play within a single move of capture.'

▼ *South Carolina, always the most bellicose of the Southern states, declared itself separated from the United States in December 1860, soon after hearing the news that Lincoln had been elected President of the Union. Six more Southern states were quick to follow South Carolina. They proclaimed themselves a new country – the Confederate States of America – and by the time the First Battle of Bull Run was fought, there were eleven states in the CSA.*

▼ *The proud old state of Virginia agonized for many weeks over whether it should break away from the Union or not. When the decision to secede was finally taken, however, many of the Union army's best officers – who were Virginians and put their state before their country – resigned to serve in the Confederate Army. The call went out for volunteer soldiers to sign on for one year's service, and the response was enthusiastic.*

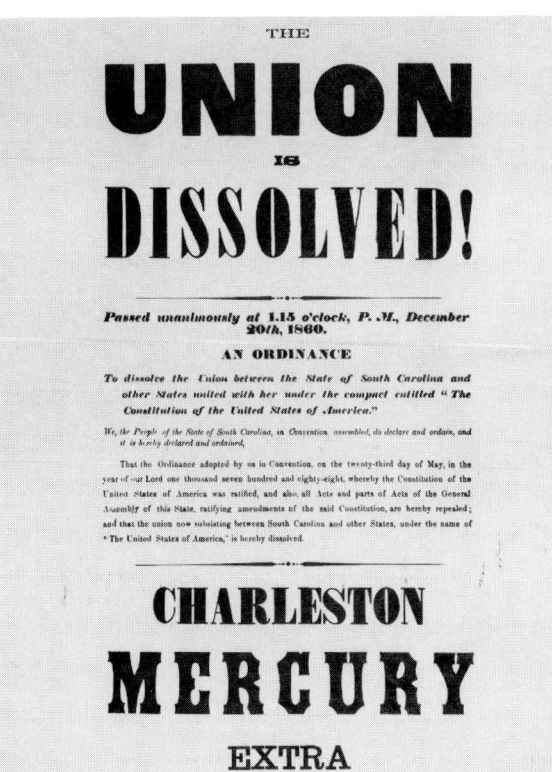

THE OPPOSING LEADERS

The two American presidents who now confronted each other had similar origins – they were both born close to the River Ohio in Kentucky, Jefferson Davis in June 1808, Lincoln some eight months later. Both grew up to be tall and lean, with the bony, angular, strong-jawed features that seem to have been fashionable at that period. They were men of intelligence and probity. Each of them went into politics and prospered and spoke, by the standards of the time, for the forces of reason and moderation. They were both family men.

But there the similarities end. Davis moved South to become a Mississippi planter while Lincoln went in the other direction and, after a variety of jobs, settled down as a small-town lawyer in Springfield, Illinois. Davis was a man of severe manner and rigid mind, with little in the way of humour or social warmth, a forbidding boss, always very sure that he was in the right. Lincoln, by contrast, was relaxed and folksy and often funny, modest in manner and – although a man of deep thought and conviction – flexible in his approach. He was the consummate politician, charming and persuasive in private meetings and committees, compelling and persuasive in his public utterances.

On the face of it, judging from their experience, Davis should have made the better war leader. At the age of 16 he had gone to study at West Point Military Academy, to emerge four years later as a second lieutenant in the US Army. He served for seven years and saw action against the 'Black Hawk' Indians. He then retired from the army to marry and become a cotton planter and a politician. He re-enlisted, however, for the Mexican War and, as colonel of the volunteer Mississippi Rifles, distinguished himself in action at the Battle of Monterey and then joined the staff of General Zachary Taylor. Returning to national politics after the war, he was President Pierce's Secretary of War in the mid-1850s. Davis had known war at many levels and in many of its aspects.

Lincoln could claim no such qualifications. He was a man of great strength and courage – a formidable opponent, by all accounts, in a fight – but his military experience was negligible. In 1833 he had volunteered for a minor Indian war, was elected captain of the local militia, marched his men about the countryside briefly but saw no action at all and was glad to get back to civilian life. But if Lincoln could point to no obvious qualifications for the task he now faced, he did have, in full measure, the qualities that Clausewitz said were of most importance to the director of a war – 'a remarkable, superior mind and strength of character'.

The Chief Military Advisers

In the event, Davis was not to prove as able a wartime commander as Lincoln, but he had one important initial advantage. His military right-hand-man from the beginning of the conflict was Robert E. Lee, a man of high distinction. Lee came from a proud Virginian family; his father had been a hero of the War of Independence. The boy studied at West Point, became an officer in the engineers, fought in the Mexican War and rose to the rank of colonel, then returned to West Point as its commanding officer. He was handsome and civilized as well as an able soldier, and won the love as well as the respect of those who served under him. He was 54 in 1861. The break-up of the United States deeply distressed him: 'I can contemplate no greater calamity for the country', he said, 'than a dissolution of the Union.' But when the dissolution came and Virginia voted to join the Confederacy, it was his love for his native state that prevailed. Had he stayed with the Union,

▲ Jefferson Davis, elected President of the CSA in February 1861, had been a professional soldier, a cotton planter, a successful politician, and in the 1850s Secretary of War to President Pierce in Washington. A man of great integrity, sincerity and resolution, he lacked Lincoln's geniality of manner and flexibility of mind. He was taken prisoner in May 1865, as the war was ending, and spent two years in gaol, for some time under threat of being tried for treason. After his release, he retired to his estates in Mississippi and took no further part in politics. He died in 1889. (From an oil painting by John Robertson)

▲ Robert E. Lee, who came from a very distinguished Virginian family, might well have become Lincoln's commander-in-chief in 1861 had he not opted for his state and the Confederacy. As it was, Jefferson Davis quickly made him his chief military adviser. He played no active part in First Bull Run, but later proved his worth as a commander in the field as well as in the realm of grand strategy. It was his determination and skill, more than any other factor, that kept the Southern cause alive and kicking for so long. He was respected by his enemies, respected and loved by his own men. He died in October 1870. (Anne S. K. Brown Mil. Coll., BUL)

it seems more than likely that he would have been offered command of Lincoln's main army in the field. As soon as he had thrown in his lot with the South, Davis made him a general and appointed him his chief military adviser. He was to serve, as adviser and field commander, throughout the war.

Lincoln's chief military adviser was another Virginian and one with an even more impressive record than Lee. Lieutenant General Winfield Scott had fought against the British in the War of 1812 and was general-in-chief of the US Army in 1847 when he brilliantly led the invasion of Mexico. When the Civil War began there was never any doubt that he would stay loyal to the Union, but he was 74 years old by that time and in poor health. A very tall man, he was now very fat as well, so much so that he could no longer get on to a horse and walked with difficulty. Sometimes his mind seemed as strong and sharp as it had ever been, but there were also times when his thoughts wandered and his orders grew vague and confused. He had less control over his temper than formerly; he could be proud and prickly; too often he let personal considerations affect his military

THE OPPOSING LEADERS

judgement. The sad fact is that Winfield Scott was too old and tired for the immense responsibilities he was now given.

Such were the four top men – Lincoln and Scott for the North, Davis and Lee for the South. Each of them had some say in the build-up to the First Battle of Bull Run but none of them was involved in the battle itself. This was the work, in varying degrees, of four generals – Irvin McDowell and Robert Patterson on the Northern side, Joseph E. Johnston and P.G.T. Beauregard on the Southern.

The Field Commanders

The action at Fort Sumter was short and simple and quite unheroic, but after it Pierre Gustave Toutant Beauregard was acclaimed throughout the jubilant South as the 'Hero of Sumter'. It was typical of the man, never one to pass up a chance for further self-aggrandisement. It was one of the qualities he shared with his own hero, Napoleon Bonaparte; strategic and tactical instruction at West Point was largely geared to the precepts and example of the great French commander, and none took the lessons more to heart than Beauregard. He loved the Napoleonic ceremonial and style. He saw himself, some said, as a reincarnation of one of the more dashing of the marshals. He was bouncing with confidence and energy, a great favourite with the ladies, and something of a swaggerer.

Beauregard came of mixed lineage, French and Welsh. He was of medium height and swarthy

▲ In 1861 the military record of General Winfield Scott was unparalleled in the United States. He had fought against the British in 1812, and his conduct of the invasion of Mexico in 1847 had made him a national hero. He was one of the few prominent Virginians who chose to stay in the Union army. Unfortunately, by the summer of 1861 he was in his mid-seventies and in poor physical shape. He was not on the field at First Bull Run, but the confused and over-cautious orders he sent to General Patterson were partly responsible for the defeat of the North. After the battle he faded from the scene and died five years later. (Anne S. K. Brown Mil. Coll., BUL)

▲ Pierre Gustave Toutant Beauregard was a general whose charismatic flamboyance, confidence and ambition were not matched by strategic skill. His schemes were often ill-advised; his orders unclear. He went to Manassas as 'the Hero of Sumter' and emerged from the Bull Run battle with his reputation even further enhanced. He continued to be actively engaged in the Civil War but never fulfilled the promise of the opening months of the war. He lived until 1893 (Anne S. K. Brown Mil. Coll., BUL)

▶ *There is nothing like war for stimulating interest in the news. Frank Vitzetelli, an artist who had been sent out by the Illustrated London News, caught something of the excitement of a mixed New York group in the weeks before Bull Run when the newspapers were calling for an attack on the South. (*Illustrated London News, *15 June 1861)*

complexion, with a touch of the exotic in his appearance and manner. His family owned slaves and ran large sugar cane plantations in Louisiana. He did well in his studies at West Point, was commissioned into the engineers and served on Winfield Scott's staff in the Mexican War. He ended the war as a major, full of ambition. But the years that followed were uneventful.

He was 43 when the Civil War broke out. This was his big opportunity. He had made no secret of his secessionist sentiments, and when Louisiana joined the Confederacy he resigned from the US Army and made the characteristically dramatic gesture of enlisting in his state militia as a private soldier. On 1 March he was made a brigadier general. After Fort Sumter he was summoned to Richmond where Davis and Lee told him they expected the Northern army to march soon towards Manassas. They asked Beauregard to go there immediately and prepare the defence of the railway junction. Arriving on 1 June, he hurled himself into the task of surveying the area, organizing his forces to repel any enemy moves across Bull Run, demanding rapid reinforcement from Richmond, and setting up a spy network behind the Northern lines. One of his proposals to Davis and Lee, typically wild and histrionic, was that he and his small army should advance to meet the enemy and 'sell our lives as dearly as practicable'. With Napoleonic hyperbole and disregard for the truth, he told civilians in the region: 'Abraham Lincoln, regardless of all moral, legal and constitutional restraints, has thrown his abolition hosts among you, who are murdering and imprisoning your citizens, confiscating and destroying your property, and committing other acts of violence and outrage too shocking and revolting to humanity to be enumerated.'

The other Southern commander was a very different personality. Joseph Eggleston Johnston was yet another Virginian of distinguished family background. They came originally from the Scottish Lowlands. His father (like Lee's) had fought in the War of Independence and later became a judge. At West Point, Jo Johnston showed an interest in academic as well as military matters – he was a keen student of French and astronomy. He fought, as an artillery officer, against the Seminole Indians under the command of General Scott, and later, as an engineering officer, against the Mexicans. He seemed to get himself wounded whenever he was in action. He was a lieutenant colonel when the Mexican War ended and had risen to be Quarter-Master Gen-

▲ *Jo Johnston was known as 'the gamecock' for his trim, erect, military bearing. Yet another Virginian, with a good army record, he was also a man of culture and courtesy. He got himself and his army on to the field at Bull Run in time to decide the issue and managed to work alongside Beauregard, though they quarrelled later on. A capable commander, he fought throughout the war. He died in 1891. (Anne S. K. Brown Mil. Coll., BUL)*

eral of the US Army, with the rank of brigadier general, by the beginning of 1861.

Once again his career ran closely parallel to that of Lee. He did not want Virginia to secede, but when it did he decided, after agonized reflection, to go with his state. Jefferson Davis welcomed him and promptly appointed him a major general, which meant that he out-ranked Beauregard.

Johnston could be a touchy and difficult subordinate, but he was an efficient, courteous and generous commander, much liked by his men. They called him 'the gamecock' in tribute to his trim, military figure and his jaunty manner.

For all that, Johnston was no hot-head. He had little time for those who thought Southerners had some sort of natural superiority as fighting men and that the war, in consequence, would be short and glorious. He knew professional soldiering and realized that his troops needed long and rigorous training before they would be ready for battle. When President Davis sent him to take charge of the army that was being formed in the Harpers Ferry region he set about drilling them hard.

On the Northern side the man who found himself facing Johnston was Major General Robert Patterson. He was a militia officer, not a regular. He had spent most of his life as a successful businessman with sugar and cotton plantations in the South, textile mills in the North and interests in railway and steamship companies. But he had fought in the War of 1812, becoming a colonel at the age of 20, and later as Winfield Scott's second-in-command on the march to Mexico City. Patterson's role at the First Battle of Bull Run was to be negative and yet highly influential. The outcome of the battle was determined, very largely, by his failure to occupy Johnston's full attention away from the main battlefield. After the defeat he was made the North's chief scapegoat. The judgement was not entirely fair; others were, in part, to blame. But Patterson was not the man for the job he was given. He was 69 years old. He had never had an independent command. He was a naturally cautious commander, always inclined to overestimate the enemy's strength. And, like the great majority of his soldiers, he was only serving on a three-month contract.

The Northern army that fought at First Bull Run was under the command of Irvin McDowell, an Ohio man. He was 42, just a few months younger than his antagonist Beauregard. In fact, they had been contemporaries at West Point, passing out in the class of 1838 – Beauregard second in a group of 45 cadets, McDowell 23rd. McDowell was not outstanding and did not seem particularly ambitious. He fought bravely in the Mexican War and was promoted to captain, but he never commanded so much as a company in action. He was a staff officer and stayed on Winfield Scott's staff after the war. By the beginning of 1861 he had risen one further rung up the promotion ladder to become a major.

So he was astonished in mid-May to be told

THE FIELD COMMANDERS

▲ Robert Patterson was not at Bull Run for the battle, and the defeat of the Northern side there is largely attributable to his failure to get himself and his army into the fight or, alternatively, to prevent Jo Johnston getting himself and his army into the fight. After the battle, Patterson was the prime scapegoat. He was neither entirely nor solely to blame, but it is undoubtedly true that his age (he was 69) and the extreme caution of his advance made it comparatively easy for Johnston to get away.

▲ Irvin McDowell was a decent, conscientious and capable commander with a wry turn of wit and a gargantuan appetite. His misfortune was to be promoted too fast. At the start of 1861 he was a major and had never even commanded a company in action. By July that year he was the general in command of the main army of the Union, charged with destroying the rebellion at its outset. His plan was sound. He fought hard. He made his worst mistakes on the field at the moment when it seemed as if the victory were his. (Anne S. K. Brown Mil. Coll., BUL)

that he had been appointed a brigadier general. Two weeks later, to his further amazement, he was given command of the Department of North-Eastern Virginia, which meant in effect that he would be in charge of the North's first attempt to subdue the Confederacy. The speed of his promotion upset many who had not been so favoured. Even Winfield Scott – an old friend – thought it had been excessive, and for some time there was a cooling-off in their relationship.

McDowell was a big, burly, square-jawed, bearded man, no drinker, but by all accounts a tremendous trencherman. He was an able officer and conscientious, but his manner was often abstracted and sometimes haughty, and this made him respected rather than liked by those subordinate to him. He was intelligent and articulate and had a cool wit. When the distinguished war correspondent of the London *Times*, William Howard Russell, arrived in Washington in early July, McDowell told him: 'I have made arrangements for the correspondents of our papers to take the field under certain regulations, and I have suggested to them that they should wear a white uniform to indicate the purity of their character.'

These were the four men who would run, as far as anyone did, the first real battle of the American Civil War. They were of varied qualities and abilities, but they all had one important thing in common: none of them had ever commanded any sizeable body of troops in battle. Even Winfield Scott had never commanded an army as large as those that were now being assembled. It was to be a formative factor.

THE OPPOSING LEADERS

THE OPPOSING ARMIES

The United States in 1860 was a profoundly unmilitary country. Its regular army was hardly more than 16,000 strong, most of them well away from the centres of population, manning scattered forts and arsenals or looking for signs of Indian trouble. It was a rare thing for a US citizen ever to see a soldier. This all changed very quickly in the spring of 1861.

Officers and Men

The outbreak of war was tumultuously welcomed on both sides. Young men rushed to enlist. Newspapers encouraged the frenzy. The long years of increasingly bitter dispute had built up into a great head of hatred and bigotry and ignorance, which now burst out into parades and public ceremonies, with much high-flown rhetoric, the waving of flags and the marching of men as the bands played on. It was a rich period for catchy marching tunes.

Most of the non-commissioned men in the US Army stayed loyal to the service of the Union, but they were – and remained – dotted about in small detachments in frontier regions. No more than 2,500 regular soldiers were in northern Virginia for the war's opening campaign. The result of Bull Run might have been very different had McDowell been able to deploy twice that number of trained men.

At the start of 1861 the officer corps of the United States army numbered just over 1,000. They were, for the most part, a highly professional body of officers, most of them the products of a four-year period of intensive study at West Point Military Academy in New York State. When the country split, more than half the officers whose homes were in the South resigned from the Union army and offered their services to the Confederacy. They included many of the best: Robert E. Lee and Jo Johnston and Beauregard; J.E.B. Stuart, the cavalry leader; Jubal Early and James Longstreet; and Thomas Jonathan (soon to be 'Stonewall') Jackson.

One of the peculiar cruelties of civil war is that it often divides families, turning blood brothers into enemies. The American Civil War also turned brother-officers into enemies. Many of them had trained, worked and fought together over many years. James Longstreet – a corps commander at First Bull Run, the son of a South Carolina planter, a tough man and little given to displays of emotion – was one of many who were deeply pained by the experience: 'It was a sad day', he wrote in his memoirs, 'when we took leave of lifetime comrades and gave up a service of 20 years.'

The recruitment of volunteers, both North and South, was done regionally through the state militia system. It was the most simple and by far the best way; regional loyalties were still very strong. Some prominent local figure would be offered a captaincy and asked to form a company of volunteer infantrymen, between 60 and 80 men

◀ *Left: an infantry private with primitive weaponry – an antiquated flintlock musket and a large Bowie knife. Flintlocks continued in use until 1862. Many volunteers brought their own Bowie knives with them but found little or no opportunity to use them in action, and they were rapidly discarded. Right, a private of the 4th Texas Infantry Regiment loads his smooth-bore percussion musket. He is hung about with a Bowie knife, bayonet, haversack and a tin canteen (water bottle) and, on his other shoulder, a canvas sling to hold his cartridge box. Centre, a First Sergeant of the Louisiana Infantry was armed with a percussion rifle and an NCO's sword. He wears a 'havelock', a cloth flap to protect his neck from the sun. These were commonly worn in the first months of the Civil War but soon abandoned and used, more effectively, as coffee strainers. (Illustration by Ron Volstad)*

23

THE OPPOSING ARMIES

ORDER OF BATTLE: THE SOUTHERN ARMY

I Corps
Commander
Brig. Gen. P. G. T. Beauregard

Assistant Adj. Gen.
Col. Thomas Jordan

1st Brigade	2nd Brigade	3rd Brigade	4th Brigade	5th Brigade	6th Brigade
Brig. Gen. M. L. Bonham	Brig. Gen. R. S. Ewell	Brig. Gen. D. R. Jones	Brig. Gen. James Longstreet	Col. P. St. G Cocke	Col. J. A. Early
Strength: 4,961	Strength: 2,444	Strength: 2,121	Strength: 3,528	Strength: 3,276	Strength: 2,620

Unbrigaded: 8th Louisiana (Col. H. B. Kelly), strength 846; Hampton's Legion (Col. Wade Hampton), strength 65

Cavalry: Harrison's Battalion (Maj. Julian Harrison), strength 209; 30th Virginia Cavalry (Col. R. C. W. Radford), strength 300; plus ten independent companies, with a total strength of 583.

II Corps
Commander
Gen. J. E. Johnston

Assistant Adj. Gen.
Brig. Gen. E. K. Smith

1st Brigade	2nd Brigade	3rd Brigade	4th Brigade
Brig. Gen. T. J. Jackson	Col. F. S. Bartow	Brig. Gen. B. E. Bee	Brig. Gen. E. K. Smith
Strength: 2,151	Strength: 2,546	Strength: 2,790	Strength: 2,262

OFFICERS AND MEN

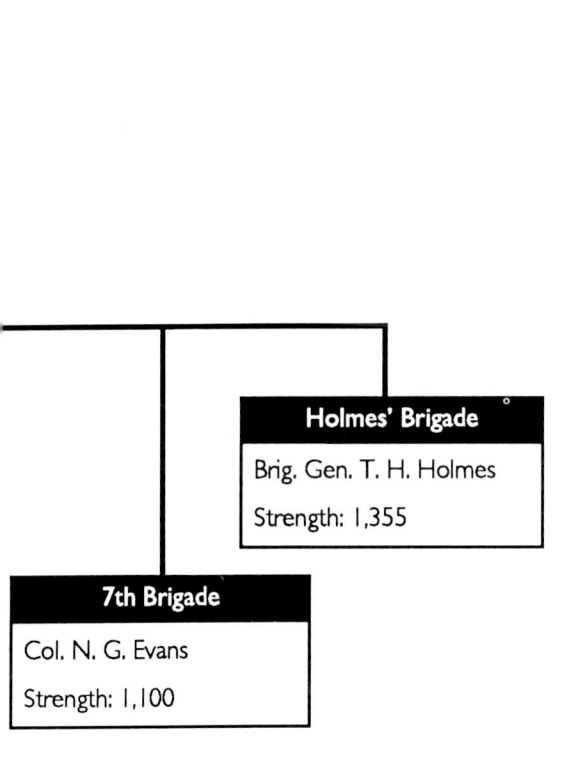

Unbrigaded:
6th North Carolina Infantry (Col. C. F. Fisher), strength 600; Beckham's Virginia Battalion (Lt. R. F. Beckham).

Cavalry:
"Jeb" Stuart's men of the 1st Virginia. There were 334 of them.

all told. He would chose two friends or acquaintances as his lieutenants, and the three of them together would then find their recruits. Generally speaking, a company would be made up of young men who had been neighbours all their lives, who had grown up together and knew each other's strengths and weaknesses. It made for *espirit de corps* but not always for good discipline.

In both armies, in theory, ten companies comprised one regiment. This would be commanded by a lieutenant colonel, who would have a small headquarters staff. The men of a regiment were usually all from the same state. In ideal circumstances a regiment meant about 1,000 men, but this number was rarely approached in practice. In very approximate terms, four or five regiments were said to form a brigade, which would be commanded by a full colonel or a brigadier general. In even more approximate terms, three or four brigades made up a division. One or more divisions could form a corps.

The key operational unit was the brigade, in theory between 4,000 and 5,000 men, in practice usually much fewer than that.

In some respects, the quality of the recruits was superb. They were young men, most of whom had grown up with enough to eat and plenty of hard physical work in the fresh air. Many of them had led tough and spartan lives. They were used to roughing it. Many were also well-used to handling weapons – shotguns, hunting rifles and pistols. They were highly motivated too. Most of them, on both sides, sincerely believed in the justice of their cause. They signed on for a wide variety of motives: because they liked fighting and did not want to miss 'the big one'; because all their friends were going; to see something of the world (most of them had never travelled outside their immediate locality); because they thought it would be exciting and different and probably fun and possibly glorious and, anyway, over quite soon. Both North and South set a minimum age limit of 18, but under-age lads on both sides wanted to join in. Many had been brought up to speak the truth so they wrote '18' on a slip of paper and put it inside one of their shoes so that when the inevitable question was asked they could honestly reply; 'I am over 18'.

They were raw material for the making of superb infantrymen. The only trouble was that they were without military training and experience of any kind, and they had, on the whole, a sturdy aversion to the kind of discipline that army life traditionally demands. This was true of the new officers as well as the men. They resented the intrusion into their lives of West Pointers with their rigid attitudes to the way things should be done, their insistence on obedience, the harsh punishments they inflicted when their orders were defied or ignored.

The streak of individualism was even stronger in the young American men in those days than it is now. They had been brought up to admire and emulate the pioneer virtues, respect for personal freedom, self-reliance, the importance of being 'your own man'. It was considered unmanly to let yourself be pushed around by someone else, to give automatic and unquestioning obedience. And these ingrained attitudes were not going to be changed the moment a man volunteered for a short spell in the army. The European armies of the twentieth century have more than once been astonished by the relaxed American way of running an army, their democratic approach to decision-making. It was even more marked in 1861, and it made things more difficult for those in command on both sides.

Uniforms

Recruitment on both sides was based on the local militia system, and over the preceding years these forces had enjoyed much local autonomy. Many had sought to attract men to their ranks by offering a lively social life, much parading about on festive

▼ *The American Civil War was the first to produce a full pictorial record, in photographs and sketches, but photography was in its early stages and could not cope with men in movement. It gave much scope to the artists. Frank Vitzetelli portrayed a regiment of New York Zouaves parading along Broadway on their way to Washington and then Bull Run. Before he went to America, Vitzetelli had covered Garibaldi's campaigns in Sicily and Italy for the* Illustrated London News. (Illustrated London News, *22 June 1861)*

▲*A sergeant of the 7th New York State Militia, one of the earliest militia regiments to go to Washington and join the Army of the Potomac.* *Many Northern units wore grey uniforms at that time, which helped to increase the confusion at First Bull Run. (Illustration by Michael Youens)*

▲*A regular army private of the 6th US Infantry Regiment. Had McDowell had more such trained and experienced men at Bull Run the result might well have been very different. (Illustration by Michael Youens)*

occasions and – above all else – by the splendour of their uniforms. As a result, a colourful and exotic variety of uniforms, reflecting foreign or historical influences, had been adopted.

Some based their designs on the costumes worn by the American colonists in the War of Independence. Others looked across the Atlantic for their models. The 39th New York Infantry, impressed by the success of the Italian freedom fighters under Garibaldi, affected the style of the *bersaglieri* sharp-shooters, including hats with flamboyant plumes. The 79th New York, recruited largely from Scottish immigrants, modelled themselves on the Cameron Highlanders with a dress uniform of kilts, sporran, silver-buckled shoes and Glengarry caps, though they changed into trousers and boots for Bull Run. But it was the French influence that predominated, North and South. If the strategic skills of the first Napoleon prevailed in West Point's battle training, it was the sartorial extravagances of Napoleon III's army that prevailed in the matter of dress, especially those of his Algerian soldiers, the Zouaves. Many militia units, on both sides, fitted themselves out with baggy trousers in bright colours (usually red), yellow or white gaiters and short blue jackets, fancifully embroidered. The men wore a red *fez* with a long tassel; the officers wore *kepis*.

In the spring of 1861, when the mass recruitment drives had been launched, each government tried to impose some measure of uniformity on its army's appearance: the North chose blue as its distinctive colour; the South opted for grey. In this way, it was hoped, in the smoky confusion of battle their soldiers would have some way of distinguishing friend from foe. Unfortunately neither

▶ *Vitzetelli's impression of 'Colonel Wilson's boys' in camp on Staten Island. One of the things the volunteers had to get used to once they were in the army was the amount of sheer 'hanging about' and waiting that military service involves. It led to a great deal of drunkenness and brawling.* (Illustrated London News, *29 June 1861*)

◀ *Vitzetelli's portraits of two members, an officer and a private, of Colonel Elmer E. Ellsworth's 11th New York Fire Zouaves (most of them had been in the city's fire brigade). Colonel Ellsworth did not get to Bull Run. He was killed in a minor skirmish at the outset of the campaign, becoming one of the first casualties of the Civil War. The 11th New York went on to face some of the fiercest fighting on the summit of Henry Hill.* (Illustrated London News, *15 June 1861*)

side was able to implement its orders immediately, so both armies marched to Bull Run displaying an astonishing mixture of uniforms. Some Southern units and many of their senior commanders were dressed in blue, while several Northern regiments wore grey tunics and trousers. It was to cost lives and affect the course of the battle at important moments.

Weapons

First Bull Run was primarily an infantry encounter, and the best infantryman's weapon was the 1855 version of the Springfield rifle-musket. Its overall length was four feet eight inches, and it weighed just over nine pounds. It was a muzzle-loader firing a .58 calibre bullet, just over half an inch in diameter. Muzzle-loading was a complicated procedure, but tests conducted in 1860 showed that a trained man could load and fire the rifle ten times in five minutes, putting six of his bullets into a two-foot square target at a distance of 100 yards. At 300 yards' range he put all ten bullets into a target that was two and a half feet square. Manufactured in the armoury at Springfield, Massachusetts, this was by far the best infantry weapon available in 1861. It meant that attackers could no longer get to within 150 yards of the enemy line, then form up and charge, confident that the defenders would have time to fire no more than one volley before they were among them with the bayonet.

The Springfield 1855 was used by both sides at Bull Run. The Confederates got many when they seized the Federal arsenals within their territories. But neither side had anything like enough to arm all their men with them, and the rest had to make do with a variety of more ancient weapons – smooth-bore muskets, like today's shotguns, which were unlikely to hit a man at anything over 200 yards, and the even more antiquated flintlocks. The only effective use for guns like this was a mass volley at short range.

The artillery had long been something of a Cinderella in both the Union army and the state militias. The equipment was expensive; the gunner's work was noisy and dirty, hard and dangerous; it called for some technical skill and

◀ *Vitzetelli makes the camp of the 2nd New York Regiment look clean, well-ordered and busy. Many of the regimental camps, in the early days of the war, were not like that. (Illustrated London News, 29 June 1861)*

much rigorous drill. To be a gunner was more demanding than to be an infantryman and was nothing like as glamorous as being a cavalryman. Perhaps for these reasons the artillery tended to attract to its ranks men of a more serious and dedicated disposition and, once in, they quickly learned to take great pride in their work. Although not many guns were taken to Bull Run – the North had 55 altogether, the South 49 – the artillery played an important role.

There was a great variety of guns, ranging from six-pounders to one 30-pounder. Most of them were smooth-bores, but some had rifled barrels, which gave greater range and accuracy. All were muzzle-loaders. The most popular was the 12-pounder 1857 Model, generally known as the 'Napoleon'. Most of these were smooth-bores, capable of hurling their missiles farther than a mile but with an effective range of about 1,500 yards. The gunner had a selection of missiles: solid iron balls weighing over 12 pounds that flew at 1,440 feet per second to cut a terrible swathe through enemy ranks; shells filled with powder that exploded on impact; grapeshot and canister, which exploded into showers of metal fragments. With a full and trained crew, a sergeant (or corporal) and seven gunners, the 12-pounder could be fired twice a minute. In ideal circumstances, a battery would comprise six guns and their supporting ammunition wagons (caissons), requiring a total of 72 horses.

The guns were influential at Bull Run chiefly because most of them were manned by regular soldiers, fully trained and animated by high professional zeal. Nine of the Northern batteries came from the regular Union army. On the Southern side many of the artillery officers were West Point men, and many more had learned their craft at Virginia Military Institute under the expert gunner and strict instructor, Major T. J. Jackson.

The Cavalry

In cavalry, the Southern forces had a marked advantage. At the end of 1860 the US army included only five regiments of cavalry (something over 1,000 mounted men to each regiment), and these were scattered about the frontier regions to the west in small units, keeping an eye on the Indians. When the Confederacy was formed, four of the five regular colonels resigned to join the South. The Northern commanders made no effort to get their cavalry units back to the Washington area in force, nor – when the call went out for volunteers – did they ask for cavalrymen. They assumed that the war would be quickly over and that it would be won by infantrymen with a little

▼ State uniforms of the South. Left, a staff captain from South Carolina. Centre, a corporal of the Alabama Volunteer Corps. Right, a private in the 11th Mississippi Infantry Regiment, which was part of General Bee's 3rd Brigade at First Bull Run. (Illustrated by Ron Volstad)

ORDER OF BATTLE: THE NORTHERN ARMY

Commander
Brig. Gen. Irvin McDowell

Assistant Adj. Gen.
Capt. J. B. Fry

1st Division
Brig. Gen. Daniel Tyler

1st Bde: Col. E. D. Keyes
2nd Bde: Brig. Gen. R. C. Schenck
3rd Bde: Col. W. T. Sherman
4th Bde: Col. I. B. Richardson

Total strength: 12,795

2nd Division
Brig. Gen. David Hunter

1st Bde: Col. Andrew Porter
2nd Bde: Col. A. E. Burnside

Total strength: 5,969

4th Division
Brig. Gen. Theodore Runyon

This division was in reserve and did not become involved in the action.

Total strength: 5,752

There was also one battalion (seven companies) of cavalry, commanded by Maj. I. N. Palmer. They marched with Col. Porter's brigade of the 2nd Division.

The North had a marginal numerical advantage. McDowell commanded some 38,000 men, though many were not engaged in the battle. The forces of Beauregard and Johnston totaled 35,000, and many of these, too, saw little or no fighting. The North had a few more guns. The South had more and better cavalry.

help from the gunners. There was no need, it was felt, to go to the considerable expense that cavalry involved. The thinking was wrong, as subsequent developments in the Civil War were to prove, but it meant that McDowell marched to Bull Run with only 500 horsemen under his command – and disposed them in such a way as to ensure that they could be of little use. There was no mounted reconnaissance screen in front of his advancing troops; no protection of the exposed flanks; no information-gathering from enemy territory; no chance of ever assembling a mobile strike force that might thrust a way through the Southern defensive lines.

two regiments. Many of them had fine mounts. They were armed with carbines, revolvers and sabres. One regiment, the First Virginia Cavalry commanded by the ebullient J.E.B. Stuart, was to play a key role at the turning-point of the battle.

Intelligence

Civil wars are complicated. There were people in the Southern states who hated slavery as much as any Northerner, who opposed secession and hoped for an early Northern victory. A few of them worked clandestinely to further the Union cause, sabotaging the military where they could, getting information to the Northern commanders. Support for the Southern cause in the Northern states was even greater. Many believed the war was a terrible mistake, that it had been brought about by anti-slavery intolerance, and that if the slave states wanted to go their own way, they should be allowed to do so in peace. In some places, in Missouri, for example, and in the city of Baltimore,

3rd Division

Brig. Gen. S. P. Heintzelman

1st Bde: Brig. Gen. W. B. Franklin
2nd Bde: Brig. Gen. O. B. Willcox
3rd Bde: Brig. Gen. O. O. Howard

Total strength: 7,232

5th Division

Brig. Gen. D. S. Miles

1st Bde: Col. Louis Blenker
2nd Bde: Col. T. A. Davies

Total strength: 6,173

Horsemanship was more highly regarded in the rural and aristocratic South. It formed a vital part in the upbringing of every young gentleman. The image of the dashing *beau sabreur* was a compelling one. As a result, the Southern forces at First Bull Run included more than 3,000 mounted men organized into seven separate companies and

▼ *A group of young Virginians who responded immediately to the state's call for one-year's service in the army. In many ways they were ideal recruits – young, strong and keen – but it was to prove difficult, on both sides, to imbue them with proper notions of military discipline.*

THE OPPOSING ARMIES

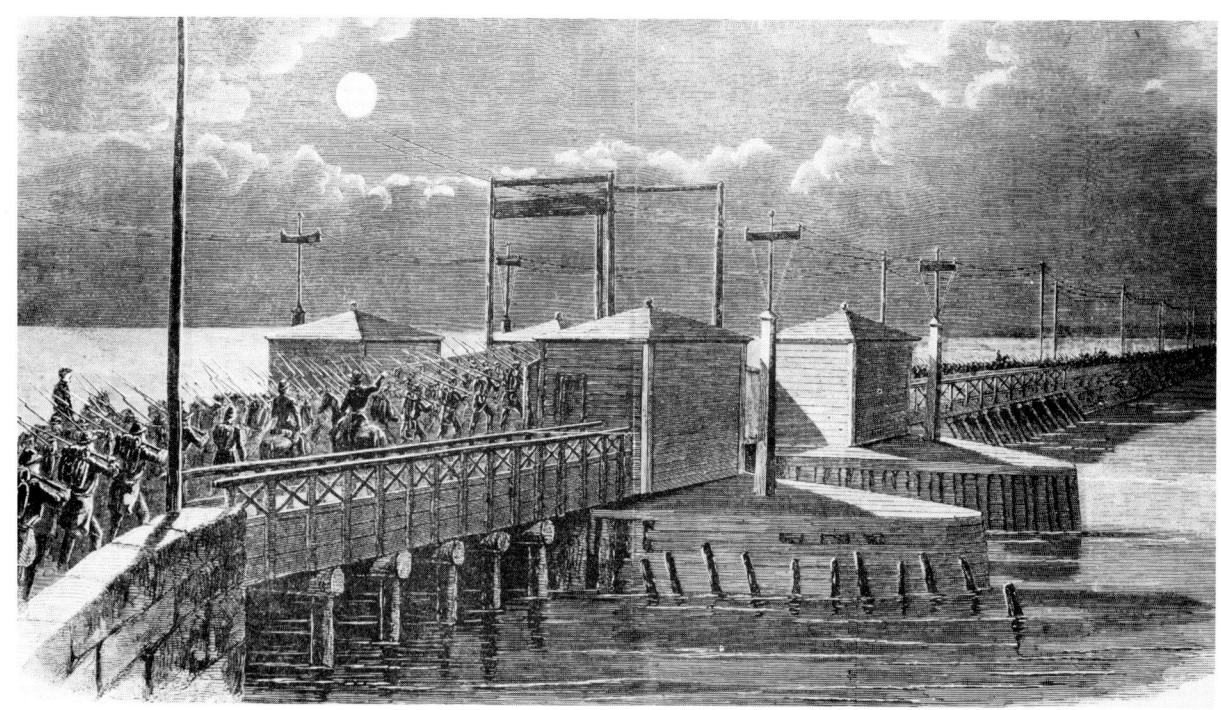

pro-South feeling was intense. It was very strong, too, in the national capital, Washington. As a result, nothing could be kept secret from the enemy for long. Troop movements of any size were noted and reported. There were Southern sympathizers with friends in very high places, and Lincoln and his top advisers soon had to accept the fact that their plans would be known to the enemy leaders within days. There was no simple way of recognizing the spies. It was impossible to police the borders effectively.

Universal Inexperience

The overriding fact about the First Battle of Bull Run is that neither side was anything like ready for it. The generals on both sides had no experience of commanding even moderately large bodies of soldiers in battle. Some had never had an independent command of any size. And the great majority of the soldiers, again on both sides, had no experience of war and had received the most perfunctory training. There were some units that had not even been taught how to load and fire their muskets. None had been properly drilled in the complex manoeuvres required to get regiments or brigades into the necessary battle formations. Few

▲ *In the early hours of the morning of 24 May 1861, Winfield Scott sent strong contingents of his army, mostly New York volunteers, out of Washington and across the Long Bridge over the Potomac and into Virginia, to seize the towns of Alexandria and Arlington. There was no resistance, though Colonel Ellsworth was killed in Alexandria – shot by an angry householder when he went on to his roof to haul down the rebel flag. (From* Harper's Weekly; *Anne S.K. Brown Coll. BUL)*

had been instilled with any real sense of military discipline.

The Times' correspondent William Howard Russell was shocked by what he found when he toured McDowell's camps in early July. He was a neutral observer and an expert one; he had seen the professional armies of Europe in action, the Prussians in Schleswig-Holstein, the French and the British in the Crimea, the British again in the suppression of the Indian mutineers. The camps, he wrote in his diary, were dirty. Discipline was criminally lax. Officers as well as men were incapable of even company drill movements. General McDowell could find no adequate map of the area he was soon to invade and had a completely inadequate staff: 'They have no cavalry, only a few scarecrow men, who would dissolve partnership with their steeds at the first serious

▼ *Full-dress infantry in the Northern army, 1861. Left to right, a first lieutenant, colonel and sergeant-major. (Illustration by Ron Volstad)*

combined movement . . . they have no carriage for reserve ammunition; the commissariat drivers are civilians, under little or no control; the officers are unsoldierly-looking men; the camps are dirty to excess; the men are dressed in all sorts of uniforms; and, from what I hear, I doubt if any of these regiments have ever performed a brigade evolution together or if any of the officers know what it is to deploy a brigade from column into line. They are mostly three months' men whose time is nearly up.'

Apart from the description of the cavalry, perhaps, and the matter of the three months' term of service, much the same account might have been made of the Southern forces.

Bruce Catton, the distinguished American historian of the Civil War, wrote: 'There is nothing in American military history quite like the story of Bull Run. It was the momentous fight of the amateurs, the battle where everything went wrong,

▲ *In the early months of the Civil War, both sides had difficulty in imposing march discipline. Their volunteer recruits saw no good reason why they should not stop and rest when they felt like it or forage about for food and drink.*

▶ *Thomas Jonathan Jackson of Virginia was a young colonel when the Civil War began. But he was a general in command of a brigade at First Bull Run, and it was on the summit slopes of Henry Hill that he won the nickname 'Stonewall'. More than any of the other commanders on the field that day, he distinguished himself and won great respect and fame. After Bull Run, he continued to fight hard and skilfully – at Antietam, in the Shenandoah Valley, at Fredericksburg – but he was severely wounded at Chancellorsville in 1863 and died soon after. (Photograph by Minnes, Fredericksburg, 1863)*

the great day of awakening for the whole nation, North and South together. It marked the end of the 90-day militia, and it also ended the rosy time in which men could dream that the war would be short, glorious and bloodless. After Bull Run the nation got down to business.'

THE ROAD TO BULL RUN

By June 1861 there were four armies in the process of formation in North-East Virginia and a general recognition that it was in this region that the war's first major encounter would take place. McDowell was creating his army in and around Washington while Beauregard did the same and prepared his defences beyond the Bull Run river. Just over 30 miles to the north-west meanwhile, in the Shenandoah Valley beyond the Blue Ridge Mountains, the rather smaller armies of Robert Patterson and Jo Johnston were sparring with each other.

The village of Harpers Ferry, at the junction of the Rivers Potomac and Shenandoah, had been abandoned by the Northern forces in mid-April. By the end of the month the region was under the control of a small Virginian force commanded by Colonel Thomas J. Jackson.

Jackson was a young man, in his mid-thirties,

but already an experienced officer. Of mixed Scottish and Irish descent, he was a Virginian by birth and loyalty. He had graduated from West Point, fought as an artillery lieutenant in the Mexican War, and later had become a teacher of military science and mathematics. More important than this, he was a man of powerful character, serious and strong-minded. He was deeply Christian: 'He lives by the New Testament and fights by the Old', someone said of him. His regard for the Bible was almost matched by his regard for army regulations and military discipline. He was one of those officers whose men dislike him initially because of his stern rule but who soon comes to command respect and affection for his fairness and integrity and his air of knowing exactly what he is about.

Jackson's force expanded rapidly as the volunteers arrived, and when their number reached some 9,000 a more senior officer, Brigadier General Joseph E. Johnston, was sent to take over. He formed the army into four brigades and gave Jackson command of the First Brigade, composed of four (later five) Virginia regiments.

Johnston had other impressive men under his command. One of them was the charismatic young cavalry leader, James Ewell Brown Stuart. In many ways Stuart was the epitome of the romantic notion of a cavalry leader – handsome, strong, extrovert in manner, flamboyant in appearance, exuding confidence and cheerfulness, full of energy and courage. Johnston called him a 'yellow jacket' which was a type of hornet. It is a tribute to 'Jeb' Stuart's qualities that he won the respect of the Presbyterian Jackson, despite the disparity in their characters.

Another junior officer who was to distinguish himself at Bull Run and earn high promotion was Captain John D. Imboden of the artillery. In his account *Incidents of the First Bull Run* Imboden said

THE ROAD TO BULL RUN

Northern Virginia and the opposing armies, mid-June 1861

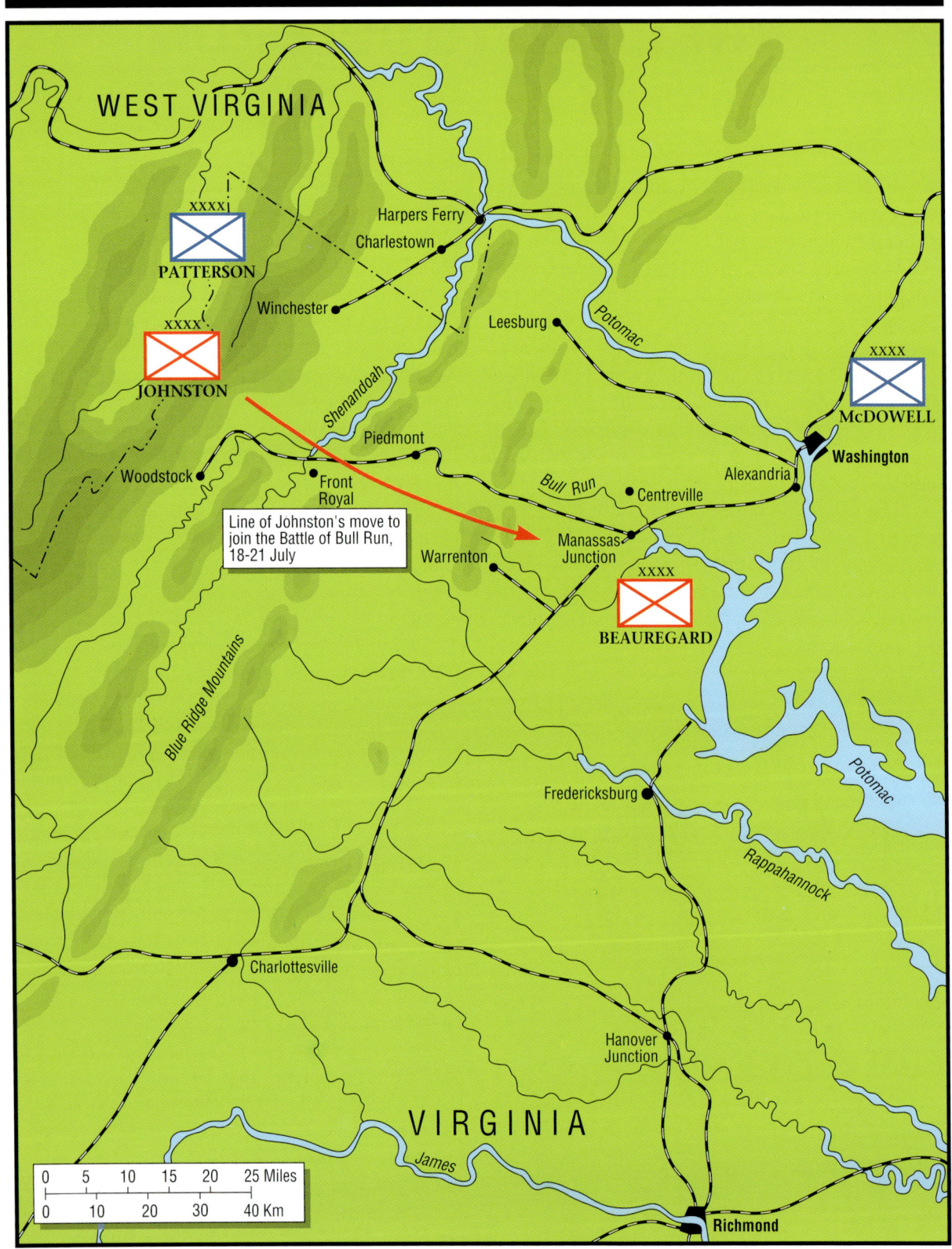

that Johnston, in these weeks before the battle, 'was ceaseless in his labours to improve the efficiency of his little army'. Johnston had Jackson's belief in the need for discipline and drill, and when circumstances allowed he carried on with Jackson's programme of intensive training. Luckily, he was given plenty of time. The commander he faced was the elderly Robert Patterson.

Patterson was beset with troubles, some of them real, some imaginary. Like most of his soldiers, he had only signed on for three months. Unlike most of them, he knew about war, enough at least to know that they were unfit for battle, inadequately equipped and insufficiently trained. He was not the man to fill them with confidence. He suffered under the constant delusion that the enemy forces facing him were much stronger than his own. This encouraged his natural caution, which was further stimulated by the orders he received from Winfield Scott in Washington. Advance slowly, he was told, and with great care; risk no reverses; make no aggressive moves unless success is certain.

In early June, Johnston decided that his positions around Harpers Ferry were scarcely defensible and of no strategic importance anyway, so he withdrew his forces to the Winchester area. He was better-placed here to deal with attacks either from the north or the west, and also, should the call come, to hurry to support Beauregard. Patterson moved towards Harpers Ferry with infinite caution. Even when he finally arrived there and found the enemy gone, he was suspicious. He was being lured, he thought, into a cunning trap. The tentative nature of his advance was increased in mid-June when Winfield Scott, without any apparent evidence, decided that Washington was in imminent danger and ordered Patterson to dispatch his only really reliable units, the regular contingents, to save the capital immediately.

Public opinion in the North, which had been so confident, was growing impatient. There was an increasing demand for decisive action of some kind. The newspapers, as usual, reflected and magnified the popular feeling. The most influential of them, the *New York Tribune*, under its eccentric and excitable editor Horace Greeley, led the chorus with its repeated headline cry 'Forward to Richmond'.

▲ *James Ewell Brown Stuart, universally known as 'Jeb', was a cavalry leader of dash and distinction who made a considerable contribution to the Southern victory at First Bull Run – first by effectively fooling Patterson in the Shenandoah Valley, then by his charges in and around Henry Hill at the turning-point of the battle. (Photograph by George E. Cook)*

President Lincoln and his top advisers felt the weight of all this pressure and were also aware that their troops' three-month term of service would begin to expire in mid-July.

Northern Plans

On 29 June the President held a meeting of his ministers and top military advisers in the White House. Winfield Scott, asked for his advice, argued against giving in to the general clamour. He was in favour of further training and preparation throughout the summer to be followed in the autumn by an attack in force down the Mississippi Valley to reach the sea and split the Confederacy in two. In this way, together with a blockade by the Union navy, the hardline secessionist states would be cut off from all help. It was called the 'Anaconda Plan', after the South American snake that squeezes its victims to death. In the event, three years later, the North was to win the war by some such method; but the idea was altogether too long-term for Northern sentiment in June 1861. Scott's ideas were dismissed with little discussion. The old general gave way without a struggle, and the meeting went on to consider the plans McDowell had already drawn up for an attack on Manassas Junction.

McDowell had made these plans a few days earlier at Scott's request. He now stuck a map on the wall and expounded them. He reckoned the enemy strength behind Bull Run at about 25,000 and, assuming that Patterson would keep Johnston fully occupied in the Shenandoah Valley, he thought they might have another 10,000 men in the field by the time of the battle. The enemy was expecting them and had been preparing his defences. McDowell proposed to advance with a force of some 30,000 men, followed by a reserve of 10,000. He would not attack frontally but hoped to work round the eastern flank of the enemy, then strike westwards along the line of the Orange and Alexandria Railroad to cut Beauregard off from his supply line from Richmond.

▼*Frank Vitzetelli was in Washington in the early summer of 1861 to observe and sketch the build-up of the Northern army. Here President Lincoln with members of his Cabinet and General Winfield Scott (seated) watch a parade of volunteer soldiers shortly before the Battle of Bull Run.* (Illustrated London News)

It was a simple and sensible plan, and no one present had anything better to suggest. McDowell stressed the importance of the coming battle and added: 'I think it of great consequence that, as for the most part our regiments are exceedingly raw and the best of them, with few exceptions, not over steady in line, they be organized into as many small fixed brigades as the number of regular colonels will admit . . . so that the men may have as fair a chance as the nature of things and the comparative inexperience of most will allow.'

Someone asked when the march to Manassas would start; Scott, without consulting McDowell, said it would begin in one week's time.

At some point, either towards the close of this meeting or immediately after it, McDowell repeated his concern about the 'green-ness' of his troops. The reply – sometimes attributed to Lincoln, sometimes to Scott – was: 'You are green, it is true, but they are green also.'

Scott's deadline for the start of the march proved impossible to meet. There was a shortage of transport wagons, horses and mules. More recruits were still on the way. McDowell complained: 'I had no opportunity to test my machinery, to move it around and see whether it would work smoothly or not.' Finally, on 15 July he called his corps commanders together and told them they would march next day. His field order warned them to proceed with caution and to remember the variety of uniforms and make sure their men did not fire on each other.

They set off on the afternoon of the next day, each man carrying three days' rations in his haversack.

Southern Preparations

Beauregard had known for weeks that they would soon be coming, and he received confirmation that they were on the way before 9 o'clock that night. A coded message was handed to him. It came from a leader of Washington society with friends in high places and intense sympathy for the Southern cause, Mrs. Rose O'Neal Greenhow. The note said: 'Order issued for McDowell to march upon Manassas tonight.' Immediately Beauregard sent orders to his outposts to fall back quietly as McDowell's men approached. Then he asked President Davis to alert Johnston and get him to start transferring his army to Manassas.

In the late afternoon of 17 July, Johnston received a telegram from Beauregard: 'War Department has ordered you to join me. Do so immediately, if possible, and we will crush the enemy.' The order from the War Department in Richmond arrived in the early hours of the next morning. Johnston summoned his brigade commanders and organized the move. Jackson's Brigade, which already had a reputation for fast marching, would go first. The men would not be told what was happening until well clear of the area so that word would not reach Patterson. One after the other, the brigades would make for the railway at Piedmont. An officer rode ahead to alert the railway authorities and arrange for trains to ferry the infantrymen the 34 miles to Manassas Junction. Artillery and cavalry would have to get there under their own steam.

When the march began the men were downhearted, believing this was another strategic withdrawal. Then they were halted and Johnston's order was read out, making it clear they were on their way to a big battle. 'The soldiers rent the air with shouts of joy', Jackson reported, 'and all was eagerness and animation.' The first men reached Manassas at 4 p.m. on Friday 19 July.

'Jeb' Stuart and his cavalry were given the job of screening the army's departure from Patterson, and in this they were completely successful. For reasons known only to himself, Patterson had moved his army to the area of Charlestown, more than 20 miles from Winchester. He had been reinforced with more volunteers, bringing the number of men under his command to about 17,000, but he persisted in his belief that Johnston was much stronger than that. He was, furthermore, getting confused and even contradictory orders from Winfield Scott. He was having to plead with the three-months' men, whose term of service was amost up, to stay a few days longer. Everything conspired to encourage his natural caution. But right until the last moment, and beyond it – when Johnston's brigades were steaming towards Bull Run – Patterson still believed he was holding Johnston in the Shenandoah Valley.

THE AFFAIR AT BLACKBURN'S FORD

McDowell's orders for the march from Washington towards Bull Run were clear and sensible, and at first all went well, though slowly. Beauregard had told his foremost units to observe the enemy columns closely but to pull back, offering no resistance. When the tracks ran through woodland, as they often did, they felled trees to delay the Nothern advance a little.

The weather was hot and sultry. Many of the advancing men, who had overloaded themselves, began to shed clothing and equipment they thought unnecessary. Some suffered from sunstroke, all from thirst. The colonel of the Third Brigade of the First Division, who had only been given that command a fortnight before, was shocked at his men's behaviour: 'The march demonstrated little save the general laxity of discipline; for with all my personal efforts, I could not prevent the men from straggling for water, blackberries, or anything on the way they fancied.' This was William Tecumseh Sherman, whose original approach to warfare was later to make a clinching impact on the course of the Civil War and influence subsequent military thinking. The historian, Sir Basil Liddell Hart, called Sherman 'the first modern strategist' for his perception that wars could be won by striking at the enemy's economic power base and undermining his morale, rather than by fighting great and bloody battles. But in July 1861 this part of Sherman's career was still to come. Sherman was just turned 40. An Ohio man, he went to West Point, was commissioned into the artillery, saw action against the Seminole Indians and the Mexicans, then resigned from the army to try his luck in business. In April 1861 he volunteered for three years' service and was made a colonel. In appearance and manner he was like many Americans of that time – tall and loose-limbed; careless of dress and restless; a cigar chain-smoker with considerable contempt for conventional thinking and a powerful, picturesque way of stating his views. He also had great energy and courage, a quick and acute intelligence. He took his soldiering seriously. He believed in marching light. On his way to Bull Run he wrote to his wife, thanking her for her letters and adding tactlessly: 'As I read them I will tear them up, for every ounce on a march tells.'

▼ *William Tecumseh Sherman was just 40 years old and the colonel commanding the 3rd Brigade of the 1st Division of the North's army at Bull Run. He showed initiative by finding a way across the river to get his men into the thick of the action, but after that did nothing to mark himself out as a man with a great military future. After Bull Run he briefly thought his army career was over, but he survived and later emerged to become one of the most innovative and important of the war's leaders. (Anne S. K. Brown Mil. Coll., BUL)*

▲ A corporal of the 1st Virginia Regiment, which was hotly engaged in the affair at Blackburn's Ford, but – as part of General Longstreet's 4th Brigade – played virtually no part in the main Bull Run battle. (Illustration by Michael Youens)

▲ Colonel Ambrose Burnside raised the First Rhode Island Infantry Regiment and became their colonel. They played an active part in the First Battle of Bull Run under his brigade command. He designed their uniform – this is a corporal – which included a red woollen blanket and, for some of the men, carbines designed by Burnside himself. (Illustration by Michael Youens)

McDowell's army pushed forward much more slowly than he and his senior commanders would have liked, though in reasonable order. There was some looting and foraging, but it was firmly dealt with. McDowell still hoped to be able to follow his original plan – to feint a frontal attack across Bull Run while a strong force marched round to the east of the enemy defences to drive in behind him on the line of the Orange and Alexandria Railroad. For the task of turning the enemy line he looked to his Third Division, commanded by Colonel Samuel P. Heintzelman. Heintzelman had been an army officer for 35 years, showing courage in action against both Indians and Mexicans. On 18

July, McDowell and Heintzelman rode out to reconnoitre the ground the Third Division would have to cover to outflank Beauregard's main force. What they saw was disappointing: 'The roads', McDowell found, 'were too narrow and crooked for so large a body to move over, and the distance around too great to admit of it with any safety. We would become entangled and our carriages would block up the way.' McDowell would have to re-think his next moves.

In the meantime he had to take the village of Centreville and push on beyond towards the River Bull Run, sounding out the enemy's strength. This job he gave to his strongest division, the First, with four brigades and a total strength of more than 12,000 men, under the command of Brigadier General Daniel Tyler.

Tyler's Attack

Tyler was 62. He had been a soldier for the first half of his career, then a successful businessman. Although he had seen no action, he had a military manner. And he was ambitious – perhaps he was

◀ Frank Vizetelli allowed himself a good measure of artistic and journalistic licence. It is not likely that he got ahead of McDowell's vanguard on the march to Fairfax (en route for Centreville), but he none the less sent his magazine this lively impression of South Carolina pickets pulling back and setting up obstacles to delay the enemy's advance. (Illustrated London News)

◀ This sketch by Vizetelli is entirely imaginary. In fact, the little town of Fairfax was taken without a shot being fired. McDowell expected stiff resistance here, but when Colonel Burnside's brigade arrived it was to find that the Southern forces had withdrawn. (Illustrated London News, 22 June 1861)

▲ Brigadier General Daniel Tyler, commander of the North's 1st Division, was highly ambitious and resented taking orders from McDowell. He did much to harm the North's chances at Bull Run. In the preliminary probing skirmish – the affair at Blackburn's Ford on July 18 – he exceeded his orders and was so badly mauled that the morale of the whole army was affected. At Bull Run itself he went to the opposite extreme and moved with such caution that half his Division never got involved in the key struggle. (Anne S. K. Brown Mil. Coll., BUL)

▲ James Longstreet, commander of Beauregard's 4th Brigade, fought a capable action at Blackburn's Ford to repulse Tyler's attack on 18 July. But on the day of the Bull Run battle, although Longstreet's men were intended to be part of the attack on Centreville and though they crossed and re-crossed the river more than once, they saw little action. (Anne S. K. Brown Mil. Coll., BUL)

one of the several officers who were offended when McDowell was promoted over their heads in May. Certainly, he had no great liking or respect for McDowell.

McDowell was clear in the orders he gave Tyler: 'Observe well the roads to Bull Run and to Warrenton,' he said. 'Do not bring on an engagement, but keep up the impression that we are moving on Manassas.'

The enemy went on falling back before him as Tyler pushed on through Centreville and beyond until he came to the crest of a hill and looked down on a well-wooded landscape and the Bull Run. There were two fords across the river immediately ahead, Mitchell's and Blackburn's. On the far side he could see some enemy soldiers. He called up two big rifled guns, 20-pounders, and got them to fire a few shots. There was a brief response, but the Southern guns were smooth-bore and lacked the range.

Beauregard's line of defence was some six miles in length, following the river from Union Mills Ford on his right to the Stone Bridge on his left. The brigade in position behind Blackburn's Ford was that of Brigadier General James Longstreet, a cool and capable officer. He had had time to prepare, and most of his men were well-concealed. He held his fire.

Tyler had been surprised by the ease of his advance so far. With a little vigorous pushing, he felt, he might march on to Manassas Junction and seize the day's glory, putting one over on McDowell in the process. He either forgot, or chose to ignore, McDowell's order that he should do nothing to bring on an engagement. He called up more guns to join him on the hilltop, then ordered two companies of the Fourth Brigade to advance towards the river.

These were men of the First Massachusetts Regiment, led by Lieutenant Colonel George D. Wells. As they moved forward, they came under scattered fire from retreating skirmishers. In a wood one of the companies, commanded by Lieutenant W. H. B. Smith, ran into a group of Southerners who were in grey uniforms similar to their own. 'Who are you?', the Southerners called. 'Massachusetts men,' they replied. There was an immediate volley and Lieutenant Smith was killed. The confusion of uniforms was to cause more trouble in the next four days.

The Massachusetts men emerged on to clearer ground just above Blackburn's Ford to find themselves under heavy fire from three sides and from an enemy they could not see. 'We were in the thick of it full 15 minutes,' Colonel Wells said, 'the balls humming like a bee-hive.' He organized his men, however, and they returned the enemy fire with sufficient accuracy to cause consternation among some of the raw Southern soldiers. Longstreet later wrote in his *Memoirs*: 'The first pouring-down volleys were most startling to the new troops. Part of my line broke and started at a run. To stop the alarm I rode with sabre in hand for the leading files, determined to give them all that was in the sword and my horse's heels, or stop the break. They seemed to see as much danger in their rear as in front, and soon turned . . .'

Colonel Wells retreated to the top of the slope, where he found his brigade commander, Colonel I. B. Richardson, together with the rest of the brigade and General Tyler. Tyler had just ordered two guns to a forward position when Captain J. B. Fry, the chief of McDowell's staff, appeared. Fry asked Tyler to cease fighting. But Tyler's blood was up by this time. He sent the guns forward and, when they were forced back by enemy fire, he ordered Colonel Richardson to lead two of his regiments into the attack. Richardson's nickname was 'Fighting Dick'. He was never one to hold back if a fight was in prospect, and now he led the 12th New York Regiment down the hill, with the 1st Massachusetts in support.

The Southern forces had used the interval to bring up reinforcements – Longstreet's reserve

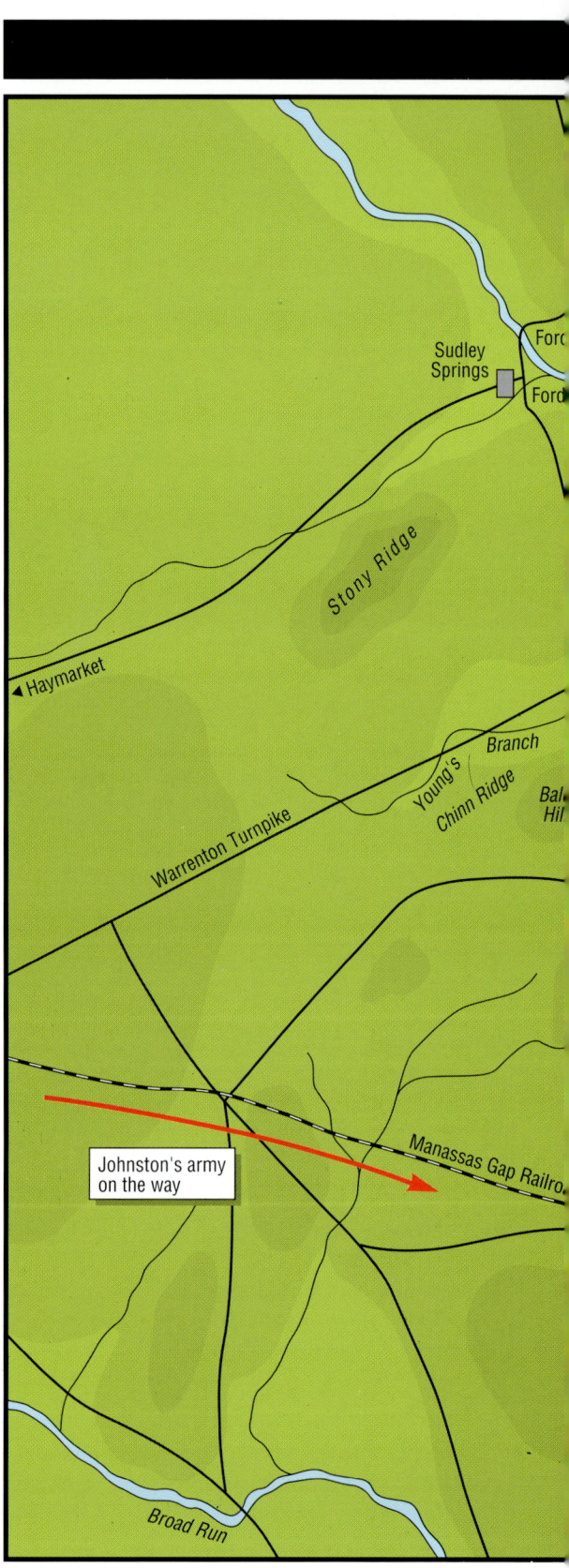

TYLER'S ATTACK

The Affair at Blackburn's Ford, 18 July

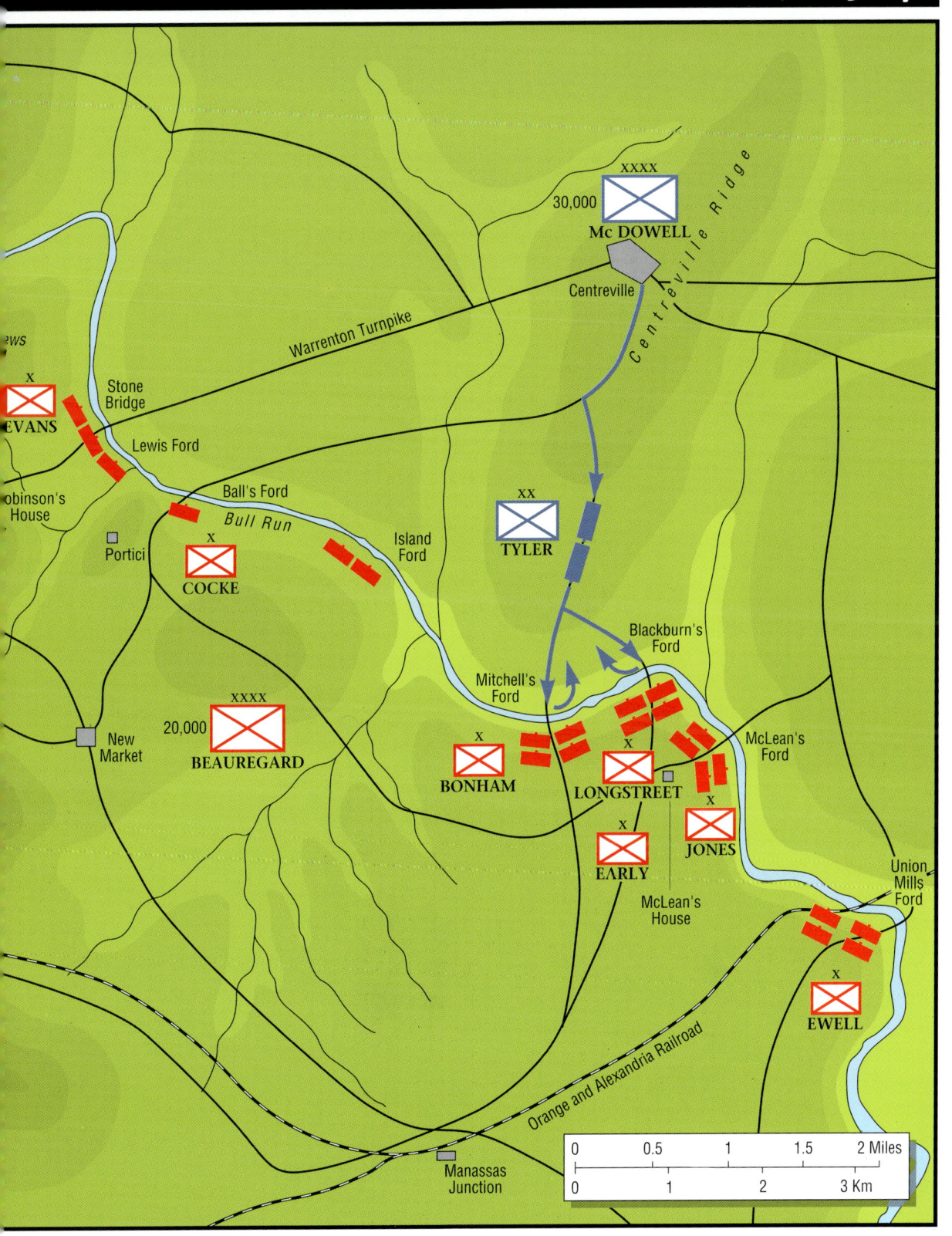

companies and men from Colonel Jubal Early's Sixth Brigade. So when the 12th New York emerged on the open ground above the river, and within range of the enemy's muskets, they came under fiercer fire than their predecessors had suffered. They took cover, returned fire and endured for half an hour. Then they ran.

When they saw this, Longstreet's men crossed the ford and launched themselves at the 1st Massachusetts Regiment, now cruelly exposed, and they too were forced to retreat back up the hill.

Richardson wanted to mount another attack. He had three regiments that had not yet been involved, and Sherman was bringing up his brigade at the double. Together, Richardson argued, they could 'clear out those fellows from the bottom in two hours'. But Tyler now felt he had gone far enough. He ordered a re-grouping behind the crest of the hill to repulse any Southern attack. No attack came.

Tyler Rebuked

Shortly before 4 p.m. McDowell rode up to make it forcefully clear to Tyler that he had exceeded his orders, and to insist that he had no intention of fighting the main battle that day.

For a while longer the guns on both sides continued firing. By chance a stray Northern shell landed in the fireplace of the McLean House, where Beauregard had set up his headquarters and where he and his staff were about to sit down to dinner. No one was hurt, but their dinner was ruined. Beauregard promptly ordered more guns to the front to exact revenge.

Altogether, the Northern army lost 83 men in this action: 19 killed, 38 wounded and 26 missing; the South lost 70: 15 killed, 53 wounded and two missing.

Beauregard had good reason to be pleased with the day's events. The Northern attack had come in the region where he had expected it. On the whole, his men had stood up well to their initiation. It had been a minor engagement, but such honours as there were certainly belonged to the South. His army's morale was strengthened. The auguries seemed good. But Beauregard was afraid that the main attack would be launched next morning, before Jo Johnston had time to bring his army to the field. The affair at Blackburn's Ford took place in the afternoon of Thursday 18 July. This was the day when Johnston started to move his army from Winchester to Manassas. They would not start to arrive until the next afternoon. In Beauregard's view, they would be too late. 'McDowell will be upon us early tomorrow', he told his staff, 'when we must fight him and sell our lives as dearly as possible.'

But McDowell, too, had much on his mind. The day had not gone well for him. General Tyler had shown a dangerous independence of spirit. Some of the volunteer soldiers had retreated in disorder. In an article he wrote later, Captain Fry, McDowell's assistant adjutant general, said: 'The Confederates, feeling that they had repulsed a heavy and real attack, were encouraged by the result. The Federal troops, on the other hand, were greatly depressed. The regiment which suffered most was completely demoralized, and McDowell thought that the depression of the repulse was felt throughout the army.'

Worst of all for McDowell was the fact that the nature of the terrain had ruled out the flanking movement he planned from the East. He now had to find an alternative, and that would take time.

THE BATTLE PLANS

The strategic advantages lay with Beauregard. His men were defending what they now regarded as their own separate homeland from the aggressor. He was operating on interior lines, well-served by railways. He had had time to survey the terrain and to prepare his defences in country that provided plenty of cover. Because the soldiers and many of the officers on both sides were largely untrained, it made best sense to hold his men in position and let the enemy charge at them, uphill, wasting strength.

But such a scheme did not accord with Beauregard's grandiloquent notions of military splendour. Time and again, in the days before the battle, he came up with impractical and potentially disastrous ideas. On 13 July he wrote to Johnston urging him to leave a token force in the Shenandoah Valley and bring the bulk of his army to Manassas, whence the two of them would advance to destroy first McDowell, then Patterson, then General McClellan's smaller army in West Virginia. Within a month, he claimed, at one brilliant stroke, the war would be won. He sent one of his staff, Colonel James Chesnut, to Richmond to present the plan to President Davis and General Lee. The listened politely, expressed admiration, then pointed out that Beauregard's assessment of his army's strength was greatly exaggerated, his assessment of its capabilities hopelessly optimistic.

A few days later, when McDowell's army started its march, Beauregard devised another aggressive scheme. He felt sure the Northerners would attack at Mitchell's Ford. As soon as this attack began, Longstreet and other brigades farther downstream would cross the river and hurl themselves at the enemy's left flank and rear, threatening Centreville. It was another wild plan. It depended on the enemy doing exactly what Beauregard expected him to do, made no provision for anything else, and exaggerated the capabilities of his own units. Fortunately, there was no prospect of its being attempted.

After the affair at Blackburn's Ford, when Johnston was at Piedmont station arranging his army's transport to Manassas, Beauregard proposed an even more unworkable scheme. Johnston should split his force in two. Half of them would go to Manassas and link up with Beauregard's army. The other half would march north of the railway, traverse the Bull Run Mountains and fall upon McDowell's right flank. Johnston later commented: 'I did not agree to the plan because, ordinarily, it is impracticable to direct the movements of troops so distant from each other, by roads so far separated, in such a manner as to combine their action on a field of battle.' At the time, he did not respond to Beauregard's suggestion. He merely sent a message to say his whole army was making for Manassas Junction.

The first of Jackson's Virginians reached Piedmont at 6 a.m. on Friday 19 July. The loading took a long time and, since there was only one locomotive available, it travelled very carefully. It was not until late that afternoon that they reached Manassas Junction. The train then hurried back for its next load, two regiments of Colonel Barstow's Brigade, men from Georgia and Kentucky. It was 8 a.m. on Saturday when they arrived at Manasss. The shuttle service speeded up when another train was commandeered. Johnston travelled with General Bee's Brigade (from Alabama and Mississippi and Tennessee) to reach Beauregard's headquarters about midday.

◀ *Colonel Israel B. Richardson, known as 'Fighting Dick', commanded the 4th Brigade of Tyler's Division, men from New York and Massachusetts. They were in action on 18 July but had little to do on the day of the main battle. (Anne S. K. Brown Mil. Coll., BUL)*

THE BATTLE PLANS

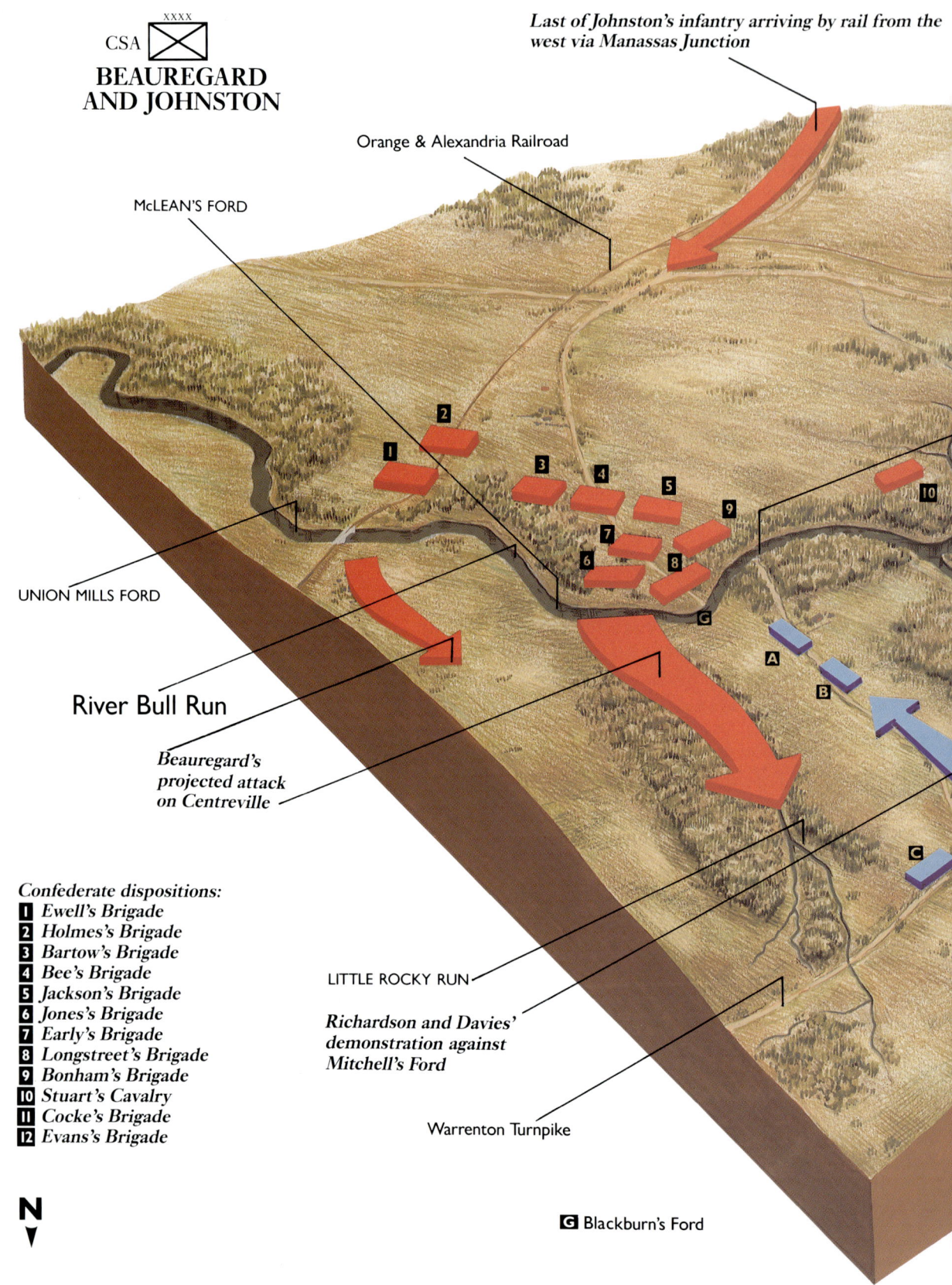

THE BATTLE PLANS

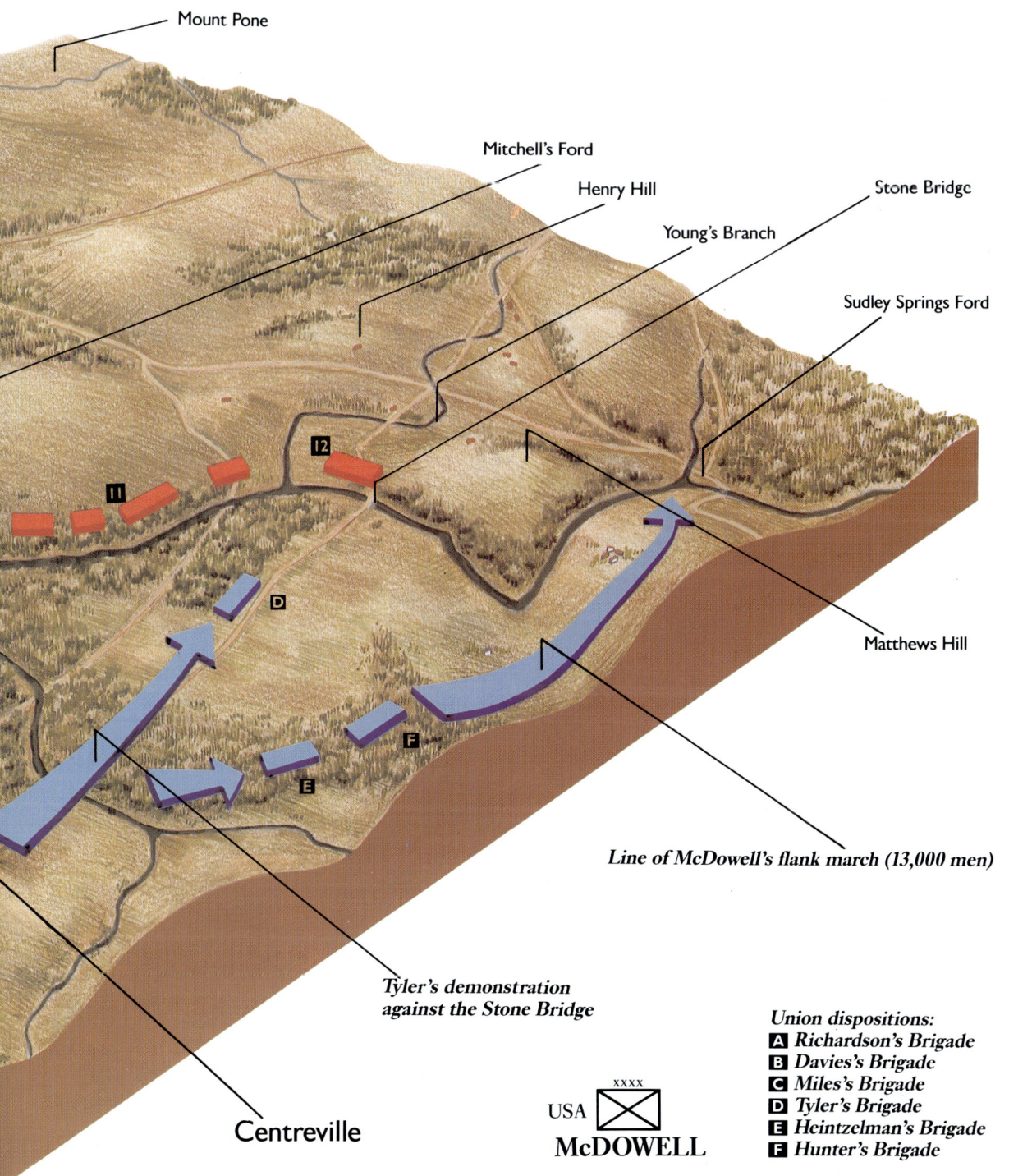

POSITIONS AND PLANS
on the eve of battle; as seen from the north.

Beauregard was a relieved man. No mention seems to have been made of his idea that Johnston should split his force in two. Half of it had now reached the Bull Run front and the rest was on the way. Further reinforcements were coming by rail from Richmond. And for two vital days, 19 and 20 July, McDowell had made no move.

There were two things McDowell had to do on the 19th. His men had run out of food, so fresh supplies had to be brought up in order that each man might go into battle with two days' rations in his haversack. The other task was to find a way, to the west, by which he might out-flank the enemy line. There was known to be a good ford, wide enough for wheeled vehicles, across the river at a place called Sudley Springs. He needed to be sure that the road to the ford would permit the reasonably trouble-free passage of two divisions, some 13,000 men.

He sent an engineering officer with a cavalry escort to find out. They rode a few miles along the road but had to turn back before reaching the ford because they ran into enemy patrols and did not want to arouse suspicion. It seemed a reasonable assumption that this was a feasible way to Sudley Springs, but McDowell wanted to be absolutely sure. So further patrols were sent, and it was not until midday on Saturday 20th that his engineers could assure him the route was practicable. In effect, a second day had been wasted.

McDowell knew he could delay no longer. Already some of his three-month' volunteers, the 4th Pennsylvania Regiment and the gunners of the 8th New York, were packing up to go, rejecting all pleas to stay for the fight. That night McDowell told his commanders his plans for the battle.

McDowell's Plan

The affair at Blackburn's Ford had convinced McDowell that it was in this area that the enemy expected his main attack. It was here, he felt sure, that Beauregard had concentrated his defences. McDowell was right. With this in mind, then, he decided to feint an attack here but send his main striking force round to the west to fall on the enemy's left flank and rear, severing the railway line before Johnston could reach the field – there were rumours that Johnston was already on the way, but McDowell dismissed them.

On the evening of Saturday 20 July, McDowell issued his orders. Tyler's First Division would stage the feint attack on the Stone Bridge, 'making proper demonstrations'. Richardson's brigade would make similar threatening gestures towards Blackburn's Ford. The Fifth Division, commanded by Colonel D. S. Miles, would stay in reserve behind them, in the Centreville area. Meanwhile the Second and Third Divisions, totalling more than 13,000 men, would march westwards in the dark, cross the river at Sudley Springs at dawn, out-flank the enemy and carry the day. McDowell himself would be with them.

It was a simple and reasonable plan. Perhaps it would have been wiser to launch his feint attacks farther downstream, more distant from the flanking movement. There was also the danger, if Johnston's army was arriving, that the flanking force would come up against Southern soldiers comparatively fresh from their train journey. But the biggest flaw in McDowell's plan lay in the detail of its timing. His first intention was that his columns should move off that evening and cover some miles before bivouacking. But several of his commanders argued that the men should be allowed to rest until the early hours of Sunday morning, and McDowell allowed himself to be persuaded. It was a mistake on two counts: the night march proved something of a nightmare; and McDowell was able to consume one of his colossal suppers, with the result that he felt seriously unwell next morning.

Southern Plans

On the farther side of the river, too, plans were being made and given for the morrow's battle. The first problem, when Johnston arrived at Beauregard's headquarters, was to determine who was in overall command. Johnston was not in any doubt about this. He out-ranked Beauregard and had taken the precaution, a few day's before, of getting confirmation from President Davis that he was to be in charge. Even so, in his account of the battle that was published after the Civil War, Beauregard gave a very different impression: 'General Johnston was the ranking officer, and entitled, therefore, to assume command of the united forces; but as the extensive field of operations was one which I had occupied since the beginning of June, and with which I was thoroughly familiar in all its extent and military bearings, while he was wholly unacquainted with it, and, moreover, as I had made my plans and dispositions for the maintenance of the position, General Johnston, in view of the gravity of the impending issue, preferred not to assume the responsibilities of the chief direction of the forces during the battle, but to assist me upon the field. Thereupon, I explained my plans and purposes, to which he agreed.' It is characteristic Beauregard. He lacked most of his hero, Napoleon's, skills as a commander but had all his assiduity in the favourable rewriting of history.

It was Johnston who took command. But he was a tired man by the time he reached Manassas and wise enough to recognize that Beauregard knew the terrain and the current dispositions far better than he did. So he listened while Beauregard expounded the situation and his plans, gave his approval and went off to catch up on some sleep. Both generals agreed that the battle would have to take place next day. Otherwise, there was a danger that Patterson might arrive to tilt the balance of strength heavily against them.

Beauregard and his staff settled down to write out the orders. His plan was, of course, an aggressive one. His line extended some six miles, from Union Bridge on the right, the point where the railway crossed the river, to Stone Bridge on the left, where the river was spanned by the Warrenton Turnpike road. Despite the setback the Northern army had suffered two days earlier at Blackburn's Ford, Beauregard still clung to his conviction that the main enemy thrust would come in that region, at Mitchell's Ford especially. So he had placed the bulk of his army, two-thirds of his men, on the right and right-centre of his line, with Johnston's men behind them in support. His left flank, where the river offered the best crossing points, he planned to guard with a brigade and a half, just over 4,000 men. At daybreak on Sunday morning, Beauregard ordered, his leading brigades in the centre would force their way across the river and, supported by the others, drive a way uphill towards Centreville in the area where he expected to find the bulk of McDowell's army.

It was a rash and ill-considered plan and the orders to his commanders were ill-written, unclear and sometimes downright impenetrable. It was a matter of the greatest good fortune for the Southern cause that it proved impossible even to begin to try and implement the plan.

That Saturday night was calm and lovely. On both sides of the river thousands of men lay on the ground, gazing at the starry sky and wondering what the next day would bring. The great majority of them, who had never been in action, tried to imagine what it would be like and worried about how they would behave under fire, whether they would disgrace themselves under the eyes of their comrades and old friends, whether they would see another night sky. All the big talk in the bars, all the parades and speeches and cheering girls were behind them now, and tomorrow they would come face to face with the reality. Even those officers who had known battle before had experienced nothing as big as this.

On the Northern side there had been many visitors to the camps during the day. The pioneer photograper, Mathew Brady, was there with his bulky equipment: 'We are making history now,' he said, 'and every picture that we get will be valuable.' There were many newspaper reporters in the camps. The editor of the *New York Times*, Henry J. Raymond, wrote to his paper: 'This is one of the most beautiful nights that the imagination can conceive. The sky is perfectly clear, the moon is full and bright, and the air as still as if it were not within a few hours to be disturbed by the roar of canon and the shouts of contending men ... An hour ago I rode back to General McDowell's headquarters ... As I rose over the crest of the hill, and caught a view of the scene in front, it seemed a picture of enchantment. The bright moon cast the woods which bound the field into deep shadows, through which the camp fires shed a clear and brilliant glow. On the extreme right, in the neighbourhood of the Fire Zouaves, a party were singing "The Star-spangled Banner", and from the left rose the sweet strains of a magnificent band, intermingling opera airs with patriotic bursts of "Hail Columbia" and "Yankee Doodle" ...

THE BATTLE PLANS

Dawn 21 July: positions of opposing forces before Tyler's gun

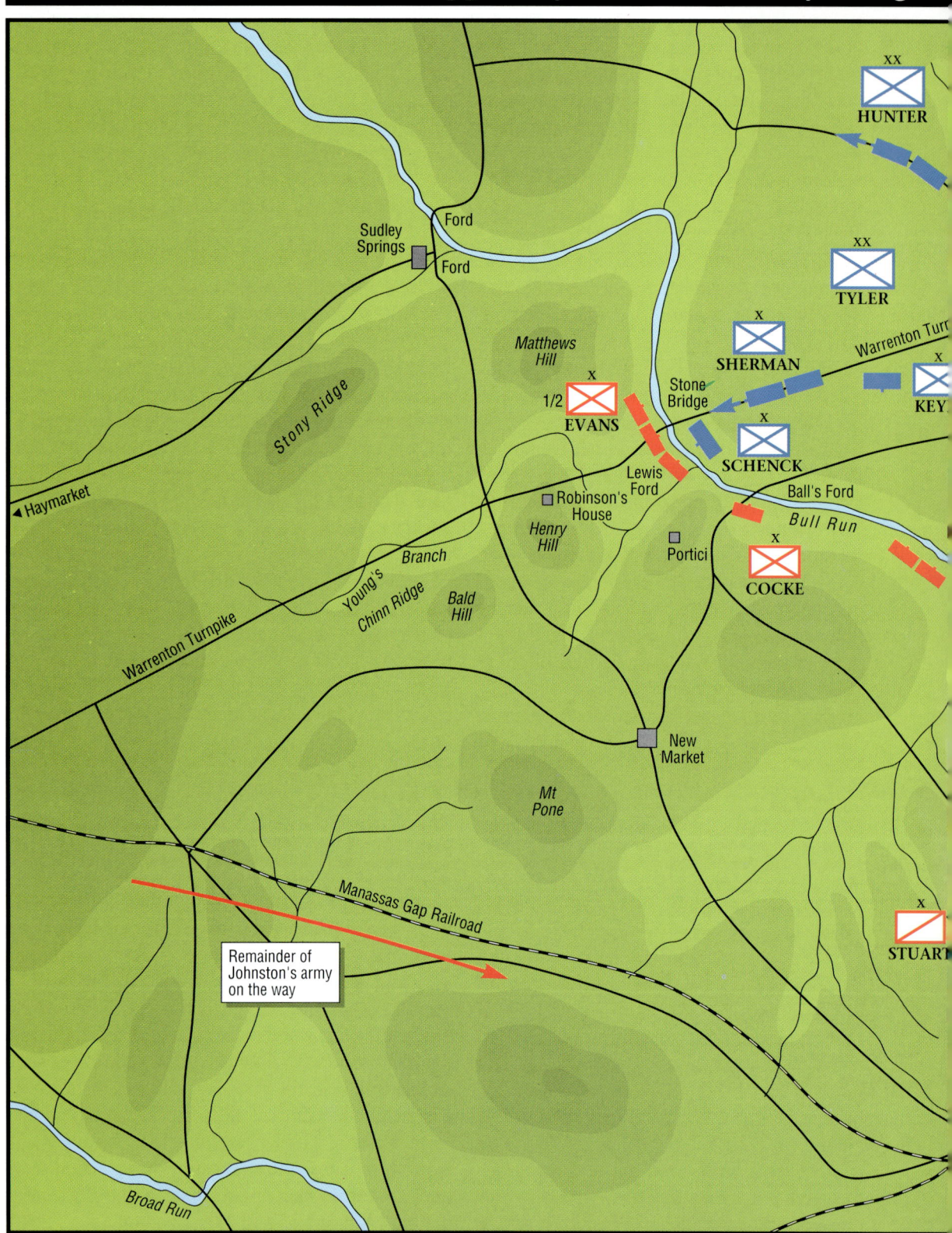

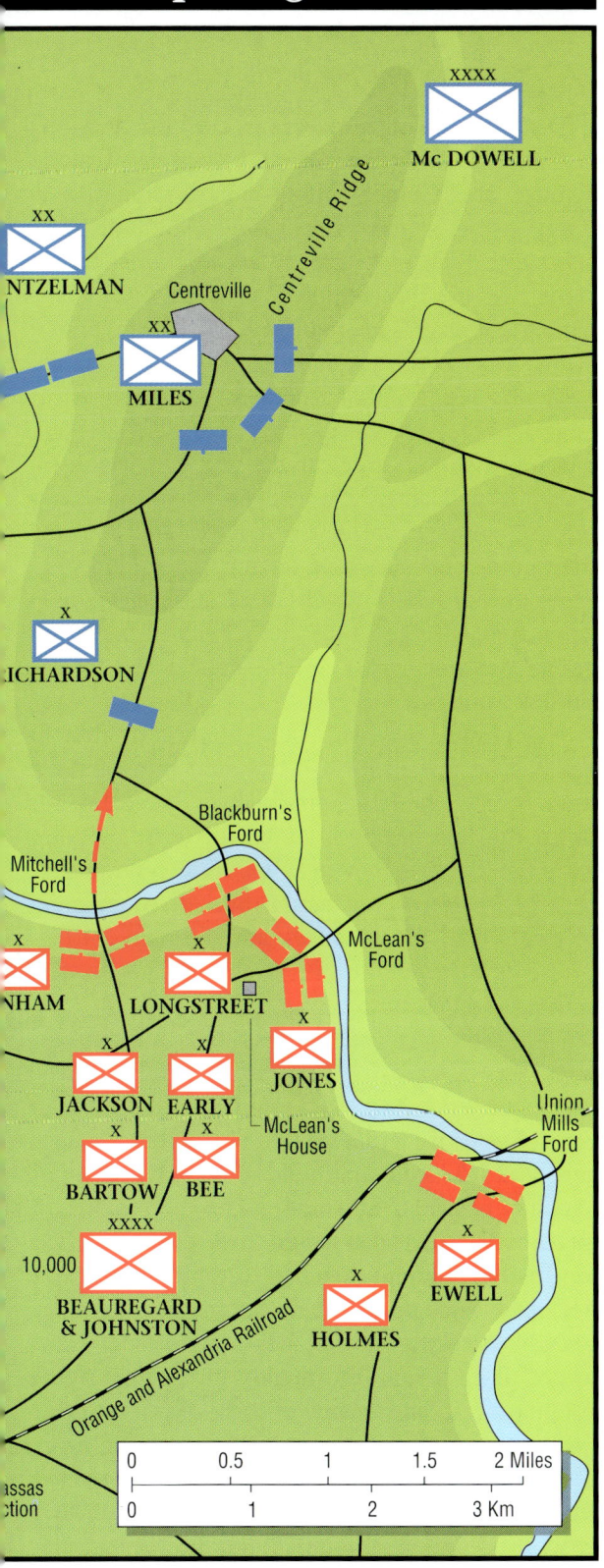

red the opening shots

THE BATTLE BEGINS

Reveille was sounded in Tyler's Division at 2 a.m. on Sunday 21 July. The idea was that Tyler's three brigades – Schenck's, then Sherman's, then Keyes' – would move off smartly and leave the road clear for the two divisions that had the long flanking march to make.

It did not work out like that. Men had trouble getting their gear together in the dark; the officers had trouble getting their men together. Schenck placed skirmishers on either side of the road, volunteer soldiers from Ohio, and they had a terrible time hacking their way through tangled undergrowth. Meanwhile his artillerymen and their horses were struggling to move their enormous 30-pounder cannon, weighing three tons, along the road. The first half mile took them an hour. For the men marching behind, it meant endless stops and starts, long periods of standing and wondering what was going on ahead, much confusion and bad temper.

As a result, it was not until long after first light, sometime after 6 a.m., that the 30-pounder gun fired three rounds across the Bull Run as a signal to McDowell that Tyler was in position at last to begin his 'proper demonstrations' at the Stone Bridge. It was also a signal to all the men of both armies that the battle was about to start.

The shells flew high over the heads of the small brigade that Beauregard had posted at the Stone Bridge on the extreme left of his line. The whole force was no more than 1,100 men – the 4th South Carolina Regiment and the 1st Louisiana, with two canon and a handful of cavalry. Their commander, though, was a formidable figure, Colonel Nathan G. Evans. Evans was a young man, 37 years old and full of fire. He came from South Carolina, graduated from West Point in 1848 and took part in a few minor Indian campaigns. He was a character, careless of reputation or rank, wild in manner, a great drinker and

▲ *Colonel Nathan G. ('Shanks') Evans was a fiery and uncouth officer, but his independent initiative on the morning of Bull Run and the skill of his fighting proved invaluable to the Southern cause. He held Tyler at the Stone Bridge, then – when he saw his army's left flank under serious threat – moved the bulk of his small brigade to Matthews Hill, where he fought another ferocious and successful defensive action. He later claimed that he 'and a few private gentlemen' had won the battle – with some help from the Almighty.*

curser and bragger. An orderly was deputed to keep close at hand, with a one-gallon drum of whisky on his back to keep the colonel well-fuelled. His nick-name was 'Shanks'. He loved a rough-house and felt unfairly starved, so far, of action. This Sunday morning was to put that right. But there was more to 'Shanks' Evans than just a bar-room brawler: he had a sharp eye for the way a battle was developing and the confidence to take important decisions promptly, on his own initiative. This acute, pugnacious personality was to have a major influence on the course of events at Bull Run. For the moment, though, as Tyler's guns thundered and his men moved gingerly down the slope towards the Stone Bridge, Evans held his fire, giving the enemy no indication of his strength or of his positions.

The Flank March

The roar of the big gun was heard by the divisional commanders of the flanking march, Colonel Hunter and Colonel Heintzelman, with dismay. They were some three hours behind their schedule. They were already late when they turned right off the Warrenton Turnpike and struck across country. The road they had been told to follow was a cart track, mostly through woods. The men who led, the 2nd Rhode Island Regiment of Colonel Burnside's brigade, had to use axes and picks and shovels to clear the way and widen the track. It was already warm, promising a day of intense summer heat. To make matters worse, their guide chose a wrong turning that added some three miles to their march. It was almost 9 o'clock when they emerged from the trees and began the gentle descent across open fields to the ford at Sudley Springs.

McDowell was with this column. At first he had felt so unwell he had travelled in a carriage; then he switched to horseback to move up and down the line urging his men forward. By going with the flank march he effectively relinquished control of the overall battle, but his other commanders had clear orders and he opted to go where he believed – rightly in the event – the vital action would take place.

The Southern commanders, too, in a different way, were already beginning to lose control over the course of events. McDowell's early start pre-empted Beauregard's aggressive plans. Beauregard and Johnston continued to hope that it might become possible, at some stage, to mount the attack with which they could threaten Centreville, but for the moment they had to wait and see what McDowell was up to. Their command system was already breaking down. Beauregard sometimes forgot to pass vital information on to his brigade commanders, and many of his messages never reached their destinations. Those that did arrive were often ambiguous and confusing. When Beauregard saw Tyler's brigades on the high ground beyond the Stone Bridge, he realized that

Evans' tiny force could not be expected to hold them at bay for long. So he ordered the brigades of Jackson, Bee and Bartow to move quickly to positions behind Evans.

On the far side of the river, General Tyler was acting with extreme caution. He had deployed Sherman's brigade on the northern side of the Turnpike, Schenck's on the South. According to Sherman's official report, they then 'remained quietly in position till after 10 a.m.'. Activity was confined to the firing of their artillery and a little tentative skirmishing towards the bridge.

Only three days before, Tyler had been admonished for exceeding his orders at Blackburn's Ford. Now he went to the opposite extreme. There seems little doubt that had he made vigorous efforts to take the bridge while it was still feebly defended – he outnumbered Evan's brigade by more than seven-to-one – he could have established a firm foothold on the far bank of the river and distracted the enemy's attention from the flank march. But he stuck to the letter of his orders and did little.

By 8 o'clock that morning Evans felt sure the enemy's move towards the Stone Bridge was a feint. Half an hour later he saw clouds of dust two miles away to the north and guessed that a big enemy column was moving round to attack from the west. Shortly afterwards the flank march was spotted by Beauregard's Chief Signal Officer, Captain Alexander. Edward Porter Alexander was an intelligent and conscientious officer. He had been the star pupil of the pioneer of visual signalling in the field, Dr. Albert J. Myer, an army surgeon who had devised a method of sending messages considerable distances by flag signals ('wigwagging') in daytime, by torches at night.

▼ *The Stone Bridge carries the Warrenton Turnpike across River Bull Run. It played a vital part in the battle. At the start of the day it marked the extreme left of the Southern defensive line and was guarded by Colonel 'Shanks' Evans's small brigade. Unfortunately for the Northern cause, Tyler's attack was so feebly maintained that Evans was able to hold the bridge and move farther left to delay the advance of McDowell's flank movement.*

THE BATTLE BEGINS

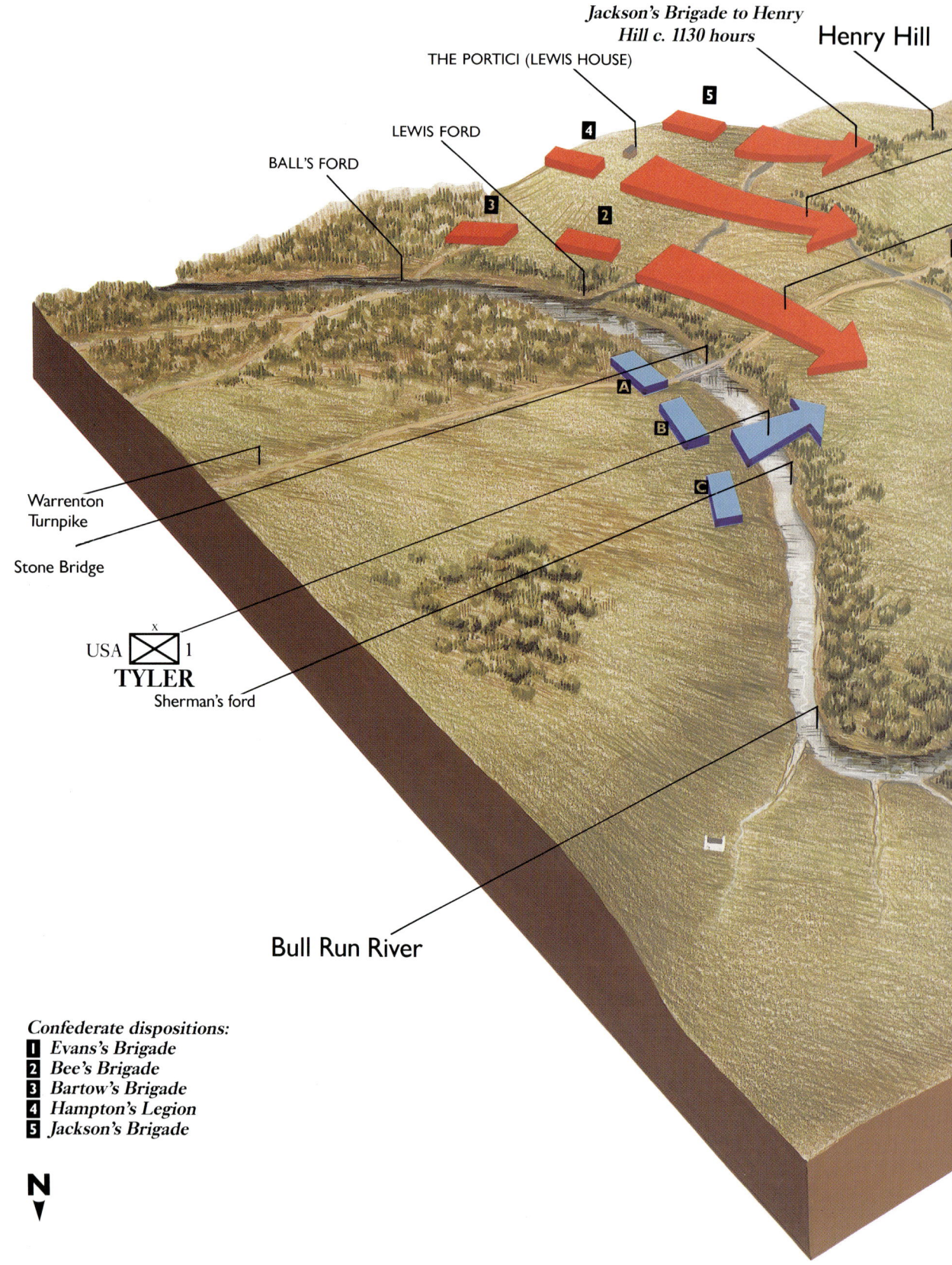

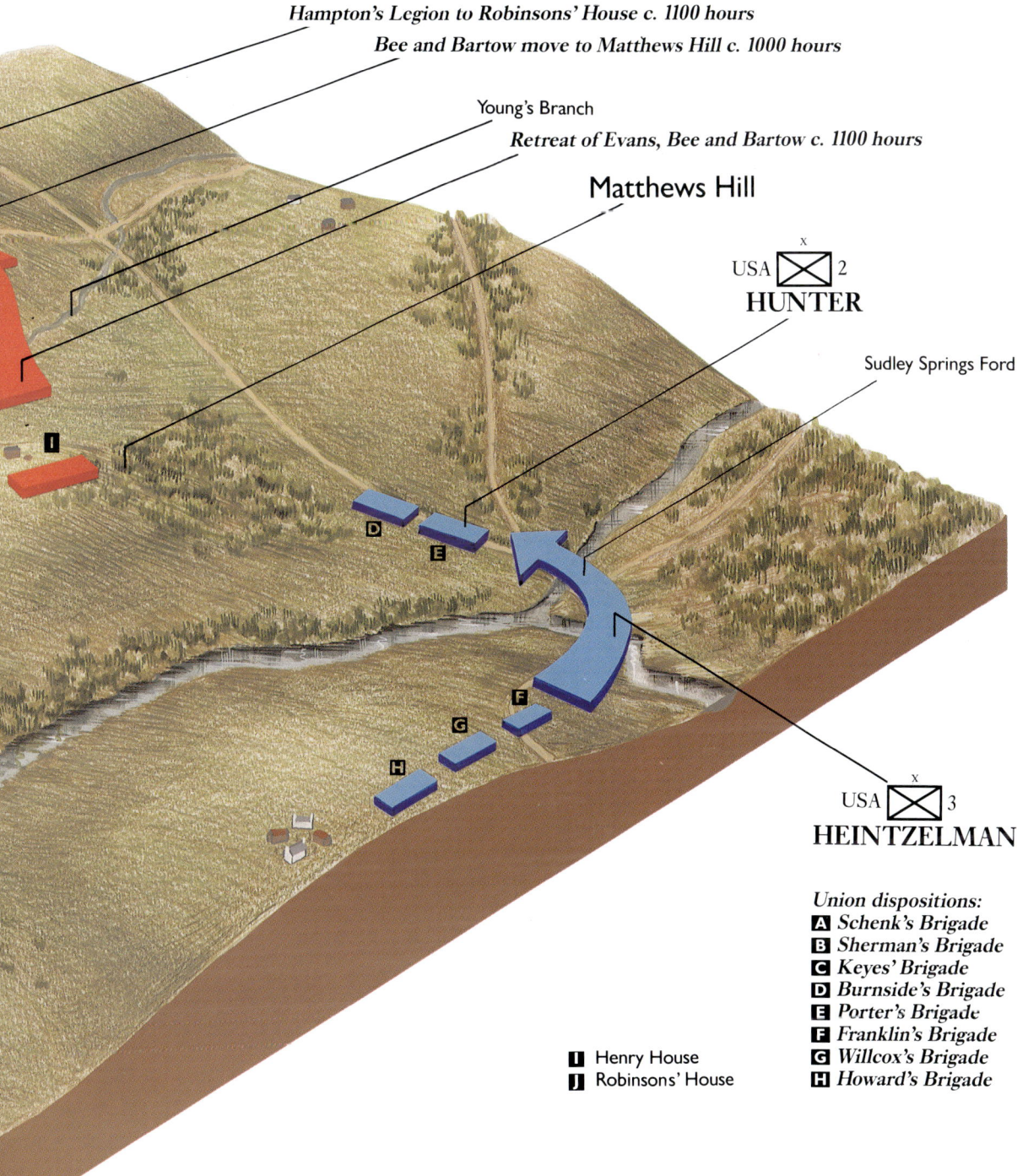

MATTHEWS HILL

as seen from the north. The situation at 0915 hours (and subsequently) when Evans's firing on Hunter's leading brigade announced the beginning of the main battle.

▲ Colonel Ambrose E. Burnside is oddly immortalised in the English language by the word that now designates his style in whiskers – 'sideburns'. It was his brigade that was first halted by 'Shanks' Evans in position on Matthews Hill. From then on, they were in the thick of the action until the retreat in the late afternoon. (Anne S. K. Brown Mil. Coll., BUL)

▲ David Hunter commanded the 2nd Division of the Northern army, which led the big flanking movement. 21 July marked his 59th birthday: he celebrated by getting wounded in the initial engagement at Matthews Hill and had to hand over his command to Burnside. (Anne S. K. Brown Mil. Coll., BUL)

Alexander was a young man – he had graduated from West Point only four years before – and ambitious. For weeks before the battle he had been busy setting up lookout and signal platforms and training his men in the codes. He had been rudely awakened that morning when the second shell from Tyler's 30-pounder tore through the roof of his tent. Now, shortly before 9 a.m., he was surveying the scene by telescope from his headquarters signal tower when he saw the morning sunlight glinting on cannon and bayonets far away to the north. Immediately he signalled to Evans: 'Look out for your left. You are turned.'

Evans Moves

It confirmed what Evans already suspected, and he acted immediately. Leaving only four companies to cover the bridge, he took the rest of his men and two six-pounder guns as rapidly as possible to his left and found an excellent position on Matthews Hill. There was good tree cover for his riflemen and his guns as well as a fine view across the open ground the Northerners would have to cross. He placed the 4th South Carolina Regiment on the left with one gun; the 1st Louisiana on the right with the other. Soon after that, the 4th Alabama Regiment arrived to help. They were just in time.

It was about 9.15 when the leading column of McDowell's flanking force, men of the 1st Rhode Island Regiment, emerged from the woods below Matthews Hill. Evans immediately fired a volley. The real battle had begun.

The commander of the Second Brigade of the Second Division, which now came under fire, was a most imposing military figure, Colonel Ambrose E. Burnside. He sported a magnificent black moustache and luxuriant side-whiskers so impressive that he gave a new word to the English language – 'sideburns'. He was a West Point graduate who had seen action against the Apaches, but that was years ago. He retired from the army in 1853 to go into business, manufacturing a breech-loading rifle. When the Civil War broke out he re-enlisted, raised the 1st Rhode Island Regiment, took command as its colonel and soon afterwards was in charge of a brigade. There were two Rhode Island regiments in the brigade and the young governor of Rhode Island, William Sprague, although a civilian had come along too, to see how the boys acquitted themselves.

Evans' initial volley took them by surprise. They were not expecting to meet the enemy so soon. And they were tired. The day was already hot and they had been on their feet, stopping and marching and clearing a way, for more than six hours. It was with difficulty that Burnside got his riflemen spread out into line. They began to return the enemy's fire, though he was not easy to see.

The divisional commander, Brigadier General David Hunter, was on the scene very quickly. He had served nearly 40 years in the army but had never been in action. It was his 59th birthday, and he was to see more than enough action in the next few minutes. He struggled to get the rest of Burnside's brigade into battle line and the batteries into position to answer the fire of Evan's guns, then led infantry and artillery towards the enemy, up the gentle lower slopes of the hill. They came under intense fire, and Hunter was badly wounded in his left cheek and neck. As he was being carried from the field, he told Burnside, 'I leave the matter in your hands.'

The general standard of infantry marksmanship at Bull Run was poor. Most of the raw recruits made the mistake of firing too high. But the fire that Colonel Evans brought to bear was unusually effective. Colonel John Slocum of the Second Rhode Island was mortally wounded in this fierce little action. Burnside had his horse shot from under him. The Northern forces, superior in numbers to Evans's from the start and increasing in strength all the time as fresh columns arrived, were effectively halted. For the second time that day 'Shanks' Evans proved he had the knack of giving the enemy the impression that his forces were far stronger than they were – Burnside thought he was dealing with at least six infantry regiments and two, probably more, full batteries of artillery.

But Evans knew he could not hold out indefinitely against the force that was building up against him. He had two guns and about 900 men, holding off Hunter's two brigades, a total of nearly 6,000 men and several batteries. On top of that, Heintzelman's brigades were rapidly approaching. Evans played for time cleverly. Sending urgent messages requesting reinforcement, he launched the men of the 1st Louisiana Regiment, known as 'Wheat's Tigers', in an attack on the re-forming Northern line. Major Roberdeau Wheat, a very tough individual, led the charge and was severely wounded. They were beaten back but not before they had further hardened the Northerners' belief that they were dealing with a considerable and confident body of men.

Reinforcements Arrive

Evans was vastly relieved when he saw support arriving: General Barnard E. Bee with two-and-a-half regiments, closely followed by Colonel Francis Bartow with two regiments of Georgians. The arrival, at the double, of some 2,800 men did much to redress the imbalance. It was shortly after 10 a.m..

Evans had stalled the Northerners' advance for almost an hour and endured much, especially from the expert gunfire of Charles Griffin and J. B. Ricketts. It was time to hand over to fresh men.

General Bee had all of Evans's relish for a good fight. He had distinguished himself in the Mexican War but had been starved of fighting since then, and his great concern on the morning of Bull Run was that he might miss the action. He was furious when he was moved to the Stone Bridge area because he was sure the real fight would be elsewhere. He waited as patiently as he could, listening to the noise of the intensifying battle a mile or more to his left, and finally determined, on his own initiative, to double towards the sound of the guns. Together with his artillery commander, Captain John D. Imboden, he galloped to the top of Henry Hill, surveyed the scene and said: 'Here is the battlefield and we are

▲Brigadier Barnard E. Bee of South Carolina commanded the 3rd Brigade of Johnston's army, the first unit of that army to get into the fight proper. As Evans had done before him, he shifted his men to the far left of the line when he saw that that was where the action was. He arrived in the nick of time to save Evans, and from then on he and his men were at the heart of the fight. It was he who likened Jackson's stand to a stone wall. Soon after that, Bee, riding at the head of his brigade, was mortally wounded.

▲Colonel Francis Bartow, commander of Johnston's 2nd Brigade, was quick to follow Bee's Brigade to the threatened left of the line, with two regiments of Georgians, He took part in the desperate charge against the Northern lines at Matthews Hill, then in the battle for Henry Hill. He was killed on Henry Hill. (Anne S. K. Brown Mil. Coll., BUL)

in for it! Bring up your guns as quickly as possible, and I'll look round for a good position.'

Bee marched his men (volunteers from Alabama and Mississippi) down the hill, formed them into line and established them on Evan's right. Behind him came Bartow with his Georgians, and they positioned themselves with their guns on Bee's right. Now the line of Southerners – Evans, Bee and Bartow – planned to launch themselves in a desperate attack, hoping to overrun and silence the Northern batteries that had been pounding them hard.

They charged downhill towards the brigades of Burnside and Porter who, as the senior, was now in command. One of Bartow's Georgians said two days later: 'This bold and fearful movement was made through a perfect storm.' When they had fired a volley, the Northern line rose and advanced. Within moments the battle dissolved into a confused, short-range turmoil. 'It was a whirlwind of bullets,' one man remembered. Many men fell, killed or wounded. The toll was heaviest among the officers. Units found themselves leaderless and lost. In the end, as it had to do, the sheer weight of the Northern numbers turned the scales, and the Southerners retreated back up the hill in disarray.

McDowell was anxious. The stubborn resistance of the Southerners had now held up his outflanking movement by nearly two hours, and clouds of dust in the distance towards Manassas meant the enemy had more units on the way. But he too could summon up reinforcements. He sent orders to Tyler, still virtually becalmed above the Stone Bridge, to press his attacks much more vigorously. And at last (it was now about 11 a.m.) the leading brigades of Heintzelman's Division – men from Massachusetts and Minnesota – were moving up to the front.

Heintzelman was 56. He had fought with distinction against the Mexicans and the Indians, but he was a prickly, short-tempered man, and the morning so far had been a succession of frustrations. He arrived on the scene just as the Southern regiments were pulling back up Matthews Hill. At first the Northern line was in almost as much confusion as that of the retreating Southerners. Heintzelman could find no one who seemed to be in command. Then McDowell appeared and immediately ordered Heintzelman to use his fresh regiments to keep up the pressure on the enemy. He tried a frontal attack, but it was beaten back. He sent two regiments – the 11th New York and Ellsworth's Zouaves – round to the right to attack the enemy flank, but they were held off by Evans, who had managed to re-group his diminishing force. Heintzelman was planning a third assault when he saw the enemy pulling back from the top of Matthews Hill. Bartow had seen another powerful enemy force approaching from the north – this was Sherman's brigade, 3,400 strong.

Sherman Joins In

After the initial march down the Warrenton Turnpike in the early hours, Sherman's men had had a quiet time. Sherman used it to reconnoitre along the river bank, upstream from the Stone Bridge, to see if there was a possible crossing place. He was in luck. As he watched, a Southern horseman rode down the slope on the opposite side of the river, disappeared briefly, then reappeared on the near side to shout some words of taunting abuse. Sherman did not react. He had found out what he wanted. Close at hand, here was a fording place not so exposed to the enemy as the

▲ Brigadier General S. P. Heintzelman commanded the 3rd Division of the Federal army, which marched behind Hunter's Division on the flank march by way of Sudley Springs. As a result, his brigades were into action later than Hunter's, but they were very heavily involved in the fight for control of Henry Hill. (Anne S. K. Brown Mil. Coll., BUL)

▲ The point on the River Bull Run, slightly upstream of the Stone Bridge, where Sherman's sharp eyes had noticed a Southern horseman fording the stream earlier in the morning. He got his brigade across here without difficulty when the order came to join the battle on Matthews Hill.

Stone Bridge itself and which did not involve the long detour to Sudley Springs. When the order came, shortly after 11 a.m., to join the battle on Matthews Hill, he took his brigade – with the 69th New York in the lead – comfortably across the ford, though he had to leave his artillery behind.

Sherman's initial worry was about the problem of identification. Some of his regiments were in grey uniforms, and he was afraid they would be fired upon by their own side as they advanced. In the event, the first sizeable force they came upon were the enemy, General Bee's 4th Alabama Regiment. The Alabamans were deceived and held their fire. The volley from the 69th New York killed the colonel of the 4th Alabama and seriously wounded the major, leaving them leaderless. They retreated hastily.

The retreat was very close to being a rout, but Sherman did not pursue the enemy as he fell back across the Warrenton Turnpike and up the slopes of Henry Hill beyond. It was necessary first to find his fellow commanders and work to a concerted plan. He deployed his brigade behind that of Colonel Porter, who told him Hunter had been wounded and that McDowell was in the area. He found McDowell, who was feeling much better than he had been earlier that morning.

Victory, McDowell felt, was now within his grasp. The enemy was on the run. The arrival of Sherman, with Keyes' Brigade close behind him, meant that he had succeeded in concentrating more than half his army on the weak and now sorely battered left flank of the enemy line. One more push, it seemed, and the day was won. Sherman's regiments were moved in line to take the centre position, with Burnside on his right and Porter on his left. The advance was sounded and, as the men moved forward, McDowell rode along the line shouting, 'Victory! Victory! The day is ours.'

▲An artist's impression of the battle, entitled 'Gen. Burnside's Brigade at the Battle of Bull Run'. Presumably, it is an effort to recapture the moment when Burnside, together with Porter's Brigade, had driven Evans, Bee and Bartow from Matthews Hill, and was preparing to attack Henry Hill. (Anne S. K. Brown Mil. Coll., BUL)

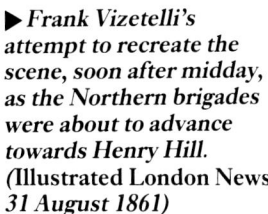

▶Frank Vizetelli's attempt to recreate the scene, soon after midday, as the Northern brigades were about to advance towards Henry Hill. (Illustrated London News, 31 August 1861)

THE FIGHT FOR HENRY HILL

Matthews Hill, between River Bull Run and the Warrenton Turnpike, declines southwards to a small tributary stream called Young's Branch, which presented no obstacle to advancing soldiers. Beyond the stream the ground rises gently, mostly through woodland, to the Warrenton Turnpike that crossed the Northern line of advance from East to West. Beyond the turnpike rise the steeper slopes of Henry Hill, dotted with trees but with much open grassland as well. It is not a particularly steep incline, but it gains height steadily for some 800 yards to reach a wide, undulating plateau with woodland on its farther side. It was here that the key encounter of the First Battle of Bull Run was to take place, a long and fierce and fluctuating struggle.

In July 1861 there were two modest houses on this hillside. A hundred yards above the turnpike, at the top of a grassy lane with split-rail fencing on each side, stood Robinson's House, the clap-board cottage of a freed slave. Almost at the top of the hill, just where it begins to level out to the summit plateau, there was a slightly grander place called Henry House. This had been the farm and family home of the man who gave his name to the hill, Dr. Isaac Henry, a retired naval surgeon. By 1861 he had been long dead, but his widow, Judith, a helpless invalid of 84, and two of their sons who were both semi-invalids, were still there, being looked after by a young Negress called Rosa Stokes. They were all in the house as the Northern army approached.

The advance of McDowell's line towards Henry Hill brought the sounds of battle closer to the two Southern commanders, Johnston and Beauregard. They were stationed at the centre of their line, on a small hill just south of Mitchell's Ford and nearly two miles to the south-east of Henry Hill. From Beauregard's point of view this was the proper place to be. He expected Mc-

Dowell's main attack in this area and planned to launch his own assault, towards Centreville, with the brigades on his immediate right.

Unfortunately, nothing seemed to be happening as he had expected. Soon after first light the enemy had appeared on the slopes beyond Mitchell's Ford, but since then, bewilderingly, he had made no strenuous effort to press ahead with his advance. At the same time, Beauregard's own orders for a push across Bull Run by the brigades on the right wing of his line – Longstreet's at Blackburn's Ford, Jones's at McLean's Ford and Ewell's (with Holmes's in support) at the railway crossing – were clearly not being implemented. In fact, Longstreet and Jones had moved their forward units across the river and formed them into line; then they waited for Ewell to join them on their right. He did not arrive. Beauregard's courier had never reached Brigadier General Ewell with the orders. The courier dispatched to

▲ Henry House as seen from the back of the Robinson House.

◀ The lane, with split-rail fencing either side, that leads from the Warrenton Turnpike to Robinson's House. It was here that Colonel Wade Hampton made the gallant and successful stand that further delayed the Northern advance.

▶ A private of the 1st Virginia Cavalry, the riders who distinguished themselves before and during (and long after) First Bull Run, under the command of Colonel 'Jeb' Stuart. Far right, a private of the 23rd Virginia Regiment. (Illustration by Michael Youens)

▲ Brigadier General Richard S. Ewell, commanding Beauregard's 2nd Brigade, was desperately keen to get into the fight and was continually frustrated. It was intended that he should be part of the drive on Centreville, but – through administrative incompetence – Beauregard's orders never reached him. Like the Grand Old Duke of York, Ewell marched his men up and down all that hot summer's day and never got anywhere. (Anne S. K. Brown Mil. Coll., BUL)

▲ Wade Hampton was outstanding even in an era of remarkable men. Some said he was the greatest landowner in the South. In the South Carolina state legislature he spoke out for secession. And when the Civil War came he threw everything – his fortune and his considerable energies – into raising and training his own Legion. He took 650 men to Bull Run. They only just arrived, in time, by railway from the South, but played an important part in holding up the North's attack on Henry Hill until Jackson had organized his defensive line on the summit plateau. (Anne S. K. Brown Mil. Coll., BUL)

Brigadier General Holmes also failed to deliver. Since no one on Beauregard's staff had noted the couriers' names, these failures in communication were never explained. So both generals held their positions and waited, with mounting and ill-concealed impatience. Ewell especially, 44 years old and desperately eager for action, made no secret of his feelings. Finally he got orders to advance, moved fast across the river, and then got orders to pull back again and resume a defensive position. By the end of the day, it was reckoned, Ewell's Brigade had marched and counter-marched more than twenty miles in the heat of the day without once coming to grips with the enemy. Holmes's Brigade, too, saw no action.

Johnston and Beauregard grew more and more concerned as the morning wore on and, while little was happening in front of them or to the right, a great deal was clearly going on to their left. Sometime between 11 a.m. and noon, the Signal Officer, Captain Alexander, reported that he had seen a great cloud of dust in the sky to the north-west. The two generals were afraid this marked the approach of General Patterson from the Shenandoah. At last Johnston determined to take matters into his own hands.' The battle is there,' he said to

Beauregard, pointing to the left. 'I am going.' He rode off.

Beauregard issued rapid orders. The brigades of Holmes, Early and Bonham should move, with speed, towards the sound of battle. Those of Longstreet, Jones and Ewell should resume their defensive positions south of Bull Run. Then Beauregard too galloped towards Henry Hill.

The situation on their left flank looked desperate. Evans, Bee and Bartow had been driven back from Matthews Hill in considerable disorder. For the North, reinforcements were arriving in strength. McDowell and his brigade commanders worked hard to form them into line for what they hoped would be the final big push to victory. Sherman was posted by the Sudley Springs road; what was left of Burnside's brigade was on his left; Keyes's brigade to the left of them. To the right of Sherman, Porter re-grouped his men. Two of Heintzelman's brigades, those of Colonel W. B. Franklin and Colonel O. B. Willcox, were directed to extend the right flank as they came up. It was a formidable force.

The South also had reinforcements on the way, but for the moment the only new men in the field were the 650 infantryman from South Carolina of Colonel Wade Hampton's Legion. The colonel, one of the great landowner/planters of the South, was an immensely wealthy and charismatic man. He was patriotic too for the Confederacy. The Legion was his own, raised and financed and led by him. Theirs had been an eventful day already. Shortly after first light their train from Richmond had pulled into Manassas Junction. They had made a quick breakfast and then orders came to hurry to the relief of Evans on the extreme left flank. It was a three-hour cross-country march and much had happened before they reached the summit of Henry Hill. They arrived just in time to see their own forces falling back and the enemy preparing to advance in line. Colonel Hampton led the way rapidly down the hill to the area of Robinson's House. They took position and almost immediately found themselves attacked from three sides by vastly superior numbers. They held their ground stoutly and had time to fire several volleys before they were forced to retreat back up Henry Hill. It was a purely holding operation, but a

▲ *It was shortly before noon when General Jackson arrived at the summit of Henry Hill with his 2,000 Virginians. He rapidly grasped the situation and organized his men into a superb defensive position, so good that the attacking Northern regiments were unable to break through and, in the end, wore themselves out in their repeated attempts. (Anne S. K. Brown Mil. Coll., BUL)*

successful one. It gave time for another new arrival to take position – General T. J. Jackson.

'Stonewall' Jackson

Jackson's Brigade – just over 2,000 Virginians with four cannon – had started the day before dawn. First they were moved forward to support Longstreet; later they were ordered two miles to the left to support Bonham and Cocke. When he arrived there, Jackson heard the din of the real battle going on even farther to the left and, as Bee and Bartow had done before him, immediately pressed on. He

THE FIGHT FOR HENRY HILL

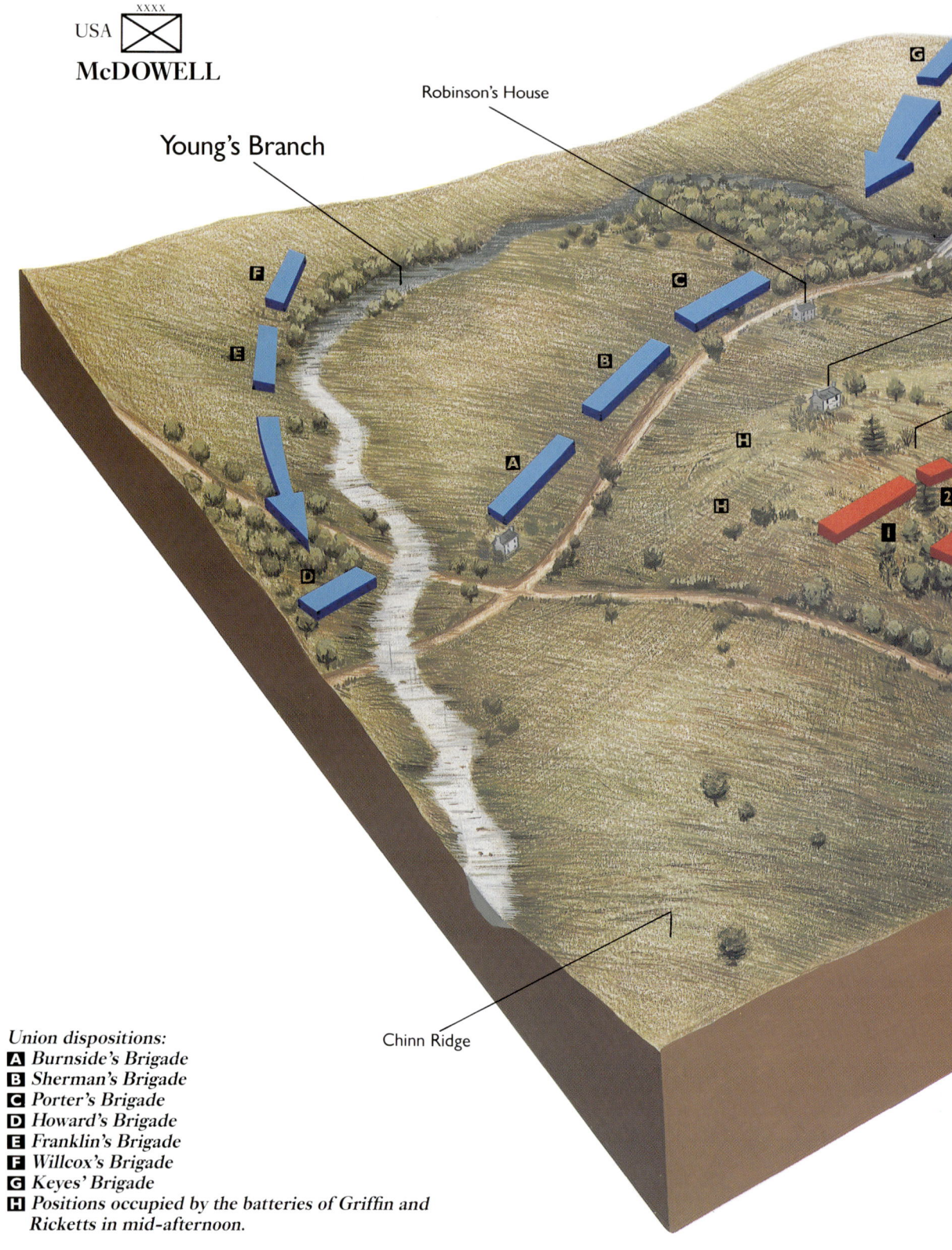

Union dispositions:
- **A** Burnside's Brigade
- **B** Sherman's Brigade
- **C** Porter's Brigade
- **D** Howard's Brigade
- **E** Franklin's Brigade
- **F** Willcox's Brigade
- **G** Keyes' Brigade
- **H** Positions occupied by the batteries of Griffin and Ricketts in mid-afternoon.

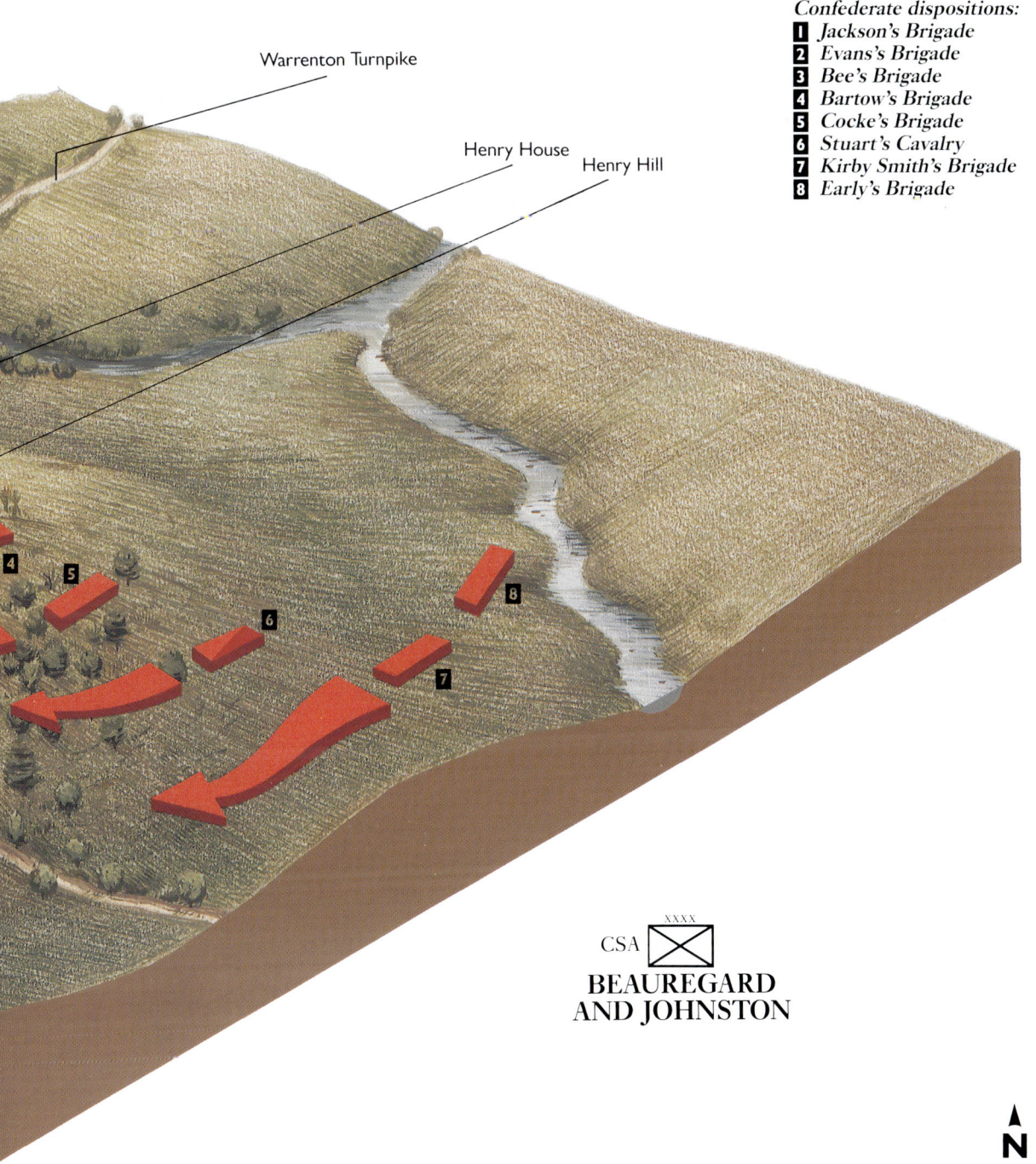

THE FIGHT FOR HENRY HILL

as seen from the south. Dispositions at midday, at the commencement of the battle for Henry Hill.

emerged from the woods on to the summit plateau of Henry Hill at about 11.30 a.m.

At that moment there was a brief lull in the fighting, both sides hurriedly re-forming their lines. Many of Bee's men – some of them wounded, others shattered by their first experience of battle – were stumbling through to the rear, speaking of defeat. As one of the Jackson's men said, it 'was not an encouraging sight to brand-new troops'.

Jackson organized his brigade into line, 150 yards or so behind the forward crest of the hill. It was an excellent position, of the type often used and recommended by the Duke of Wellington. The woods immediately behind offered good cover. The men would be invisible to the enemy guns and invisible to their infantry too until the moment when they emerged on to the plateau, within close range. In the centre of his line Jackson placed one of his own batteries and the four smooth-bore six-pounders of Captain John Imboden that had been busily pounding the enemy at the foot of the hill.

Before long they heard the battle resume. Then, to their right, they saw Bee's men in flight. To give some cover to Wade Hampton's beleagured Legion, Jackson got his guns firing.

The infantrymen on the right of the line, lying on the grass and waiting, saw a single horseman galloping towards them. One of them described the moment: 'He was an officer all alone, and as he came closer, erect and full of fire, his jet-black and long hair, and his blue uniform of a general officer made him the cynosure of all.' It was General Bee. He asked who their commander was, then rode along the line. An orderly sergeant of Jackson's, Henry Kyd Douglas, later wrote: 'General Jackson was sitting on his horse very near us. General Bee, his brigade being crushed, rode up to him and with the mortification of an heroic soldier reported that the enemy was beating him back.

"Very well, General," replied Jackson.

"But how do you expect to stop them?"

"We'll give them the bayonet," was the brief answer.

Bee galloped away and General Jackson turned to Lieutenant H. H. Lee of his staff with this message:

"Tell the colonels of this brigade that the enemy are advancing; when their heads are seen above the hill, let the whole line rise, move forward with a shout and trust to the bayonet. I'm tired of this long-range work!"'

Bee rode off to see what was left of his brigade. He could only find one of his regiments, the 4th Alabama, and they were disorganized and dispirited, all their senior officers gone. Bee appealed to them to return to the fighting under his command. It is not certain what his exact words were. The first published account appeared in *The Charleston Mercury*, quoting General Bee's principal aide. According to this, Bee turned to the Alabamans, gestured with his sword towards Jackson's line and shouted: 'There is Jackson standing like a stone wall. Let us determine to die here, and we will conquer. Follow me!' Beauregard, in his account of the battle, gives the words that are usually quoted: 'Look! There stands Jackson like a stone wall. Rally behind the Virginians!' Three days after the battle, back in Richmond, one of Beauregard's staff officers, Colonel Chesnut, was reunited with his wife and told her, and she wrote it into her diary, of 'Colonel Jackson, whose regiment stood so stock still under fire that they are called a stone wall'. Whatever the precise wording and circumstance, an enduring and legendary name had been given. And Bee's call worked. The men of the 4th Alabama followed him back towards the enemy. Bee, still on horseback, was at the head of the leading company when they came under fierce fire from the Northern artillery. Bee was severely wounded, and an aide carried him to the rear. He died before the day was out.

It was about this time, half an hour into the afternoon, that the commanding generals, Johnston and Beauregard, finally arrived at the summit of Henry Hill. For the first time that day they were under heavy fire, but they calmly disregarded it and set about reorganizing their shattered units and getting them back into a defensive line around Jackson. Beauregard wrote: 'We found the commanders resolutely stemming the further flight of the routed forces, but vainly endeavouring to restore order, and our own efforts were as futile. Every segment of line we succeeded in forming was again dissolved while another was being formed: more than two thousand men were shouting each some suggestion to his neighbour, their voices mingling with the noise of the shells hurtling through the trees overhead, and all word of command drowned in the confusion and uproar. The disorder seemed irretrievable, but happily the thought came to me that if their colours were planted out to the front the men might rally on them, and I gave the order to carry the standards forward some 40 yards which was promptly executed by the regimental officers, thus drawing the common eye of the troops. They now received easily the orders to advance and form on the line of their colours, which they obeyed with a general movement; and as General Johnston and myself rode forward shortly after with the colours of the 4th Alabama by our side, the line that had fought all morning, and had fled, routed and disordered, now advanced again into position as steadily as veterans.'

Johnston's account of the same incident is less colourful but almost certainly more reliable: 'When we were near the ground where Bee was re-forming and Jackson deploying his brigade, I saw a regiment in line with ordered arms and facing to the front, but 200 or 300 yards in rear of its proper place. On inquiry I learned that it had lost all its field officers; so, riding on its left flank, easily marched it to its place. It was the 4th Alabama, an excellent regiment, and I mention this because the circumstance has been greatly exaggerated.'

Division of Command

In their subsequent accounts the two generals also gave rather different versions of a vital issue that now arose. Beauregard wrote: 'As soon as order was restored I requested General Johnston to go back to Portici (the Lewis house) and from that point – which I considered most favourable for the purpose – forward me the reinforcements as they would come from the Bull Run lines below and those that were expected to arrive from Manassas, while I should direct the field. General Johnston was disinclined to leave the battle-field for that position . . . I felt it was a necessity that one of us should go to this duty, and that it was his place to do so, as I felt responsible for the battle. He considerately yielded to my urgency . . . '

Johnston's description of this conversation agrees that the suggestion came from Beauregard and that he accepted it, but makes it firmly clear that he retained command of the whole battlefield: 'I gave every order of importance,' he said.

The incident reveals their contrasting characters. Johnston was insisting that it was he who was in charge of the battle. Beauregard was claiming that, once he had arrived on the scene, the key action of the day was his. In effect, however, the division of duties was both sensible and successful. Johnston rode the mile or so back to the Portici, which gave him a wide view of most of the field of action, a more central position and readier access to the other brigades. Those that were being hurried towards Henry Hill had to pass close by the Portici, and Johnston was able to give them precise directions. Beauregard, meanwhile, was in his element – in the heat of the action, riding along the lines to shout words of praise and encouragement as the vision of glory inspired him. The men cheered him as he passed. A bursting shell killed his horse under him. General Bartow, rallying the men of his 8th Georgia Regiment and putting them in position on Jackson's left, fell with a bullet through his heart. 'With 6,500 men and 13 pieces of artillery', Beauregard wrote, 'I now awaited the onset of the enemy, who were pressing forward 20,000 strong, with 24 pieces of superior artillery and seven companies of regular cavalry.'

Beauregard was exaggerating the disparity in strengths and, in the interest of promoting his heroic image, made no mention of the very real advantages he enjoyed. There had been time to organize his line; his men were in the defensive role; the enemy had to attack uphill, across mostly open ground. And now he had 'Jeb' Stuart and his cavalrymen, who had ridden hard from the Shenandoah to be in time for the fight and had now been placed on the left of Jackson's line.

In fact, though it was not realized until much later, the Northern commander, McDowell, had already missed the best chance he was to get that day. He had imposed his plan upon the battle. He had succeeded in getting more infantrymen and

The Battle for Henry Hill, 1400 hours 21 July

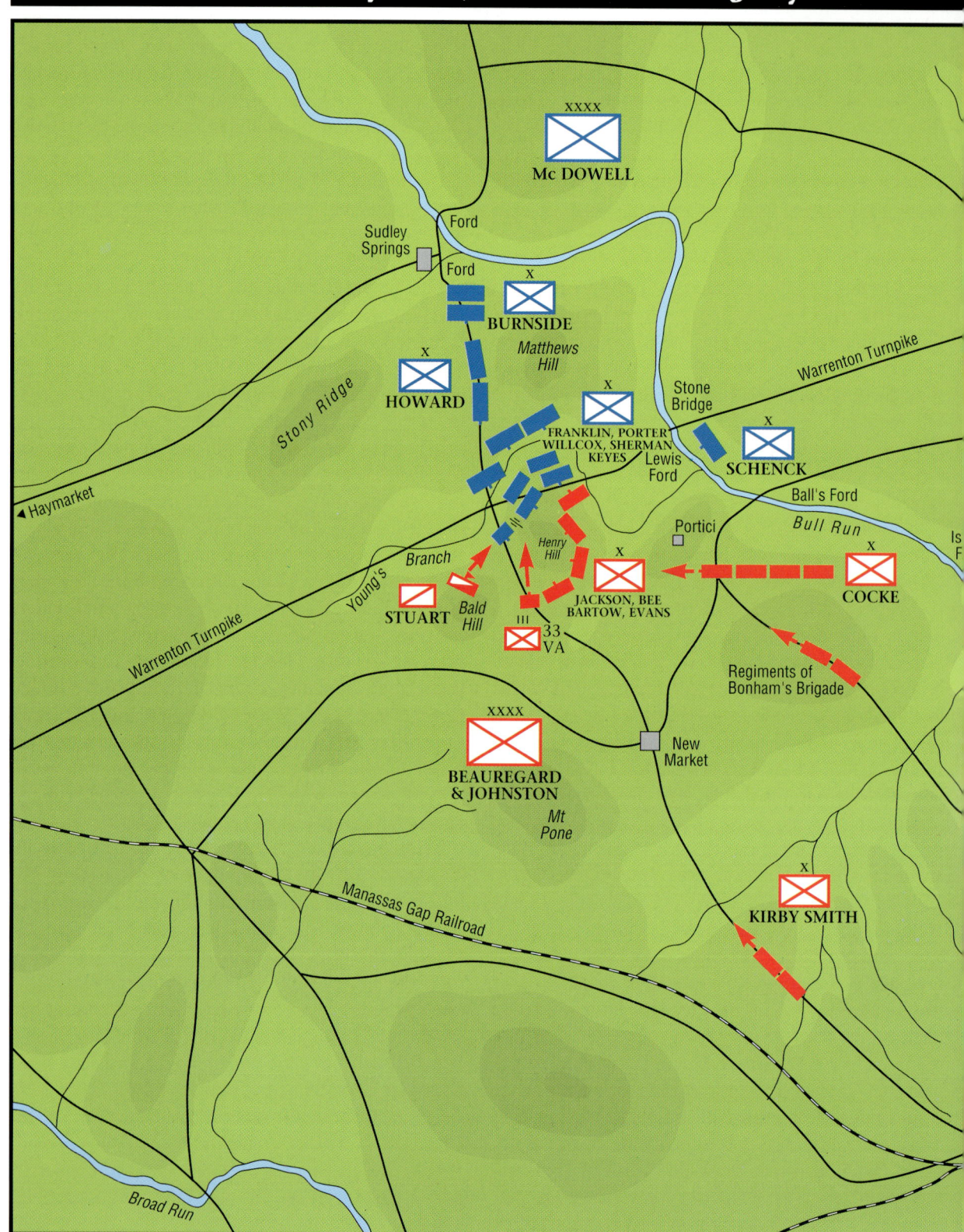

BELEAGUERED BATTERIES

more guns to the vital place than the enemy had. Then, unaccountably, he had delayed his attack. And when he did attack, it was piecemeal. He had whole brigades available to him but he launched his men up the hill by the regiment only. One by one the regiments advanced, to be pounded by the enemy artillery as they struggled up the hill, then, as they emerged on to the plateau, to be met by a tremendous volley of fire from the infantry at short range. They would be driven back and, after a pause, giving the enemy time to reload, another regiment would be hurled forward to meet the same reception. Jackson had no need to order his threatened bayonet charge. They simply had to maintain their position, fire and re-load. He was a calming, reassuring influence, moving along the line and saying, 'Steady, men! Steady! All's well!'

Beleaguered Batteries

Early on in the Henry Hill engagement, McDowell made a serious tactical error. He ordered two of his best batteries, those of Charles Griffin and

▲ *The irrepressible 'Jeb' Stuart, who led the only effective cavalry unit involved in the battle, turned up on the left of Jackson's line; charged and dispersed the 11th New York Regiment; and later told Jubal Early that if he attacked now the enemy might well break, which is exactly what happened. (Anne S. K. Brown Mil. Coll., BUL)*

75

▲ This drawing by W. Momberger gives a spirited impression of the scene on the lower slopes of Henry Hill during the long afternoon, as one by one the Northern regiments marched up the hill in an attempt to break Jackson's line. (Anne S. K. Brown Mil. Coll., BUL)

J. B. Ricketts, to advance to a position near to the Henry House, from which they could batter the Southern line at close range. These were batteries of the regular US army, efficient and ably commanded. From the very beginning of the battle they had been actively engaged, directing their fire at Evans's Brigade on Matthews Hill, then advancing on to that hill to hit the enemy positions on Henry Hill. Griffin had had one of his guns disabled, but Captain James Ricketts's battery was intact – six ten-pounder rifled guns.

When they got the order to advance, the two captains asked what infantry support they would have. They were told that the 11th New York Regiment, the Zouaves, were on their way at the double. They were dubious, but the order was firm, so they dutifully limbered their guns and set off.

The Southern battery commander John Imboden could hardly believe what he saw from the top of Henry Hill. There had been a lull in the action. 'My men lay about', Imboden wrote, 'exhausted from want of water and food, and black with powder, smoke and dust.' Then he saw the enemy batteries advancing, *unaccompanied*: 'It was at this time that McDowell committed, as I think, the fatal blunder of the day, by ordering both Ricketts's and Griffin's batteries to cease firing and move across the turnpike to the top of the Henry Hill, and take positions on the west side of the house. The short time required to effect the change enabled Beauregard to arrange his new line of battle on the highest crest of the hill . . . If one of the Federal batteries had been left North of Young's Branch, it could have so swept the hilltop where we re-formed, that it would have greatly delayed, if not wholly have prevented, us from occupying the position.'

Ricketts was first up the hill, but as he approached Henry House he came under fire from sharpshooters. 'I turned my guns upon the house', he said, 'and literally riddled it.' One of the shots smashed the bed on which the widow Henry was lying. She died a few hours later, the only woman casualty of the battle. Soon after – it was now about 2 p.m. – Griffin's battery arrived, and they turned their combined fire on Jackson's line, only 200 yards away.

But the batteries were completely unprotected. The 11th New York Regiment, in their bright red Zouave trousers, moved up the hill, at the double, to support them. The Southerners held their fire until the Zouaves were on the plateau, then let them have a thunderous volley. It was frightening rather than anything else. One Virginian witness commented wryly on his comrades' marksmanship: 'I recollect their first volley. It was apparently made with guns raised at an angle of 45 degrees, and I was fully assured that the bullets would not hit the Yankees, unless they were nearer heaven than they were generally located by our people.' After that, however, the Southerners' shooting improved, and the Zouaves found themselves pinned down in a hail of fire. The two companies on their right pulled back down the hill, escaping the rifle fire but running into 'Jeb' Stuart's cavalrymen who charged among them, slashing with sabres and firing their carbines. The plateau and slopes of Henry Hill had become an inferno of fire, smoke and confusion.

Captain Imboden, firing shrapnel at the advancing Northerners, forgot to step away from the gun's muzzle: 'Heavens! what a report. Finding myself full 20 feet away, I thought the gun had burst. But it was only the pent-up gas, that, escaping sideways as the shot cleared the muzzle, had struck my side and head with great violence. I recovered in time to see the shell explode in the

▲ *Captain Charles Griffin commanded the battery of the 5th US Artillery. They were in action early, against Evans on Matthews Hill. Later, when McDowell ordered two batteries to take position near Henry House, Griffin made no secret of his doubts about the move but obeyed the order. The result was disaster. (Anne S. K. Brown Mil. Coll., BUL)*

▲ *Captain James Ricketts, commander of the 1st US Artillery, went up Henry Hill ahead of Griffin and drove the enemy out of Henry House. When the batteries were overrun he was wounded and captured. He recovered, was released, became a brigadier general and took part – as did many of the officers on the field at First Bull Run – in the Second Battle of Bull Run in August 1862. (Anne S. K. Brown Mil. Coll., BUL)*

THE FIGHT FOR HENRY HILL

▲ *Another of Frank Vizetelli's sketches for the Illustrated London News. It was captioned: 'Attack on the Confederate batteries at Bull Run by the 27th and 14th New York Regiments – from a sketch by our special artist'. (Illustrated London News)*

▼ *The fight for the guns of the two Federal batteries at Henry House became a popular subject for American artists. This was a painting by E. Jahn. (Anne S. K. Brown Mil. Coll., BUL)*

◀ A private of the Louisiana Tigers, a regiment raised in New Orleans. (Illustration by Michael Youens)

▲ A private of the Charleston Zouave Cadets. (Illustration by Michael Youens)

enemy's ranks. The blood gushed out of my left ear, and from that day to this it has been totally deaf.'

Imboden's battery had run out of ammunition. He ran to Jackson to ask permission to retire: 'The fight was just then hot enough to make him feel well. His eyes fairly blazed. He had a way of throwing up his left hand with the open palm toward the person he was addressing. And as he told me to go, he made this gesture. The air was full of flying missiles, and as he spoke he jerked down his hand and I saw the blood was streaming from it. I exclaimed, "General, you are wounded." He replied, as he drew a handkerchief from his breast pocket, and began to bind it up, "Only a scratch – a mere scratch," and galloped away along his line.'

Jackson was enjoying himself, getting cooler as the fighting grew hotter. The Northerners were still attacking in waves, and there were moments when it looked as though they would break through. An officer rode up to Jackson and said, 'General, the day is going against us.' 'If you think so, sir,' Jackson replied, 'you had better not say anything about it.'

A further case of mistaken identity did much to

▲ *Brigadier General William B. Franklin, commander of the 1st Brigade of Heintzelman's Division, had a distinguished army career: first in his class at West Point, promoted in the Mexican War, an accomplished surveyor and engineer. At Bull Run his men, from Minnesota and Massachusetts, did not reach the front until the struggle for Matthews Hill was over, but after that they were continuously under fire throughout the struggle on Henry Hill. (Anne S. K. Brown Mil. Coll., BUL)*

help the Southern cause. Colonel Arthur C. Cummings's 33rd Virginia Regiment wore blue uniforms. The Colonel, afraid that his men would break and run if they were held in position any longer, ordered them to advance towards the guns of Ricketts and Griffin. Griffin saw them coming and swung two of his guns round and had them loaded with canister. Just as he was about to fire, his superior officer, Major William F. Barry, shouted, 'Captain, don't fire there; those are your battery support.' 'They are Confederates', Griffin shouted back, 'as certain as the world, they are Confederates.' But Barry insisted, and the guns were swung back to their original line of fire. The Virginians, meanwhile, marched ever closer, in line; then halted, raised their rifles and fired a volley. 'And that', Griffin told a subsequent Board of Inquiry, 'was the last of us. We were all cut down.' Most of their horses and many of the gunners were killed. Ricketts was severely wounded. Griffin struggled to save what he could, but Cummings and his Virginians were among them quickly to capture ten field guns and much ammunition.

McDowell was not prepared to abandon such a prize. Two regiments of Franklin's brigade, men from Massachusetts who had just reached the scene after a long march, were sent charging up the slope. They re-took the guns, but only briefly, before being driven back by Jackson and his Virginians – Beauregard with them, shouting, 'Give them the bayonet! Give it to them freely!' When the enemy fell back, he rode along his line, crying, 'The day is ours.' Moments later Heintzelman, the commander of McDowell's Third Division, led the 1st Minnesota Regiment in a counter-attack, and the Virginians were driven back yet again.

The battle swayed to and fro. Another of Heintzelman's brigade commanders, Brigadier General Orlando Bolivar Willcox, led his own regiment, the 1st Michigan, up the hill to retake the guns. Then Jackson charged and drove them down again. Willcox's men were to be in the thick of the action from now on. But Willcox himself was quickly wounded and then captured. He ran towards a line of men in blue uniforms to tell them they were firing on friends, discovering too late that they were the enemy.

Fluctuating Fortunes

So it went on for nearly two hours, at the hottest time of a very hot day – a brutal, interminable slogging-match, devoid of military finesse. The premium was on courage and endurance. Even Jackson was impressed: 'It was the hardest battle I have ever been in,' he said a few days later.

Sherman's brigade was heavily involved and his official report written four days later, gives a vivid impression of what it was like: 'This regiment [the 2nd Wisconsin] ascended to the brow of the hill steadily, received the severe fire of the enemy, returned it with spirit, and advanced, delivering its fire. This regiment is uniformed in grey cloth, almost identical with that of the great bulk of the secession army; and, when the regiment fell into confusion and retreated toward the road, there was a universal cry that they were being fired on by our own men. The regiment rallied again, passed the brow of the hill a second time, and was again repulsed in disorder. By this time the New York 79th had closed up, and in like manner it was ordered to cross the brow of the hill and drive the enemy from cover. It was impossible to get a good view of this ground. ... The fire of rifles and musketry was very severe. The 79th, headed by its colonel, Cameron, charged across the hill, and for a short time the contest was severe; they rallied several times under fire, but finally broke ... This left the field open to the New York 69th, Colonel Corcoran, who, in his turn, led his regiment over the crest, and had in full, open view the ground so severely contested; the fire was very severe, and the roar of cannon, musketry and rifles, incessant; it was manifest the enemy was here in great force, far superior to us at that point. The 69th held the ground for some time, but finally fell back in disorder.'

The commander of the New York 79th, Colonel James Cameron (his brother was President Lincoln's Secretary of War) was killed in this action. A few days later, describing the action in a letter to his wife, Sherman said, 'I do think it was impossible to stand long in that fire.' One Southern officer turned to a friend and said, 'Them Yankees are just marchin' up and bein' shot to hell.' The key factor in all this was the admirable defensive line that Jackson had chosen when he first arrived: set back from the rim of the plateau, semi-circular in shape, allowing converging fire from various directions; backed by woodland that gave the defenders good cover.

It is hard, at least with the benefit of hindsight, to see why intelligent commanders like McDowell and Sherman persisted so long with their costly, piecemeal, frontal attacks. Sherman would not have done so later on in his fighting career. McDowell had the resources, initially, to mount a frontal assault in brigade strength – one wave of men following the other too quickly to allow the enemy time to reload and reorganize. Or he could have sent Heintzelman's fresh brigades farther round the western flank to attack the enemy's side and rear. Either of these tactics, or both applied simultaneously, would almost certainly have won him the day. But none of these options was tried. The men had not been drilled in large-formation movements. Their commanders had never handled units of this size before. McDowell simply went on hoping that his next regimental attack would bring the breakthrough.

And he was, in effect, on a diminishing spiral. His new regiments, moving up to the front, could

▶ *Another artist's impression of the scene at the height of the struggle. It depicts Colonel Michael Corcoran leading a charge of the 69th Regiment against Southern batteries. (Anne S. K. Brown Mil. Coll., BUL)*

THE FIGHT FOR HENRY HILL

see what was happening to their predecessors. They marched past many wounded or demoralized men, scurrying to find safety. The morale impact was powerful. It is a tribute to the calibre of these young, untried, volunteer soldiers that so many of them went on fighting for so long. But all the time, the North was losing men and confidence.

About 3 p.m. the last of Heintzelman's brigades arrived – Howard with three regiments from Maine and one from Vermont. They were hurled into the attack, then hurled back by the enemy.

McDowell had no more reinforcements on the way.

For Beauregard, on the other hand, things were very different. General Johnston was feeding him with a constant stream of support – Virginian regiments from Cocke's Brigade, two of Bonham's South Carolina regiments. Some were used to strengthen Jackson's line. Others were sent to extend his western flank. And there were more on the way.

The tide of the battle was turning.

The Battle for Henry Hill, 1600 hours 21 July

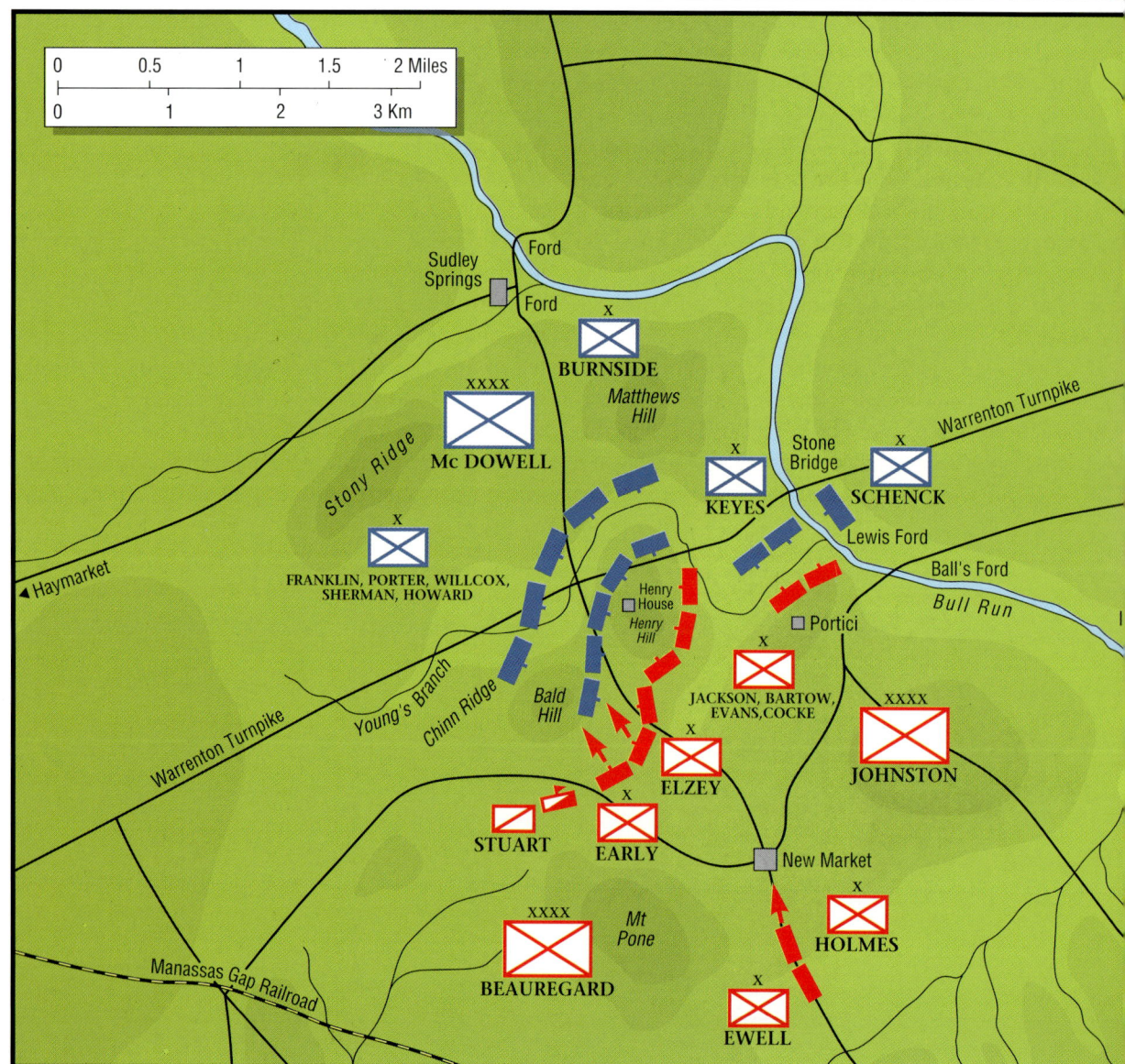

RETREAT AND ROUT

The final, clinching factor for the South was the arrival of two comparatively fresh brigades, a total of nearly five thousand men. One of these brigades was commanded by Colonel Jubal Early, the other by Brigadier General E. Kirby Smith.

Kirby Smith's Brigade, regiments from Virginia, Maryland and Tennessee, was the last part of Johnston's Shenandoah Valley army to be ferried over by train. Their journey had been much delayed, and it was not until after midday that they pulled into Manassas Junction. There they dumped their knapsacks and moved off at the double towards the battle. General Johnston ordered them to the far left of the line. It was about 4 p.m. when they arrived on the summit of Henry Hill and came under fire. Within minutes Kirby Smith had been hit in the chest by a bullet and badly wounded. His place in command was promptly taken by Colonel Arnold Elzey, a Maryland man and a graduate of

▲ Brigadier General E. Kirby Smith commanded the 4th Brigade of Johnston's army. They were the last contingents of Johnston's to arrive at Bull Run, but they moved quickly to the left of the Southern line and got there just in time to launch a critical attack. Unfortunately, Kirby Smith could not lead the charge: he was wounded and had to hand over to Elzey. (Anne S. K. Brown Mil. Coll., BUL)

West Point who had given distinguished service in the Mexican and Seminole wars. He led the brigade through the woods to the Chinn Ridge. Under cover of the trees they were formed into line, then advanced into the open to see the enemy directly ahead. It was what was left of Howard's Brigade after it had been driven off Henry Hill, still shaken and disorganized. Elzey ordered a volley, then a charge. Howard's men broke and ran. A few moments later a jubilant Beauregard rode up and – seeing himself for once as Wellington rather than Napoleon – cried, 'Hail, Elzey! Thou Blücher of the day.'

Jubal Early's brigade were not far behind Elzey's. Even by the standards of the day, Early was an odd man, a lonely bachelor with a short temper and a rasping tongue. His men (regiments from Virginia, South Carolina and Mississippi) called him 'Old Jube' or 'Old Jubilee'. In fact, he was no more than 44, a West Point graduate who had fought the Seminole before retiring from the army to try his hand as a lawyer and politician. He was a Virginian, another of those who argued against secession but, when it came, threw in his lot with his state. He was to prove a very able leader in the Civil War.

So far his day had been a frustrating one with much marching to and fro, crossing and re-crossing the Bull Run without any real action. Then he was ordered towards Henry Hill. Johnston directed him to follow Kirby Smith's route and push the line even farther westwards. No sooner was he in place there than he received a message from the cavalry leader, 'Jeb' Stuart, that it looked as if the enemy were about to break and he should advance straight away. He did so, meeting minimal resistance. Beauregard now ordered the whole of his line, from the right of Henry Hill to the left of the Chinn Ridge, to move forwards. It was the beginning of the end for McDowell.

The whole of the Northern line in the Henry Hill area fell back in considerable disorder. They had been on their feet for 14 hours or so. Many had been under fire for six or seven hours. They were hot, weary and very thirsty. They had seen horrors that would haunt their memories for the

▲ *Colonel Arnold Elzey, from Maryland, led the charge that marked the end of all Northern hopes. They scattered the already-disorganized remnants of General Howard's Brigade. It was at this moment that Beauregard realized victory was within his grasp. (Anne S. K. Brown Mil. Coll., BUL)*

▲ *The eccentric but effective officer, Colonel Jubal A. Early, commanded Beauregard's 6th Brigade. Together with other commanders on the right of the line, he had spent much of the day doing little and listening, with mounting frustration, to the sounds of battle over to the west. His chance came at the last moment. It was his downhill charge from the Chinn Ridge that flung the whole Northern line into retreat. (Anne S. K. Brown Mil. Coll., BUL)*

▲ Frank Vizetelli's version of the panicky scene on the road to Centreville as Northern soldiers dropped their weapons and ran, getting tangled up with fleeing wagons and civilians. The flight was all the more impetuous because everyone thought the Southern cavalry were close on their heels. In fact, despite the evidence of this drawing, the cavalry never appeared. In his caption, Vizetelli wrote: 'Retreat is a weak term to use when speaking of this disgraceful rout, for which there was no excuse.' He was refused permission to accompany the next Northern army to attack into Virginia, that of General McClellan, and spent the rest of the Civil War with the Southern armies. (Illustrated London News)

▶ Another artist's view of the scene when the Northern soldiers turned and fled.

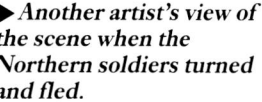

RETREAT AND ROUT

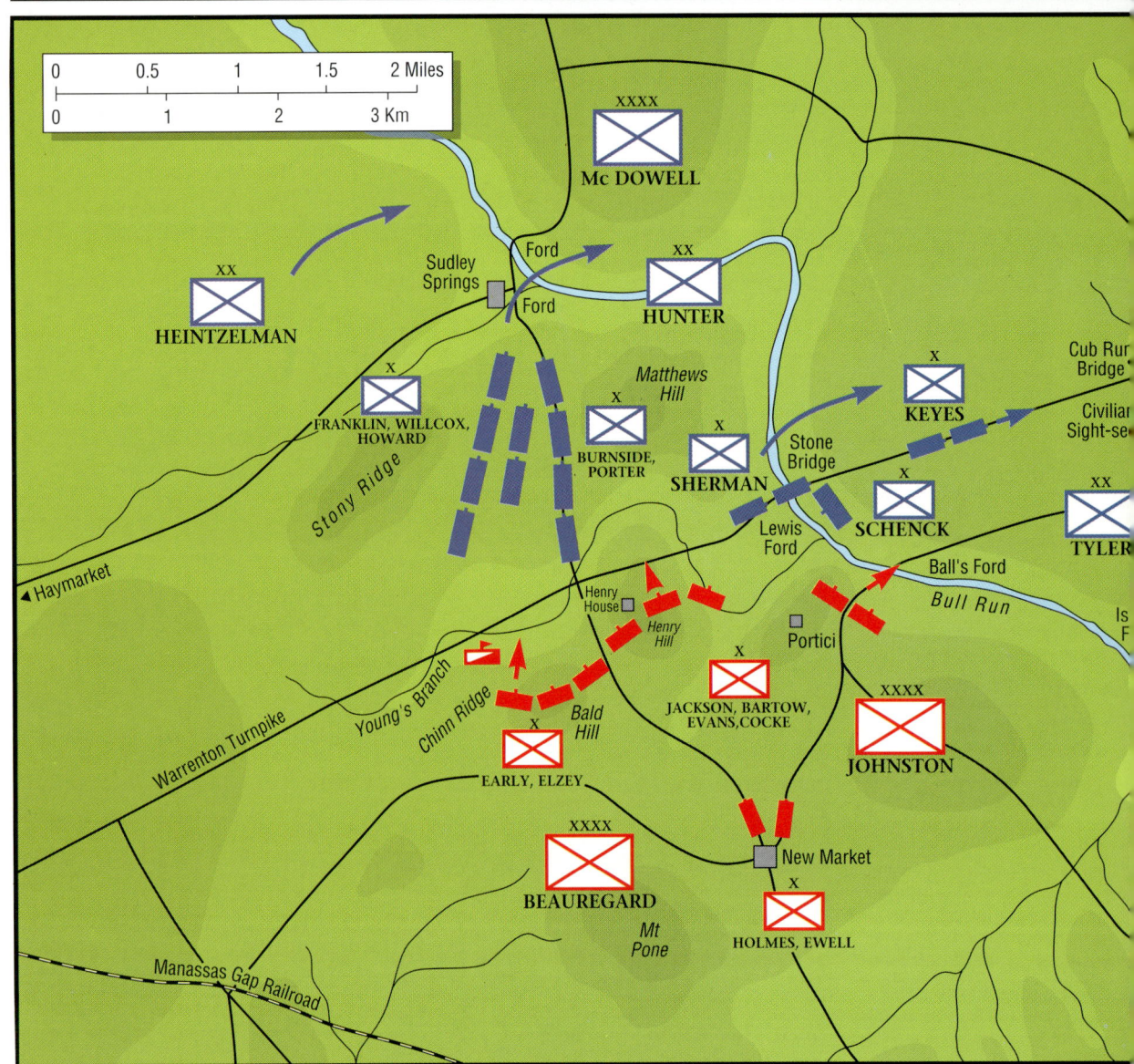

Final Retreat and Rout of Union Forces

rest of their lives. Many were lost. Units were dispersed and leaderless. McDowell struggled to restore some kind of organization, but he was virtually powerless. He described the conclusion of the battle in these words: 'It was at this time that the enemy's reinforcements came to his aid from the railroad train (understood to have just arrived from the valley with the residue of Johnston's army). They threw themselves on the woods on our right, and opened a fire of musketry on our men, which caused them to break, and retire down the hillside. This soon degenerated into disorder, for which there was no remedy. Every effort was made to rally them, even beyond the reach of the enemy's fire, but in vain ... the plain was covered with the retreating groups, and they seemed to infect those with whom they came in contact. The retreat soon became a rout, and this soon degenerated still further into a panic.'

The picture was not all as black as McDowell painted it. A battalion of regular infantry maintained its order and covered the others' more

THE CIVILIAN COMPLICATION

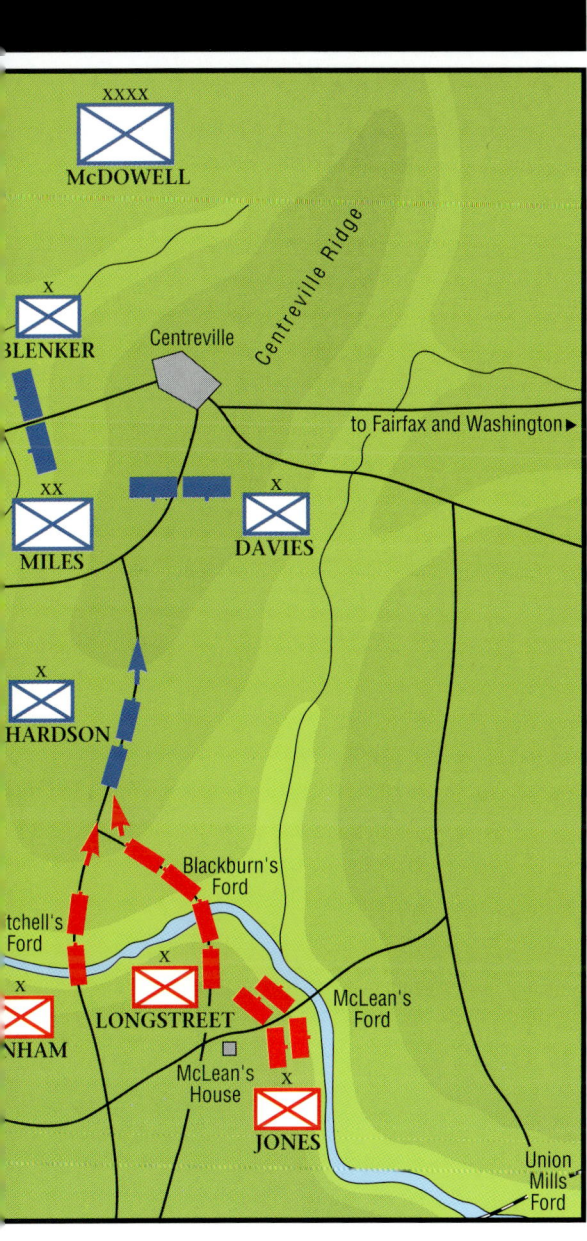

confined to my own company, and I am sure my vision was not particularly clear. General Jackson said the Second and Fourth Regiments pierced the enemy's centre. I have no doubt he knew. I have been surprised that I cannot remember any of my sensations during that turmoil, but I have a vague recollection of personal discomfort and apprehension, followed by intense anxiety for the result of the battle. Since then it has not been difficult for me to understand how much better it is for a war correspondent, in order to describe a battle vividly and graphically, not to be in it at all. I know we went in. My part of the line was driven back at first; then we went in again and fought it through, and found, when the smoke cleared and the roar of artillery died away and the rattle of musketry decreased into scattering shots, that we had won the field and were pursuing the enemy. This is not very historical but it's true.'

Most of the Northern soldiers who had been engaged in the Henry Hill fighting escaped the way they had come – by the ford at Sudley Springs or the one that Sherman had found. The real chaos, the rout, occurred a mile to the east in the area where the Warrenton Turnpike crossed a stream called Cub Run.

The Civilian Complication

The situation here was made worse by the presence of many civilian day-trippers who had driven out from Washington to spend Sunday enjoying a country picnic and a grandstand view of their army's victory. Among them were several Congressmen with their wives and families, and at first it had all been exciting and enjoyable. They were too far away to see any detail of the action, but the noise was impressive and clouds of dust and smoke assured them that they were witnessing the biggest battle that had ever been fought in North America. It was not so entertaining, however, in the late afternoon when the action suddenly and rapidly swirled towards them. They ran for their horses and carriages, fighting to get away to safety. The Southern artillery was doing all it could to encourage the confusion, and one shell hit the Cub Run bridge, overturning an army wagon and blocking the road completely. Now the

precipitate retreat. Sherman too – although he spoke bitterly about his men after the battle – made what Beauregard called 'a steady and handsome withdrawal', holding the enemy at bay.

The Southerners were also exhausted by this time, too tired and shattered to pursue the fleeing enemy with any great vigour. One of Jackson's company orderly sergeants, Henry Kyd Douglas, gave an honest and bewildered account of what it felt like to fight the battle of Henry Hill: 'I confess that I remember very little; my observation was

panic was total. Soldiers threw away their rifles and equipment and ran. Army wagons and civilian carriages were abandoned. The rumour flew that the enemy cavalry were right behind them. Senator Lyman Trumbull of Illinois wrote: 'Literally, three could have chased ten thousand ... It was the most shameful rout you can conceive of. I suppose two thousand soldiers came rushing into Centreville in this disorganized condition.'

McDowell was in Centreville before 6 o'clock that evening. The news was telegraphed to General Winfield Scott in Washington: 'The day is lost. Save Washington and the remnants of this army... The routed troops will not re-form.'

As the bulk of his army continued its headlong flight, McDowell struggled to organize those brigades that remained intact, that had hardly been

◀ *This painting by Alonzo Chappel depicts Colonel Louis Blenker organizing the rearguard to cover the retreat of the rest of the army and stop the enemy reaching Centreville.* *Blenker commanded the 1st Brigade of the 5th Division, and this was his only taste of action throughout the day. (Anne S. K. Brown Mil. Coll., BUL)*

▲ *William Howard Russell, the distinguished 'special correspondent' for The Times of London, went to Matthew Brady's photographic studio in Washington shortly after First Bull Run to sit for this portrait. For some reason he wore the uniform of a Deputy Lord Lieutenant of Ireland. Russell was on the scene too late to see much of the fighting at Bull Run, but he saw the retreat and rout and wrote a vivid account of it. As a result he was not allowed to march with the next Northern advance, and for a time he was in serious danger of being lynched by outraged Northerners. He returned to England in April 1862.*

engaged at all in the day's fighting, to form a line to defend Centreville. It proved impossible, chiefly because Colonel Dixon S. Miles, whose Fifth Division had been held in reserve, had passed much of the day swigging brandy to console himself for missing the action. Miles was 57 years old, an impressive military figure with a good combat record against the Mexicans and the Indians. But he was not suited to the inactive, supporting role. By mid-afternoon he was too drunk to issue coherent orders and, in trying to mount an attack, succeeded only in offending his fellow commanders. As soon as McDowell saw the state of the man, he relieved him of command. Darkness began to fall and the stream of shattered soldiers and terrified civilians continued to claw their way along the road back to Washington. McDowell decided there was nothing he could do but follow them.

President Lincoln had gone for his usual evening carriage ride, cheered by the reports from the battlefield. After half an hour he returned to the White House to be told that a new and terrible message had been received – the army was broken and routed. According to one of his staff, 'he listened in silence, without the slightest change of feature or expression, and walked away to army headquarters'.

The Confederate President, Jefferson Davis, had not been able to wait for the news to come to him. He took the train to Manassas where he found many soldiers who had fled from the battle and who assured him that the South had been beaten. He pushed on, however, and finally found General Johnston who told him that, on the contrary, it was the North that had been defeated and routed. He was just in time to see the final moments: 'In riding over the ground, it seemed quite possible to mark the line of a fugitive's flight. Here was a musket, there a cartridge box, there a blanket or overcoat, a haversack, etc., as if the runner had stripped himself, as he went, of all impediments to speed.' Davis rode around the battlefield, congratulating the brigades of Elzy and Early, getting food sent to men who were very hungry, trying to cheer the wounded. Later, he returned to the headquarters and questioned Johnston about the day's fighting.

Beauregard arrived about 10 p.m. Between them they composed a telegram to the War Department in Richmond: 'Night has closed on a hard-fought field. Our forces have won a glorious victory . . . ' Davis signed it, to Beauregard's chagrin.

Davis asked if the enemy were being pursued. Being answered in the negative, he wondered if it were now too late. They decided to order General Bonham, whose brigade of nearly five thousand men had been least wearied by the day's work, to push towards Centreville. Then they had second thoughts, fearing it would be too risky to send them forward in the dark. So Bonham was ordered to take up the pursuit at first light. By then, however, it had been raining steadily for several hours, turning streams into rivers and the roads into quagmires. There was no pursuit.

Counting the Cost

During the next few days the battlefield was combed for equipment left behind by the fleeing Northerners. There were 27 guns, including the great 30-pounder, and a lot of ammunition; more than 500 rifles and half a million rounds of ammunition; and much else besides – wagons and horses, hospital stores and food.

On both sides the losses in men were high. The South lost almost 2,000 men altogether: 387 killed; 1,582 (possibly more than this) wounded; 13 missing, either killed or captured. The losses were particularly bad among the officers. Colonel Wade Hampton's Legion was worst hit, sustaining almost twenty per cent casualties. The brigades of Bee and Jackson were not far behind with about sixteen per cent. 'Shanks' Evans's brigade, which was in the battle from start to finish, got off more lightly: 146 casualties among 1,100 men. For the North, the figures were worse: 460 men killed; 1,124 wounded; 1,312 missing, killed or captured, mostly the latter. Sherman's Brigade was worst hit, with 107 killed, 205 wounded and 293 men missing. Andrew Porter's Brigade suffered a total of 464 casualties; that of Willcox 432. Here too there were many officers among the casualties, though the proportion was not as high as in the Southern armies.

THE 'MIGHT-HAVE-BEENS'

Every major event, certainly every battle, has its intriguing imponderables – the 'if onlys' and the 'might-have-beens' that could have transformed the whole scene. First Bull Run had more than its share of them.

If the regular army of the United States had been, say, 30,000 strong at the beginning of 1861 (twice its actual size), and if – as seems likely – the great majority of the soldiers had remained loyal to the Union, Bull Run would not have happened at all. It is unlikely that the South would have dared to take up arms.

If McDowell had had, say, 5,000 regulars under his command, he would probably have won the battle. In fact, he had only one professional unit, the 14th US Infantry, a thousand men or so under the command of Major George Sykes. They fought hard and well in the battle for Henry Hill and when, in the end, the volunteer units broke and ran, it was they who held firm and covered the retreat. A brigade of such soldiers would have made a world of difference.

In all likelihood, the North would have won the battle if General Robert Patterson had been a younger and more vigorous man and if his orders from Winfield Scott had been more forceful. Patterson failed to engage Johnston's army and hold it in the Shenandoah Valley. And, having let the enemy slip away, he failed to get his own army to the battle. It was Johnston's brigades – those of Bee and Bartow, Jackson and Kirby Smith – that clinched the issue. Indeed, it is arguable that the North would have broken through and won the day if Johnston's men had not had the railway to speed their march across. Even with the help of the railway, Kirby Smith only arrived on the battlefield in the nick of time.

McDowell's battle plan was better thought-out than Beauregard's and much more efficiently implemented. In a sense, McDowell was the victim of his own superior competence. Had he failed to get his flanking movement under way – or had Beauregard's attack gone according to Beauregard's plan – the main action would have been fought in the centre of the line, with the Northern forces in a defensive role and the Southerners having to attack across the river and then uphill. Almost certainly, the North would then have prevailed.

McDowell made three very serious mistakes. Had he taken only one day, instead of two, to reconnoitre the ground and re-provision his men, he would probably have broken through the enemy line on Henry Hill and won the battle. He might well have broken through if he had ordered the first stage of the flanking march to take place on the Saturday evening. These self-generated delays gave the enemy just enough time to get brigades into position to protect his flank. Even in the early afternoon of Sunday, when he had preponderant strength around Henry Hill, McDowell might have broken the Southern line if he had attacked in brigade strength instead of piecemeal, regiment by regiment. At this vital time the Southern cause was saved by the independent initiatives of a few brigade commanders – 'Shanks' Evans, Bee and Bartow, Wade Hampton and Jackson.

The South had most of the luck. Again and again, its brigades appeared at the right spot and at the opportune moment. The best example was the final one, when Elzey's onslaught was followed immediately by that of Jubal Early, provoking the retreat that soon became a rout. Before that, for two or three hours, the issue was delicately poised and could have gone either way.

The commanding generals on both sides knew that it all hinged, in the end, on timing. McDowell said: 'Could we have fought a day – yes, a few hours – sooner, there is everything to show that we should have continued successful.' Johnston said

McDowell's plan would have worked 'if it had been made a day or two sooner'.

Consequences

The North had been entirely confident of victory and was now utterly shocked by defeat. Some clergymen said they had been punished by God for starting the battle on the Sabbath. Most people looked for someone to blame. Patterson was the obvious scapegoat. He was roundly condemned, then allowed to disappear into retirement – his three months' service was up anyway. Miles, too, was disgraced. A court of inquiry found him guilty of drunkenness, and he never again received a command of any importance. General Tyler was luckier. His performance before and during the battle had been studiously unhelpful – aggressive at Blackburn's Ford when his orders told him to be cautious, over-cautious when the battle was on and aggression was called for. But he kept his rank and remained in the army for three more years, never distinguishing himself but doing what he could along the way to discredit McDowell.

McDowell himself was demoted within four weeks and replaced by the North's new hope, General George B. McClellan. McDowell continued to serve, though he was never again given an independent command of any significance. He took it with his usual good grace. Meeting *The Times* correspondent, William Howard Russell, who was greatly hated for his vivid account of the rout, he said: 'I must confess I am much rejoiced to find you are as much abused as I have been. I hope you mind it as little as I did. Bull's Run was an unfortunate affair for both of us, for had I won it, you would have had to describe the pursuit of the flying enemy, and then you would have been the most popular writer in America, and I would have been lauded as the greatest of generals.'

Most of the Northern commanders lived to fight another day, none of them more effectively than Sherman. Initially Sherman felt sure his military career was over. He wrote to his wife: 'Well, as I am sufficiently disgraced now, I suppose soon I can sneak into some quiet corner.' But soon afterwards he was promoted to brigadier general and on his way to greater things.

In the South all was jubilation at first. Many of the soldiers thought their victory meant the war was over – the North would not dare invade again – and simply went home. The commanders, Johnston and Beauregard, issued a proclamation the grandiose style of which suggests that Beauregard was its author: 'Soldiers! we congratulate you on an event which ensures the liberty of our country. We congratulate every man of you, whose glorious privilege it was to participate in this triumph of courage and of truth – to fight in the battle of Manassas. You have created an epoch in the history of liberty and unborn nations will rise up and call you "blessed".'

Beauregard was promoted to full general the day after the battle and made the most of the lionizing that followed. Songs and marches were composed in this honour, and atrocious verses:

'Oh, the North was evil-starred, when she met thee, Beauregard!
For you fought her very hard, with cannon and petard, Beauregard!
Beau cannon, Beauregard! Beau soldat, Beauregard!
Beau sabreuer! beau frappeur! Beauregard, Beauregard!'

Johnston took a less self-glorifying line. 'The credit', he said, 'is due to God and our brave southern soldiers, not to me.'

Both commanders were involved in many more Civil War battles, but neither succeeded in establishing himself as a great leader. Before long they were wrangling with each other – and with Jefferson Davis – about the conduct of the battle and the failure to pursue the enemy.

One Southern commander, Brigadier General Thomas J. Jackson – who attained fame at Bull Run, earned his nickname there and was to further enhance his reputation – refused to be swept away by the prevailing euphoria. Henry Kyd Douglas wrote: 'And yet Jackson afterwards was never enthusiastic over the results of that battle; on the contrary, he said to me that he believed a defeat of our army then had been less disastrous to us. The South was proud, jubilant, self-satisfied; it saw final success of easy attainment. The North, mortified by defeat and stung by ridicule, pulled itself together, raised armies, stirred up its people, and prepared for war in earnest.'

That is precisely what happened. The Civil War went on for nearly four more years. By April 1865 more than 600,000 men had died, more than the United States has lost in any other war; much of the land, especially in the South, had been laid waste. The distrust and hatred that were created took many decades to disperse. The First Battle of Bull Run marked the end of America's innocence.

▶ *In June 1865 a monument, built by Northern soldiers, was dedicated. Its inscription reads: 'In Memory of the Patriots who fell at Bull Run.'*

▶ *Behind Henry House stands the grave of Mrs. Judith Henry who was killed, as she lay on her sick bed, by Northern gun fire.*

THE BATTLEFIELD TODAY

The Americans conserve and cherish their historical sites, and Bull Run is a good example of this. The important places in First Bull Run – Henry Hill and Matthews Hill, Chinn Ridge and the Stone Bridge – are included in what is called the Manassas National Battlefield Park in Prince William County, Northern Virginia. It is looked after by the National Park Service of the US Department of the Interior.

On the summit of Henry Hill stands the Visitor Centre, with a handsome Grecian entrance. This is open daily except at Christmas. It offers audio-visual programmes giving an outline account of both Bull Run battles, as well as maps, prints, colour slides and a range of books about the battles and the Civil War as a whole. The staff are friendly and well-informed.

You can take, free of charge, a leaflet that gives a map of the area and details of two suggested walks. The first, no more than a mile of easy going, takes you to Henry House, past the point from which the Southern guns fired on Matthews Hill in the late morning, to the Robinson House where Hampton's Legion delayed the Northern advance; then back up the hill to the spots where Jackson organized his 'stonewall' line, where Bee and Bartow were mortally wounded, and where Griffin's battery was overrun by the Virginians.

The second tour is some six miles long, a pleasant walk along gravel paths through pine-scented woods to the river and the Stone Bridge, along the riverside passing the ford that Sherman crossed, through woods and open fields to Matthews Hill, then turning southwards to return to Henry Hill along the line where McDowell's forces advanced and then retreated. There are information boards at the key points, and some of them give you, at the press of a button, taped information about the action there.

Today the route is dotted with monuments. Henry House is rather bigger than the building there in 1861. On one side of the house is Judith Henry's grave: on the other is a stone monument – 'In memory of the Patriots who fell at Bull Run' – built by the US Army and dedicated on 13 June 1865. Some 200 yards away, an inscribed stone marks the spot where Colonel Bartow, 'The first Confederate officer to give his life on the field', was killed. This was placed here in 1936. Two years later the State of Virginia commissioned the equestrian statue of 'Stonewall' Jackson that dominates the plateau. Close by is an inscribed memorial stone to General Bee, set here in 1939.

Across the battlefield, six-pounder canon of the period, smooth-bore and rifled, attended by their caissons, indicate the positions from which Ricketts, Griffin and Imboden and others pounded the enemy.

There is a house where the Robinson House stood, again slightly bigger than the original. The house of the freed slave survived First Bull Run surprisingly well, but was badly damaged and looted by Northern soldiers during the Second Battle of Bull Run. After the war Robinson asked for compensation, and Congress voted him $1,249. The lane up the house from the Turnpike is much as it must have been in the late morning of 21 July 1861 when Heintzelman's regiments fought their way forward, convinced that victory would soon be theirs.

▶ *Henry House today, rather bigger than it was in 1861. The guns and caissons are sited where the great struggle took place in the mid-afternoon.*

THE BATTLEFIELD TODAY

▶ *A fine equestrian statue of 'Stonewall' Jackson marks the spot where he formed the defensive line that repelled all Northern assaults.*

A GUIDE TO FURTHER READING

The American Civil War was the first war in history to be exhaustively described by men of all ranks. A library of books has been written about it, and the process still goes on. The war's oustanding modern, non-academic historian was Bruce Catton. The most detailed account of First Bull Run is that given by William C. Davis. The key primary source is *Battles and Leaders of the Civil War (volume 1)* edited by Robert Underwood Johnson and Clarence Clough Buel of *The Century Magazine*. First published in New York in 1887, it gives accounts of the battle by General Johnston, General Beauregard, General Fry as well as that of the artillery captain, John D. Imboden.

Other valuable sources are:

CATTON, B.	*The Penguin Book of the American Civil War*, London, 1960: a brief and balanced survey of the whole war.
–	*The Coming Fury*, London, 1966: a more detailed account of the battle and the events that led up to it.
–	*Reflections of the Civil War*, New York, 1981.
DAVIS, W.C.	*Battle at Bull Run*, Baton Rouge, 1977: a thoroughly researched and well-written description of the whole battle, with an excellent bibliography.
–	*The Fighting Men of the Civil War*, London, 1989.
EARLY, J. A.	*War Memoirs*, Indiana, 1969.
HANSON, J. M.	*Bull Run Remembers*, Manassas, Virginia, 1953: an entertaining and reliable account of both the Bull Run battles.
LOSSING, B. J.	*Pictorial History of the Civil War (volume 1)*, Philadelphia, 1866.
SANDBURG,	*Abraham Lincoln: The War Years*, New York, 1939.
SHERMAN, W. T.	Memoirs of General William T. Sherman, Indiana, 1875.

▶ *After the battle a memorial was erected on the spot where Colonel Bartow received his death wound, on the summit plateau of Henry Hill. It was dedicated 'to the people of Savannah, Georgia', and inscribed with what were said to be his dying words: 'They have killed me, boys, but don't give up the fight.' (Anne S. K. Brown Mil. Coll., BUL)*

▲ A dramatic 'artist's impression' of the clash between Stuart's cavalry and the New York Zouaves on Henry Hill. (Anne S. K. Brown Mil. Coll., BUL)

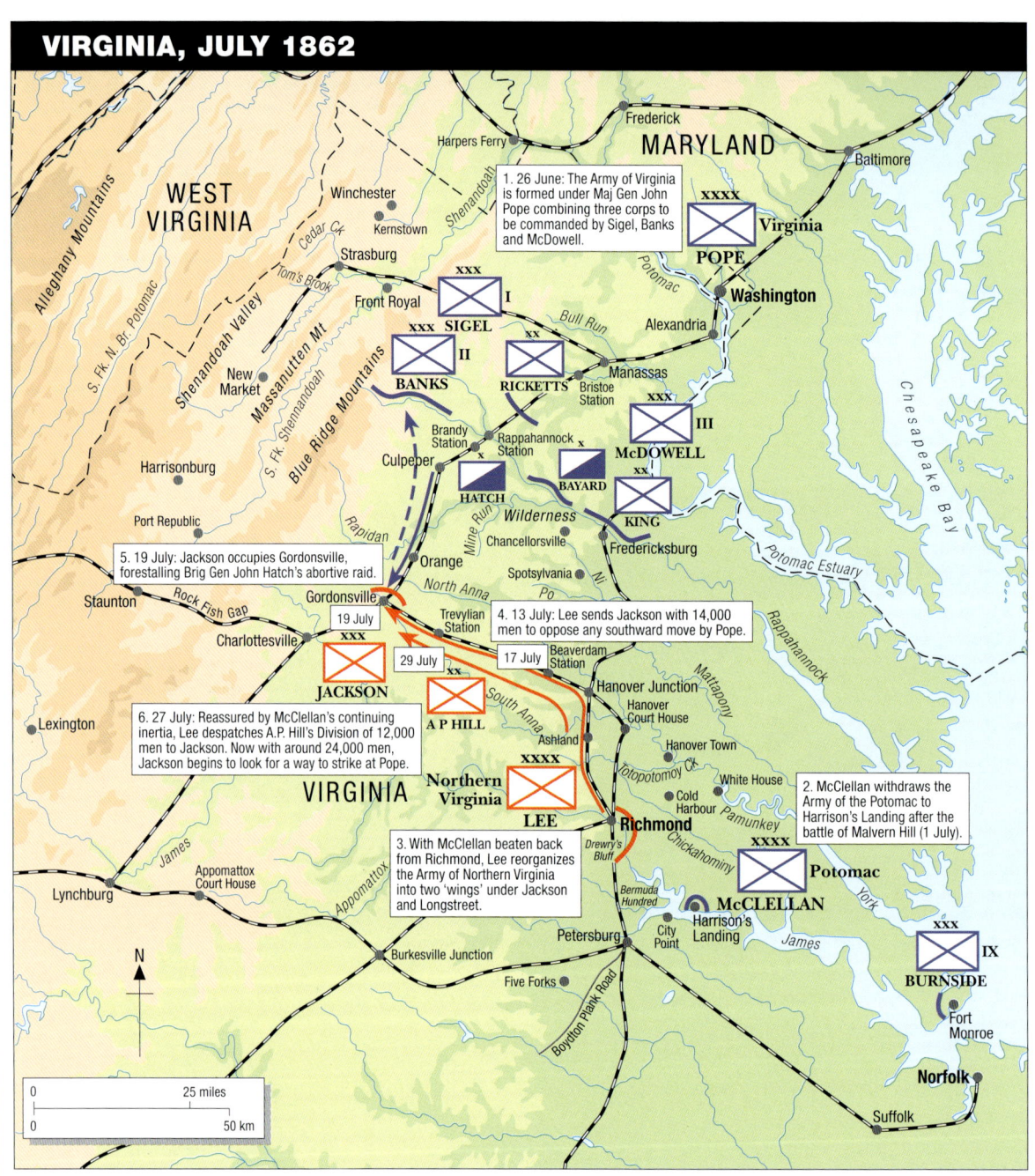

PART TWO
Second Manassas 1862

BACKGROUND

On the night of August 22 to August 23, 1862, a Confederate cavalry raid on Union General John Pope's headquarters near Catlett Station, Virginia, produced considerable booty – the general's tent and dress coat, more than $300,000 in cash and, most importantly, his dispatch book.

The orders within that book confirmed the fears of Confederate General Robert E. Lee: that Pope's army was trying to link up with that of General George B. McClellan. Were that to happen, the combined 180,000 men would certainly overwhelm Lee's army of 60,000. The race was on.

On August 25, Lee sent General Stonewall Jackson and 24,000 men on a hard march that culminated 36 hours later at a Virginia crossroads known as Manassas Junction. Pope realized what was happening, and endeavored to engage Jackson and destroy him before General James Longstreet and his army could arrive to reinforce Jackson.

The stage was set for the South's greatest victory. Here is the complete story.

Confederate General Thomas "Stonewall" Jackson would lead his men with distinction at Manassas (the Southern name for the two battles known in the North as Bull Run) both in 1861, and again in 1862. Religious fervor was among his many traits. Here some of his loyal men join their colorful commander in prayer. NA

ORIGINS OF THE CAMPAIGN

Reserved Virginian Robert E. Lee's masterful handling of operations, during the Second Manassas campaign, did much to establish him as the premier military leader of the Confederate States of America. NA

From the fall of Fort Sumter in South Carolina on 14 April 1861, the first year of the Civil War had gone badly for the Union. The first major engagement between the two untested armies demonstrated the Federals' typical poor showing during the course of the early fighting. On 21 July, Major General Irvin McDowell's Yankees fled from the Confederates under the overall command of General Joseph E. Johnston at the Battle of Bull Run, as the North called it, or the Battle of Manassas, as the Southern victors referred to the brief encounter.

After this débâcle President Abraham Lincoln immediately set out to find a military man who would not fail him as McDowell had. He also sought a winning strategy to crush the Rebels. "Old Abe" quickly settled upon one key strategic goal – the capture of the capital of the Confederate States of America at Richmond, Virginia. And the man who Lincoln thought could achieve this was a self-styled "Napoleon of the New World," Major General George B. McClellan. During late July 1861 the diminutive major general had been responsible for establishing Washington, DC's defenses. This was much to Lincoln's relief because he was apprehensive about his own capital becoming the target of the Confederate forces.

With this accomplishment to his credit, Northern officials tasked "Little Mac" with the creation of what would become the Army of the Potomac. Once he had forged the Federal soldiers into this mighty weapon McClellan proposed to move by sea and assemble at Fort Monroe, Virginia. This Federal bastion was about seven days' march from Richmond, and thus a logical staging area for McClellan's proposed invasion.

By March 1862 McClellan had assembled a sufficiently powerful force to begin his move to the Virginia Peninsula. He had hoped for more troops, but Lincoln, fearing for Washington's security, refused McDowell, who was by now relegated to the command of a corps, permission to send his 40,000 soldiers with McClellan. Instead McDowell's I Corps was retained in the vicinity of Manassas where the defeat of the previous year doubtless remained fresh in his mind.

This was only one of the problems that plagued McClellan's bid to capture Richmond. Indeed, his own inability to take decisive action resulted in a month's delay in the unnecessary siege of Yorktown. That costly decision allowed Confederate General Johnston to bring up his army to face McClellan. McClellan had ordered siege artillery to be brought up from Washington, but two days before his bombardment was due to begin Johnston withdrew toward Richmond. McClellan pursued the retreating Johnston slowly to within a few miles of the seat of the Confederate government. McClellan still hoped that McDowell, by now at Fredericksburg, would join him and further bolster his numbers. This would only be possible if another Union command under General Nathaniel Banks, could secure northern Virginia's strategic Shenandoah Valley. The valley was both a valuable source of food and materials for the Confederacy and a possible route for a Southern attack on Washington. McDowell's forces at Fredericksburg would not be released to McClellan until any potential threat from the Shenandoah Valley had been dealt with.

General Thomas "Stonewall" Jackson's lightning Shenandoah Valley campaign in May and June 1862 showed the threat was far from dealt with. With 18,000 men, Jackson ran rings around numerous separate Union commands that in total outnumbered him almost four-to-one. In the spring, Jackson rode roughshod over not only Banks's men but also those of McDowell and a third command under the original standard bearer of the Republican party, John Charles Frémont. Attacking the fragmented Union corps in the Valley, Jackson won a series of victories at McDowell (8 May), Front Royal (23 May), Winchester (25 May), Cross Keys (8 June) and Port Republic (9 June).

Such was the effect of the victories won by Stonewall Jackson and his "foot cavalry", an honorific bestowed on Jackson's men as a result of their lightning movement and aggressive tactics during the Valley campaign, that they were able to rejoin the Army of Northern Virginia to assist in the defense of Richmond. With General Johnston having been wounded at Seven Pines (Fair Oaks), General Robert E. Lee had now taken command.

It became clear to Lincoln that he had to address a number of issues as the summer of 1862 brought further bad news to the Northern cause. After the intensive Seven Days campaign, in which McClellan failed to overwhelm the Confederate defenders of Richmond, Lincoln considered new candidates for the post of general-in-chief. A well respected West Point graduate, Henry Halleck, was seen as the heir apparent, but he would be cast more as a chief of staff than a field leader.

Furthermore, the president realized the disjointed commands that Jackson had humiliated needed to be consolidated under one man. This individual might also be a potential replacement for McClellan as the field commander of the Union Army. As such, it was necessary to find a contender with the right qualities, not the least of which was actual victory against a major Southern force. There was no one who could make that claim in the eastern theater, but fighting in the western theater had been less one sided. There, some Northerners had demonstrated grit and the ability to win. The western theater seemed to Lincoln the most fertile ground to seek a fighting general during that bleak summer of 1862.

Union survivors built an obelisk near the Brawner farmhouse to commemorate the deadly contest at Second Bull Run, the Northern name for this engagement. The opposing sides often gave different titles to battles.

OPPOSING COMMANDERS

UNION

John Pope

When Lincoln reached the conclusion that McClellan was not the man to bring the war to an end, he turned to a fellow native of Kentucky – John Pope. Pope, like Lincoln, had left this state and relocated to Illinois, and it was from here that he received an appointment to the United States Military Academy. After graduation in 1842, his class standing (17 out of 56) was high enough to secure a posting to the prestigious Corps of Topographical Engineers.

Pope eventually ended up apparently trapped in the backwater of Maine, but he was rescued by the outbreak of the Mexican War in 1846. His service and valor in this conflict earned him promotion to brevet captain.

By 1 July 1856 Pope had advanced to a captaincy in the Topographical Engineers, a rank he held until 14 June 1861. On that day, having had the good fortune to serve as an escort officer accompanying Lincoln to the inauguration, and because of other ties to the new chief executive, he was advanced to a brigadier of volunteers. During the next year he held various commands in Missouri, serving under John C. Frémont. His performance was such that he ultimately was put in charge of operations along the Mississippi River.

By early 1862, after victories at New Madrid and the Mississippi River's Island No. 10, he was made commander of one of the three field

During July 1861, at the Battle of First Manassas, Jackson made "Portici" his headquarters. Over 12 months later, the din of muskets and cannon could again be heard in the vicinity of this stately home. LC

armies led by Henry W. Halleck toward Corinth, Mississippi. He soon added a second star to his shoulder straps when he was appointed a major general of US Volunteers on 21 March 1862. All this put him in line for consideration when Lincoln decided to combine the three divided Union commands in northern Virginia, which had all failed to bring Jackson to bay in the Shenandoah Valley.

With the disparate corps combined into the Army of Virginia, Pope took charge of the organization on 26 June 1862. Frémont would not serve under his former subordinate, and was replaced by another officer. He was not the only one to disdain Pope, who became unpopular with many of his fellow officers, as well as the rank and file. This bad feeling could be traced to the early days of Pope's command of the Army of Virginia. He issued a pompous communiqué to his new command boasting: "Let us understand each other. I have come to you from the West, where we have always seen the backs of our enemies; whose business it has been to seek the adversary, and to best him where he was found; whose policy had been attack and not defense." Not only did these words grate with McClellan and his supporters, but they also raised the hackles of the troops in the Army of Virginia, many of whom had been serving in the theater for some time and resented being portrayed as ineffective or even worse, cowardly!

In another unfortunate piece of bombast, Pope claimed his headquarters would be in the saddle. This boast backfired with several of Pope's peers maintaining he had his "headquarters where his hindquarters" ought to be.

Lincoln unilaterally selected Pope as a "western man" who could prosecute the war, but his choice of champion did more than antagonize the forces of the eastern theater, however. Pope became a target for particular hatred in the South by prescribing harsh treatment of Confederate sympathizers. Virginians in areas controlled by his troops were to be brought in and instructed to take the oath of allegiance to the United States. If they balked, they were to be turned out from their homes and expelled to enemy territory. Additionally, not only did he order his troops to live off the land, but also directed that guerrillas were to be executed as traitors when captured. Furthermore,

TOP **Major General George B. McClellan (center) had been hailed as the man who would bring swift victory for the North. "Little Mac" did not live up to expectations, although he continued to command the Army of the Potomac after he failed to capture Richmond. Many other generals in this group portrait would serve at the Battle of Second Bull Run. NA**

ABOVE **Known as "Old Brains" Major General Henry Wagner Halleck assumed duties as general-in-chief of the Union Army during the summer of 1862. He was a good administrator, but lacked strategic capabilities and the strong leadership needed to direct his fellow Union generals during the campaign that brought the Northern and Southern armies back to Bull Run. NA**

five local civilians of prominence were to be rounded up and put to death if partisans shot at his men.

In this foretaste of the total war concept practised so effectively later by Ulysses Grant, Pope provoked the usually mild-mannered Lee in a way that no other adversary ever had. Lee developed a personal enmity toward Pope, referring to him as a "miscreant" who had to be "suppressed."

In response, the Confederate government made it known that Pope and his officers would not be accorded consideration as soldiers. If caught they would be held prisoner so long as Pope's odious dictates remained in effect. Should Southern civilians be killed, a like number of Federal prisoners would be sent to the gallows.

These harsh measures were not carried out and after the Second Manassas campaign the point became moot. In fact, at that time Lincoln also lost faith in his protégé and shortly after Pope's defeat in northern Virginia he was transferred.

For most of the remainder of the war Pope oversaw the Department of the Northwest, and among other things dealt with the 1864 Sioux uprising in Minnesota. Having redeemed himself in the eyes of the administration, in 1865 he received a brevet as a regular army major general in recognition of his actions at Island No.10. The following year he mustered out of the volunteers, but returned to the regulars where he served as departmental commander in various locations until his retirement in 1886. Six years later he died.

Henry Halleck

At the same time that Lincoln was looking for an alternative to McClellan as his eastern field commander, he was also seeking to replace McClellan as general-in-chief. On 11 July 1862 Henry Halleck, a New York native and Military Academy graduate (1839), was given the mantel previously worn by Winfield Scott and George McClellan.

An engineer officer who had been breveted for his performance in Mexico, Halleck previously had overseen construction of coastal

Disappointed with McClellan's performance, President Abraham Lincoln cast about for a new head for his army. He now pinned his hopes on John Pope, who despite much bravado was no match for the opposition he encountered at Second Bull Run. Pope's shortcomings proved costly, opening the way for the Confederates to bring the war north. NA

Major General Irvin McDowell had commanded at First Bull Run, but his reputation suffered greatly as the Union Army left the field in disarray. During the summer of 1862 McDowell, seen here (center) with his staff, was to return to the scene of this earlier Federal defeat. NA

LEFT **During both battles at Manassas, Henry P. Matthew's solid stone house on the Warrenton Turnpike would be pressed into service as a hospital. USAMHI**

In 1852 Franz Sigel journeyed from his native Baden in Germany to the United States. He was outspoken and held liberal views, leading him to support the unsuccessful Revolution of 1848 against Prussia. The former army officer fled his native land, which brought him to St. Louis, Missouri. His influence among the German community led to him being commissioned as a brigadier general of volunteers soon after the Civil War began. NA

fortifications, served as a member of the faculty at West Point, and conducted a study of France's military. These endeavors and his writings *Report on the Means of National Defense* and *Elements of Military Art and Science*, along with a translation of the influential French volume *Vie Politique et Militaire de Napoleon* by Henri Jomini, earned him the nickname of "Old Brains" but this sobriquet became derogatory during the Civil War.

Although Halleck had left the army in 1854 to establish a law practice in California, he continued his interest in the profession of arms. When the war broke out, Winfield Scott recommended Halleck be given an important assignment, and as such, on 19 August 1861, he was commissioned a major general in the US Army.

After modest accomplishments in the western theater of operations he was called to Washington, where it was believed his administrative capabilities would bear fruit in galvanizing the Union army into a viable force. This was not to prove the case, however, and a number of his subordinates criticized him for a failure to clearly communicate both what was expected of them and the actions of the various commands. To some degree both of these characteristics were evident during the Second Manassas campaign.

Furthermore, Halleck tended to attribute failures to others, thereby alienating most of his fellow generals. Consequently, he was finally reassigned as the army's chief of staff, and in this role performed well, although he remained one of the most unpopular men in Washington.

At war's end he remained in uniform, first as commander in Virginia and later as head of the Military Division of the Pacific. In 1872 he died while serving in Louisville, Kentucky.

Nathaniel Banks

Massachusetts governor "Bobbin Boy" Banks, who had been speaker of the state's lower house, and for a time one of its US congressmen, was just one of many political appointees to be named a general in the Union volunteers. With no military background, he remained in divisional and departmental commands near the capital during the early stages of the war, but was then sent to the Shenandoah Valley. The Confederates under Stonewall Jackson outfought the politician-turned-

Massachusetts governor Nathaniel P. "Bobbin Boy" Banks was just one of many political appointees to be named a general in the Union volunteers. Lacking a military background, he remained in divisional and departmental commands near the capital during the early stages of the war, but by the time of Second Manassas was II Corps commander in the Army of Virginia.

soldier, and after capturing a significant cache of his supplies jokingly referred to him as "Commissary Banks".

Not long after Banks was assigned to the Army of Virginia, Jackson goaded him again at Cedar Mountain, then once more faced him at Second Manassas. After a short assignment in Washington, the administration shipped him to New Orleans as Benjamin F. "Beast" Butler's replacement. In that command Port Hudson was his first target, but he failed to overcome the defenses until after Vicksburg had been taken by Grant.

His effectiveness during the Red River Campaign of 1864 was little better. Despite such lackluster martial performances, Congress decided to honor him with a resolution of thanks. Banks mustered out of the volunteers on 24 August 1865 and returned to politics.

Irvin McDowell

As a young man Irvin McDowell attended the Collège de Troyes in France, then went on to the US Military Academy where he graduated 23rd of 45 cadets in his class of 1838. He was commissioned in the artillery, with a stint of frontier duty before returning to West Point as a tactics instructor and adjutant.

During the Mexican War he became General John Wool's aide de camp and adjutant, followed by another posting to the frontier. He ultimately secured a transfer to army headquarters in Washington. While serving there, Winfield Scott introduced him to a number of influential members of Lincoln's administration. Secretary of the Treasury Samuel Chase particularly championed his cause and was instrumental in obtaining Major McDowell a promotion to brigadier general in the Regular Army on 14 May 1861. Two weeks later he assumed command of forces south of the Potomac and in the vicinity of the capital.

McDowell was not to remain encamped for long, however. Political pressures and the short term of enlistment of some of his troops, forced him to lead his unprepared army to Manassas. Part of his command marched against Blackburn's Ford along Bull Run. A few days later McDowell launched his main attack, which resulted in the First Battle of Manassas (Bull Run). The failure of Union arms at First Manassas brought an end to his rapid rise. Four days after this defeat, McClellan assumed control, while on 3 October McDowell was assigned a division. After the Army of the Potomac was organized, he gained a better berth, being entrusted with I Corps. His first assignment was the protection of Washington as McClellan began the Peninsula Campaign. In due course his men were to proceed overland to support McClellan in his drive against Richmond, but as events transpired McDowell and his men were diverted to face Jackson in the Shenandoah Valley.

Following this unsuccessful effort, he was assigned III Corps in Pope's Army of Virginia. In that capacity he participated in the actions at Cedar Mountain and Rappahannock Station. Several years later the former engagement gained him a major-general's brevet in the Regular Army.

In the wake of Second Manassas he was relieved from his command, being singled out as one of the parties responsible for the Union defeat. He requested a court of inquiry, and was absolved of blame for the débâcle; a fate not shared by fellow Union general Fitz John Porter, who became the scapegoat for the loss, not clearing his name until many years after the war.

South Carolinian James Longstreet began his military career as a cadet at West Point, graduating in 1842. Commissioned as a second lieutenant in the infantry, he served in the Mexican War where he was wounded at Chapultepec. He subsequently became a major in the US Army Paymaster Department. On 1 June 1861, Longstreet, who would come to be known variously as "Old Pete" and "Old War Horse", resigned his commission to join the Confederate forces. Longstreet's performance in various engagements during the early stages of the war gained him Lee's confidence, as a result of which he was given command of a "wing" of the Army of Northern Virginia. NA

Although McDowell managed to lift this cloud from his record, he would not receive another field command. Instead he served on commissions and boards in Washington until 1 July 1864 when he was sent west to take over the Department of the Pacific, which was then headquartered in San Francisco.

On 1 September 1866, McDowell mustered out of volunteer service, but secured a billet as a brigadier general in the Regular Army, and six years later advanced to major general, the grade at which he retired in 1882. He ultimately became park commissioner for the City of San Francisco.

Franz Sigel

In 1852 Franz Sigel left his native Baden bound for the United States. He was an outspoken liberal, and had supported the unsuccessful Revolution of 1848 against Prussia. This former army officer was subsequently forced to flee his native land, and not long after landing in his new country, he made his way to St. Louis, Missouri. He worked there for nearly a decade as a schoolteacher. Then, in 1861, having become something of a pillar of the influential German population in the area, he attracted Lincoln's attention. The president desired to win support among transplanted Europeans with an anti-slavery, Unionist bent. With this objective in mind, during the summer of 1861, Sigel was commissioned as a brigadier general of volunteers.

Thereafter he became active in Missouri, fighting at the Battle of Wilson's Creek. On 8 March 1862, he commanded two divisions at the Battle of Pea Ridge, helping defeat Southern troops under Major General Earl Van Dorn.

Promotion to major general followed on 22 March 1862. Soon afterwards he was brought to the eastern theater to face Jackson in the Shenandoah Valley. When Pope was selected to command the Army of Virginia, Sigel was appointed commander of I Corps. Following the Second Manassas campaign he briefly commanded XI Corps in the Army of the Potomac, but his military career was lackluster at best after that. Sigel's defeat at the Battle of New Market (15 May 1864), led to his removal from field command. Almost a year later he resigned his commission, returning to civilian pursuits until his death in 1902.

CONFEDERATE

Robert E. Lee

As the son of a Revolutionary War hero it came as no surprise when young Robert E. Lee obtained an appointment to West Point. He entered the academy in 1825, and after four years as a cadet had managed to avoid receiving even one demerit. In addition, he graduated second in his class of 1829, which earned him a commission as second lieutenant in the Corps of Engineers.

His first assignment to work on fortifications at Hampton Roads was followed by a detail to serve as an assistant to the chief of engineers, a duty that began in 1834. This posting to Washington allowed him to live in a fine home that his new bride's family had given the couple. The stately home still stands overlooking Arlington National Cemetery.

Lee then went on to other duties, not the least of which was on Winfield Scott's staff during the Mexican War, where he served at both Cerro Gordo and Churubusco. He conducted reconnaissance during this period that greatly assisted the movement of Scott's forces. His services brought three brevets and Scott's highest accolade. He ultimately pronounced Lee "the very best soldier that I ever saw in the field."

Lee went on to become the commanding officer of the 2nd US Cavalry, and later the superintendent of West Point. Soon after the Civil War began, Lee's first-class reputation prompted Lincoln to offer him command of the Federal Army. He declined then resigned his commission, offering his services to his native state of Virginia.

On 23 April 1861, his offer was accepted with the rank of major general in the Virginia state forces. By 14 May he was also commissioned as brigadier general in the Confederate Regular Army. A month later he jumped to full general.

Jefferson Davis quickly appointed him as his military advisor, but after Joseph Johnston was wounded at Seven Pines, Lee departed Richmond to replace him. Thereafter, he remained in the field for the duration of the war, gaining many laurels and a legendary status. President Jefferson Davis ultimately appointed him general in chief of the Confederate States Army on 31 January 1865. It was, however, far too late for even Lee's prodigious talents to turn the tide.

Lee was a very different type of military leader from Pope, except in one respect. He, too, sought a classic confrontation in the mold of Austerlitz. According to eminent military historian Russell Weigley, at Second Manassas Lee "came as close as any general since Napoleon to duplicating the Napoleonic system of battlefield victory by fixing the enemy in a position with a detachment, bringing the rest of the army onto his flank and rear, and then routing him from the flank." It was a perfect textbook execution, but as Weigley concluded: "Lee was too Napoleonic. Like Napoleon himself, with his passion for the strategy of annihilation and the climactic decisive battle as its expression, he destroyed in the end not the enemy armies, but his own."

James Longstreet

South Carolinian James Longstreet began his military career as a cadet at West Point, graduating in 1842, as one of John Pope's classmates. He then received his commission as a second lieutenant in the infantry, and his first field duty was in Florida. After that he served in the Mexican War where he received a wound at Chapultepec. His actions in this conflict brought two brevets. Duty on the frontier followed, but eventually he transferred to the Paymaster Department and there he secured the rank of major.

On 1 June 1861, he resigned his US Army commission and sought a post as paymaster with the Confederate forces. Instead, on 17 June, he was made a brigadier general and placed in command of a brigade. By early October, he rose to the rank of major general, at which time he became a divisional commander. He subsequently participated in the Peninsula Campaign, Yorktown, Williamsburg, Seven Pines, and the Seven Days.

His performance in these various engagements gained Lee's confidence. Because of this he was placed in charge of a "wing" of Lee's

Except for Robert E. Lee, no other Confederate commander gained such renown or was more exalted than Thomas J. Jackson. A graduate of the class of 1846 at West Point, Jackson had served in the artillery in the Mexican War, where he earned two brevets. After the war he resigned his commission, and took up a post at the Virginia Military Institute, where the humorless professor no doubt would have remained in obscurity had it not been for the Civil War. Certainly an eccentric he was undoubtedly one of the South's boldest and most aggressive commanders. He played a key role in the Confederate prosecution of the war until his tragic death following the battle of Chancellorsville. NA

At the outbreak of the war some Union troops appeared in gray uniforms, as shown in this portrait of Henry H. Richardson, a subaltern with Company F of the 21st Massachusetts Volunteer Infantry. This regiment fought at Henry Hill on 30 August 1862. USAMHI

forces, a term that was pressed into service at that time to evade a piece of early Confederate legislation that disallowed organizations larger than a division. Ultimately Lee was able to have this prohibition repealed, and at that point Longstreet officially took command of I Corps of the Army of Northern Virginia, which in addition to other elements contained over 50 per cent of that army's infantry.

Although he was not as aggressive in pressing the enemy at Second Manassas as Lee may have wished, Longstreet nevertheless generally served his superior well. In fact, Longstreet's seizing of Thoroughfare Gap proved pivotal in the ultimate routing of Pope's troops. This accomplishment and his actions at Sharpsburg soon thereafter, led to his promotion to the rank of lieutenant general.

His friends sometimes called him "Pete" but to others he became Lee's "Old War Horse". Despite this latter title, his inclination toward strategic offense and tactical defense differed from that of his superior. While Longstreet's philosophy was correct in some instances, such as at Gettysburg, his incapacity for independent operations marred his reputation. Whatever Longstreet's shortcomings, he remained at Lee's side until the final surrender at Appomattox.

Thomas J. Jackson

Except for Robert E. Lee, no other Confederate commander gained such renown or was more exalted than Thomas J. Jackson. A graduate of the class of 1846 at West Point, Jackson had served in the artillery in the Mexican War, where he earned two brevets. After the war he resigned his commission then took up a post at the Virginia Military Institute, where the humorless professor no doubt would have remained in obscurity had it not been for the Civil War. Cadets considered him peculiar to

Some of Irvin McDowell's men encamped at Culpeper, Virginia, a town that boasted a key depot on the Orange & Alexandria Railroad. The seated man appears in the typical combat uniform that came to be associated with the Union Army – the dark blue "bummer's" cap, with dark blue, four-button sack coat and sky-blue kersey trousers. USAMHI

say the least, and they gave him such nicknames as "Tom Fool Jackson" and "Old Blue Light", in the latter instance because of his penetrating blue eyes.

When war came he accepted a colonelcy in the Virginia forces. He was soon ordered to the Union arsenal at Harpers Ferry. From there he marched with Joseph Johnston, as commander of 1st Brigade, Army of the Shenandoah. Newly promoted to brigadier general on 17 June 1861, Jackson was part of Johnston's army that moved to unite with Brigadier General Pierre Beauregard's troops at Manassas. Jackson's conduct during the subsequent First Battle of Manassas gained both he and his brigade the name "Stonewall".

By the fall he was a major general with responsibility for the strategically important Shenandoah Valley. He would again sting the enemy, but not always with the desired results. For instance, at Kernstown (23 March 1862) he suffered a defeat, for which the pious soldier partially blamed himself because he had fought on a Sunday. Nevertheless, he was able to divert Federal reinforcements to the valley and away from the attack on Richmond.

In May Jackson's performance improved. He halted Major General John C. Frémont's advance from West Virginia at McDowell, then took the offensive against a number of other Union commanders, none of whom could bring him to bay. His victories in the Valley Campaign behind him, Lee ordered Stonewall to assist in the defense of Richmond.

Once George McClellan had withdrawn after the Seven Days battles, Lee sent Jackson north, informing him in a letter, "I want Pope to be suppressed … " Knowing Jackson's propensity to keep his plans to himself, Lee's missive also suggested, "advising with your division commanders as to your movements, much trouble will be saved you in arranging details, and they can act more intelligently." Unfortunately, Jackson never took this sage counsel to heart.

At Cedar Mountain he committed his forces piecemeal, suffering unnecessary casualties in his eagerness to engage General Banks's Corps. His flanking movement later in the Manassas campaign was executed with great daring and threw Pope's Army of Virginia off balance. He then held firm in the face of determined attacks until Longstreet was able to roll up the Union left flank.

After Second Manassas, Lee once again detached Jackson and charged him with the seizure of Harpers Ferry. He subsequently rejoined Lee at Sharpsburg. Then came another promotion and command of II Corps.

Fredericksburg followed; then Chancellorsville, where his men outflanked the Union right and devastated the XI Corps of the Army of the Potomac. Later that night, as Jackson was returning from a reconnaissance, some of his own men opened fire, striking him in the arm which was amputated. Complications set in, and on 10 May 1863 he died of pneumonia, depriving the South of one of her greatest commanders.

Matthew Brady captured another gray uniform worn by a Northern officer, in this case an ornate example donned by the one-time commander of the 5th New York, Abram Duryée. Early in the war Duryée put aside this outfit for a brigadier general's uniform. At Second Manassas he commanded the 1st Brigade, 2nd Division of III Corps, under McDowell. During the battle he received two wounds, but nevertheless continued on active duty. USAMHI

OPPOSING PLANS

Lee's Strategic Envelopment
Despite McClellan's failure to capture Richmond, his powerful army remained a threat that concerned Lee and the Confederate leadership in general. It was vital that any steps taken to engage the enemy elsewhere did not jeopardize the Confederate capital. To accomplish the twin objectives of moving the fighting away from Richmond without endangering the city, Lee conceived a bold plan.

Although the enemy's 75,000 men outnumbered his 55,000, Lee decided to split his forces. One half of his army was to undertake a wide strategic envelopment with the purpose of flanking the Union line of communications and forcing the enemy to do battle at a place and time of Lee's choosing. This move would draw away forces from McClellan or at least divert other units from reinforcing him, especially if there was any hint that Washington, DC, might be threatened in the process.

Lee's scheme relied on swiftness and eluding the enemy. All the skill his subordinates could muster would be required to make the daring plan work. If he failed, however, the effect might be the opposite of that desired. The possibility existed that much of his force, if not all of it, could fall prey to the superior numbers of the Federal Army. If Lee accomplished his objective he would stand between the enemy and Washington, a position that would put the Federal Army on the

The 2nd US Sharpshooters were decked out in green uniforms, a shade long associated with riflemen. Lieutenant R.B. Calef was one of the officers in this special organization, which carried the breech-loading Sharps rifle, by the time it underwent its baptism of fire at Second Manassas. USAMHI

Weighing in at less than 100 lbs, Confederate Brigadier General William "Scrappy Billy" Mahone commanded a brigade in one of Longstreet's divisions. His pleated blouse and light-colored campaign hat offer just one example of the many variations of uniform worn by Southern officers and enlisted men alike. Note the wreath around his three stars on his collar, the common designation for most general officers in the Confederate forces. USAMHI

defensive, and in turn keep them away from Richmond. Of equal importance, a decisive victory against the North might encourage recognition of the Confederacy by European powers.

With stakes this high, Lee was willing to gamble, yet he could not afford to be reckless. Because McClellan was but 20 miles from Richmond at Harrison's Landing, and Pope's new Army of Virginia within striking distance, Lee was not in a position to take to the field himself. In fact, if Pope decided to mobilize and march on Richmond, the consequences could be disastrous. As such, not until early August, when Lee learned that McClellan was withdrawing on transports to head down river, did he have the latitude to move his immediate command for a thrust against Pope.

Pope's Mission

Jackson's success against the dispersed Union corps during the Shenandoah Campaign had resulted in the decision to create a unified command structure to better utilize the Northern forces in that area. Once Pope was in place Lincoln had two strong armies at his disposal, but the question was how best to deploy them. On taking command of the Army of Virginia, Pope was given three main priorities. He would not allow the capital to be threatened; he had to protect the Shenandoah Valley; and he should use his forces to pose a threat to the Confederates and attempt to draw Lee away from the defense of Richmond.

Pope loudly proclaimed to Lincoln and anyone else who would listen, that he was the right man for this task. If McClellan's army was added to his, Pope also felt that he would be in a position to engage in a Napoleonic-style clash that would crush the Army of Northern Virginia, leaving the road to Richmond open for his conquest. This is what the administration and many other Northerners wanted to hear.

Lincoln, in particular, paid attention to Pope's words. He and certain Northern leaders believed that harsher measures were required to quell the rebellion. To this end, the President intended to use the Confiscation Act passed by the US Senate in July 1862. This law authorized the seizure of Confederate property for the promulgation of the war, including the confiscation of slaves; a power that Lincoln hoped to exercise soon. With this end in mind he drafted an Emancipation Proclamation that would deprive the South of a major resource, namely slaves. At the same time it would send a clear message to England and other important European powers that the Confederacy was fighting for an unjust cause, which should not justifiably be supported by foreign nations.

Thus Pope received significant political support for his aggressive stance. Lincoln hoped for a major victory that would allow him to proclaim emancipation. If Pope gave him that victory he would become a national hero, and no doubt be rewarded with leadership of the Union forces.

Certainly Pope shared Lincoln's predilection to deal sternly with the South in so far as prosecution of the war was concerned. He made it clear that guerrilla activities within his area would be dealt with severely. Additionally, Pope intended to live off the land, destroy vital Confederate transportation assets, and if possible cut Lee off from Jackson. In order to accomplish all this he had to act swiftly to consolidate his forces. Although more aggressive than McClellan, who tended to have the "slows", Pope's bellicose manner would not prove any more successful.

OPPOSING ARMIES

UNION TROOPS

After the opening salvos at Fort Sumter, war fever gripped the North. At first recruiting proved easy. Thousands of men responded to President Lincoln's 15 April call for 75,000 volunteers to sign on for three months' service. Each state received a quota, and there was little difficulty in supplying the numbers required. Many flocked to the colors in part because they believed the war would be short. Indeed, a number of units had been raised for only a half-year's service.

By the summer of 1862, however, a goodly number of the original six month volunteers had returned home. They were replaced by some 640,000 volunteers who had entered the Northern ranks thereafter, usually with long enlistment periods. State troops and volunteers dominated, as indicated by the fact that Regular Army personnel totaled only 23,308 artillery, cavalry, infantry, and support troops by 31 March 1862, as opposed to 613,818 volunteers and a substantial number of militiamen. These

Some Regular Army and volunteer units alike continued to wear the long nine-button frock coat and black hat looped up on the side that had been regulation prior to the war. Men of the 2nd Wisconsin Infantry were among this group. As a consequence, they and their comrades in the 6th and 7th Wisconsin, along with the 19th Indiana, came to be called the "Black Hat Brigade". They likewise were referred to as the "Iron Brigade", a nickname they earned after stalwart performances at both Second Manassas and Antietam. NA would be the men who carried the Union banner at Second Manassas, most of whom were infantrymen clad in a variety of uniform styles and colors and carrying an array of small arms or manning numerous types of field pieces in the case of the artillerymen assigned to Pope's command.

Most of the Yankees had not seen action before. For instance, the 2nd US Sharpshooters under Colonel Henry A. Post, who had been assigned to Irvin McDowell's Corps during the Peninsula Campaign, never made it into battle during George McClellan's bid to take Richmond. Thus the specially armed regiment with its Sharps rifles had not been able to employ their breech loaders and marksmanship skills against the enemy. This situation would change soon.

The green-clad Sharpshooter regiment was formed into eight companies rather than the typical ten. Furthermore, most other regiments were made up of men from one state, but not so with these Sharpshooters. Company A had been raised from Minnesota, B from Michigan, C from Pennsylvania, D from Maine, E and H from Vermont, and F and G from New Hampshire.

The 5th New York (or Duryée's Zouaves as they were known in honor of their colonel, Abram Duryée) were more typical, in that the regiment consisted of ten companies raised from one area; New York. Duryée had seen to it that his men were attired in red fezzes and baggy trousers of a matching shade, along with white gaiters and jaunty blue jackets that reached just above the waist. Their flamboyant uniforms were based on those worn by France's famed colonial troops. Although they may have looked like dandies to the uninitiated, these colorful infantrymen from New York had seen service during the Peninsula Campaign and were considered to be excellent troops. Like many of the units who had been in that campaign as part of the Army of the Potomac, they were intensely loyal to McClellan, and not particularly pleased to have been transferred to Pope's Army of Virginia. Be that as it may, they would stand steady against the decimating fire of Hood's Brigade on 30 August, the decisive second day at Manassas.

Another veteran of Union organization, the 2nd Wisconsin, had received their baptism of fire during the First Battle of Manassas. On 28 August, when Jackson unleashed his men near Brawner's Farm, these men from the Badger State were sent forward in response, being the only regiment in John Gibbon's brigade that faced the opening Confederate volleys to have combat experience. Even then, their diminutive colonel, Edgar O'Connor, must have wondered how his command would react. Since the less than stellar Union performance at First Manassas over a year earlier, they had spent most of their time in camp drilling. "The little colonel", as he was known by some of his troops, had no reason to fear a repeat of the earlier battle, however, his men stood firm in the face of the serried ranks of the 5,000 men of Taliaferro's entire division.

William Wallace would be promoted to colonel of the 18th South Carolina after the regiment's commanding officer was killed at Second Manassas. This photograph was taken several years later, because Wallace is depicted as brigadier general, a rank he attained in September 1864. His double-breasted frock coat was of the style preferred by many Confederate officers. USAMHI

CONFEDERATE TROOPS

The Wisconsin men of "The Black Hat Brigade" waited for the advancing Southerners to come into range, little knowing their opponents had far more combat experience. Their foes were Jackson's stalwart "foot cavalry", whose first taste of combat had also been at First Manassas. They

Before his promotion to major-general and command of II Corps of the Army of the Potomac, Edwin Vose Sumner poses with his staff while still a brigadier-general. His troops would not be ordered to join Pope until 31 August, too late to participate at Second Manassas. NA

Samuel P. Heintzelman's units did see action. By the afternoon of 30 August he had assumed charge of the Union right. NA

had gained more combat experience during the Valley Campaign, and the "Stonewall Brigade" (a designation that would not become official until 30 May 1863) had paid the price for their marching and determined fighting, becoming ragged in the process. Their mixed uniforms were threadbare, shoes worn, and rations monotonous and at times sparse. Yet these soldiers were the backbone of Jackson's wing (or corps as it would later be designated).

Most were from rural backgrounds, as were a great number of Confederate fighting men, and were drawn from some 18 counties in the Shenandoah Valley. Thus, they literally were campaigning in their own backyards. Rigid training under Jackson, strict military discipline and unshakable self-belief welded them into a formidable force. They, along with James Longstreet's infantry, were more than a match for Pope's troops as they maneuvered during the summer of 1862.

Although the core of the Army of Northern Virginia was foot soldiers, Robert E. Lee's command also boasted some fine artillery batteries. Once again the men tended to come from nearby locales, and as a result had a common bond helping build unit cohesion. Some of the organizations had existed as militia before the war, which meant that their members also boasted considerable expertise as gunners.

Lee, likewise, was fortunate enough to have at his disposal some of the finest cavalry to fight on either side during the war. Southerners counted within their number numerous well-mounted and experienced equestrians. In fact, during the early part of the war Confederate horse soldiers generally proved to be more adept then their Union counterparts; performing reconnaissance and raids they became the eyes and ears of Lee's army. One of these men particularly gained fame for his exploits. A youthful Virginia-born cavalier by the name of James Ewell Brown Stuart had graduated from West Point just a little over six years before the war. Despite his junior status, he had been made a lieutenant colonel early in the conflict, and not long after participating in actions at Harpers Ferry and the Battle of First Manassas he rose to the rank of brigadier general. Flamboyant and brave, "Jeb" Stuart garnered further laurels during the Peninsula and Seven Days operations, leading to his promotion to major general on 25 July 1862, when he took command of all of the Army of Northern Virginia's cavalry. Stuart's daring leadership would plague Pope's forces in the field during that summer, although he himself was caught napping on the eve of Second Manassas, and barely escaped capture by Union cavalrymen.

CEDAR MOUNTAIN, 9 AUGUST 1862

Major General Joseph Hooker, seen here as a brigadier general, led the 2nd Division of Heintzelman's III Corps. He would meet the enemy at Kettle Run, two days before Second Manassas, and displayed an aggressive nature that helped win him the nickname "Fighting Joe". NA

On 14 July, Pope started an advance toward Gordonsville. With about 80,000 troops around Richmond, Lee had McClellan's army of 90,000 in front of him and Pope's 50,000 converging from the north. Faced with the certainty of eventual defeat unless he seized the initiative, Lee took advantage of McClellan's inactivity and sent Jackson north toward Gordonsville with 12,000 men, among other things to defend the vital Virginia Central Railroad, which connected the Valley with Richmond. On Jackson's request, Lee next sent A.P. Hill with reinforcements, raising Jackson's available manpower to 24,000.

At the same time, Federal forces made their way slowly toward Culpeper, Virginia. Jackson was delighted to learn that it was Banks, his old adversary from the Valley Campaign, who was heading his way. Jackson decided to strike rapidly toward the vicinity of Culpeper to destroy the first enemy corps to arrive, reasoning he would, thereafter, be able to operate from a central position and defeat the other two corps in detail.

Jackson's Corps was rested, their mounts in good shape, and the men had great confidence in their leaders, while they themselves were in the main battle-wise veterans. These factors and the confidence born of previous victories, made this force the best that Jackson had fielded to date. Morale was high. Jackson had every reason to think he would again carry the day. Despite his reputation for rapid marches his progress was slow, in great part because of the confusion caused once again by his penchant for keeping his plans to himself. Despite Lee's urging to maintain good communications with his subordinates, Jackson once more failed to convey his overall blueprint to his division commanders – Charles Winder, Richard "Bald Head" Ewell, and A.P. Hill. They did not know their superior's original intentions much less his subsequent modifications.

On 8 August this flaw in leadership led to chaos along the march route. Jackson had changed the order of march, and sent Ewell by an alternative route to Culpeper. This resulted in Ewell's and Hill's troops becoming entangled as the two elements crossed. Perturbed by Jackson's refusal to share his aims, Hill did little to disentangle the two columns. This meant that by day's end his units had moved only about two miles, while Ewell's men tramped only eight miles, rather than the 20 the force was supposed to make. The ability to march an army, being as much a part of generalship as actually directing the men in combat, the Confederates made a poor show.

Nevertheless, on the next day Hill woke his troops early and quickly had them on the road to make up for the lost time of the previous day. He caught up with Winder, who in turn was not far behind Ewell. As such, it was Ewell's vanguard that made first contact with Banks's advance force.

Shortly after noon some of his men ran into the Union cavalry, with a few of their guns in support on a low ridge planted with corn. Sizing

CEDAR MOUNTAIN, 9 AUGUST 1862

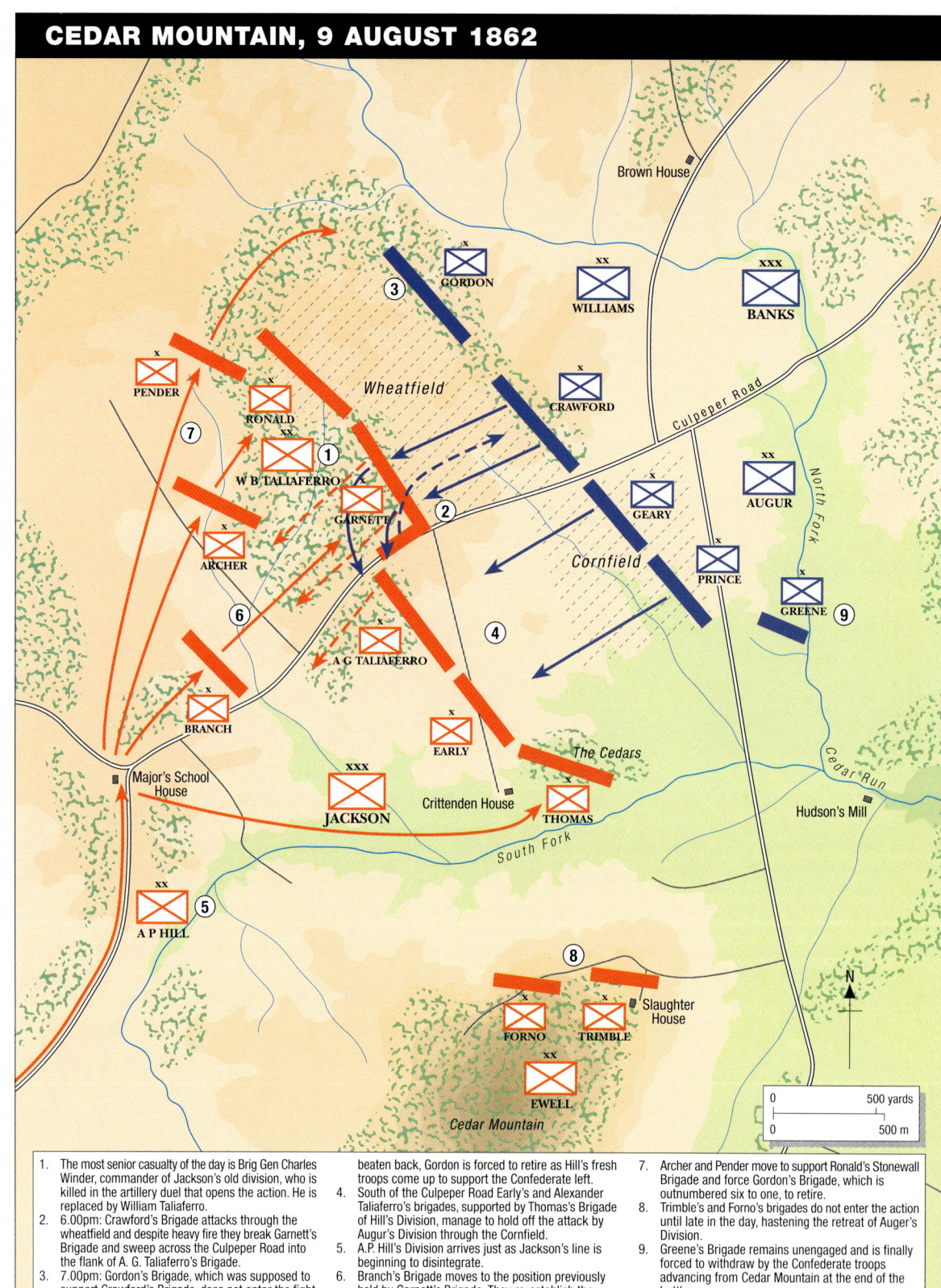

1. The most senior casualty of the day is Brig Gen Charles Winder, commander of Jackson's old division, who is killed in the artillery duel that opens the action. He is replaced by William Taliaferro.
2. 6.00pm: Crawford's Brigade attacks through the wheatfield and despite heavy fire they break Garnett's Brigade and sweep across the Culpeper Road into the flank of A. G. Taliaferro's Brigade.
3. 7.00pm: Gordon's Brigade, which was supposed to support Crawford's Brigade, does not enter the fight until an hour later. With Crawford's attack having been beaten back, Gordon is forced to retire as Hill's fresh troops come up to support the Confederate left.
4. South of the Culpeper Road Early's and Alexander Taliaferro's brigades, supported by Thomas's Brigade of Hill's Division, manage to hold off the attack by Augur's Division through the Cornfield.
5. A.P. Hill's Division arrives just as Jackson's line is beginning to disintegrate.
6. Branch's Brigade moves to the position previously held by Garnett's Brigade. They re-establish the Confederate line and help drive off Crawford's Brigade.
7. Archer and Pender move to support Ronald's Stonewall Brigade and force Gordon's Brigade, which is outnumbered six to one, to retire.
8. Trimble's and Forno's brigades do not enter the action until late in the day, hastening the retreat of Auger's Division.
9. Greene's Brigade remains unengaged and is finally forced to withdraw by the Confederate troops advancing from Cedar Mountain at the end of the battle.

up the situation, Jackson formulated his plan. He ordered a large artillery force into position on both flanks of the advancing infantry. Ewell's command was to hook around the Union's eastern flank across the slopes of Cedar Mountain. Winder was told to go to the left while Hill remained in reserve.

It took time for the troops to deploy, but eventually Confederate artillery opened up. But the bombardment had an unsuspected consequence. Crossfire from Ewell's batteries actually inhibited his advance at first. Even worse, Winder suffered a mortal wound not long after the fighting began.

Banks chose this moment to attack, his troops striking Jackson's center and left. With Winder's Division disrupted by the loss of their commander the Federals overwhelmed Garnett's Brigade and threatened to roll up Jackson's line. Every regimental commander in the brigade was killed or wounded and Winder's guns were withdrawn.

At that point Ewell attacked, Hill committed the reserves, and Jackson intervened personally to stabilize the line. Both sides of the Union line were outflanked. As the full moon rose, the Yankees retreated while their cavalry provided a screen. But Jackson had mismanaged the whole affair. His victory had been costly.

Ambrose P. Hill commanded a division in Jackson's right wing. Despite some confusion in reaching his position, Hill's forces were to play a key part in the Second Manassas clash. NA

PLAYING FOR TIME, 10–27 AUGUST 1862

Nonetheless, the battle of Cedar Mountain, as General Lee stated in his after action report, "effectually checked the progress of the enemy for the time … " Lee knew pressure from Washington would build, forcing Pope to advance. As early as 14 August, when Jesse Reno's arrival increased Pope's strength to 50,000, he made for the Rapidan with the intention of crossing his army at the historic Raccoon Ford, where "Mad" Anthony Wayne led his Pennsylvania brigade to reinforce the Marquis de Lafayette in 1781. On 13 August, in anticipation of this move, Lee ordered Longstreet's division with its two brigades under John B. Hood to move to Gordonsville. R.H. Anderson followed him, pre-empting by a day McClellan's movement from Harrison's landing toward Fort Monroe, Virginia. At the same time Jeb Stuart was ordered to move the main body of his cavalry toward Orange Court House, covering Longstreet's right.

Longstreet's troops reached the neighborhood of Gordonsville on the 16 August. The same day, Jackson quietly brought his command up behind the Clark's Mountain range, east of Orange Court House, to cover the Raccoon and Somerville fords of the Rapidan.

Lee followed and joined his army in Orange near the middle of August. On 19 August, he ordered his commanders to move against Pope and defeat him before McClellan could link up with the Army of Virginia. Longstreet advised a movement to the left in order to strike Pope's right. Lee and Jackson thought it better to turn Pope's left and put the Army of Northern Virginia between the Union troops and Washington. This would cut both Pope's line of supplies and retreat. To accomplish this, Lee directed Longstreet to cross the Rapidan at Raccoon Ford with the right wing of the army. He was to move toward Culpeper Court House, while Jackson, with the left wing, was to cross at

Former US dragoon officer Richard S. "Dick" Ewell also headed a division in Jackson's wing. His men participated in the Cedar Mountain fight, as well as at Groveton, and Second Manassas. He lost his leg as a result of a wound sustained at Brawner's Farm. NA

119

Confederate Major General John Bell Hood did double duty under Longstreet, serving as both a division and brigade commander. NA

Somerville Ford and proceed in the same direction, keeping on Longstreet's left. R.H. Anderson's division and S.D. Lee's battalion of artillery was to follow Jackson, while Stuart, crossing at Morton's Ford, was to reach the Rappahannock by way of Stevensburg. He was directed to destroy the railroad bridge, cut Pope's communications, and operate on Longstreet's right.

Ever spoiling for a fight, Jackson wanted to attack earlier. Longstreet rebutted that he was not prepared. In addition, Fitz Hugh Lee's Brigade of Stuart's cavalry, the lead brigade on the march from Richmond, had strayed too far to the right, in the direction of Fredericksburg, and was a day late in joining the army, causing another delay.

During all this activity Stuart had set out with his small staff in search of Fitz Lee. On the evening of 17 August the group reached Verdiersville. Not finding his cavalry reinforcement waiting there as expected, Stuart dispatched a rider with a message for the troops to hurry to join him. He then had his horse unsaddled while he stripped off his saber belt, hat, and other gear to get a night's sleep in the garden of the Rhodes house.

Dawn of 18 August broke with the sound of hooves, which Stuart thought must be Fitz Lee. But it was not. Pope had called for a reconnaissance in the area, and Colonel Thorton Broadhead with elements of the 1st Michigan Cavalry along with the 5th New York had obliged. Now the blue-clad troopers were riding towards the slumbering "Beauty" Stuart. The Confederate cavalier jumped on his unsaddled horse and beat a quick retreat, leaving behind his tack, cloak, and sash. Also abandoned was his plumed hat, which he had recently received from a former comrade from his days in the United States Army, Samuel Crawford. After Cedar Mountain, Crawford and Stuart had met during a brief truce and the Confederate cavalryman bet his old friend that the Northern press would declare the clash a Union victory, which it was not. When the action was reported as Stuart predicted, Crawford sent the hat to Stuart in payment of his wager. Although leaving behind many personal items, Stuart managed to vault the fence on his steed and escaped capture.

Stone Bridge across Bull Run Creek was in ruins after the first engagement fought there, as evidenced by this March 1862 photograph. Finding fords and repairing or building new bridges were all part of the game for the advancing Union troops as they sought an elusive Jackson. NA

Pontoons, such as this one at Blackburn Ford, Virginia, were one means of river crossing that could be provided by Union engineers. NA

OVERLEAF The aftermath of the battle at Cedar Mountain on 9 June left some 2,300 Federal killed, wounded, and missing on the field. Jackson's men had lost 231 dead and 1,107 wounded. By midday 11 August a truce had been arranged to allow both sides to remove their wounded and bury their dead. The Confederate troops also took the opportunity to gather up some 1,000 Northern firearms that had been left on the ground, in contravention of the terms of the truce. Although Federal commanders were incensed by this action no one was willing to renew the fighting over the matter. (Mike Adams)

The pace did not seem very hectic for these Union troops camped at Blackburn Ford, on 4 July 1862, not quite a year after the First Battle of Bull Run. Guarding crossings and other strategic spots meant that Pope's army was scattered throughout the area to counter Confederate movements. USAMHI

His adjutant general, Major Norman R. Fitz Hugh, however, was not that fortunate. He fell into the hands of the Union troops. What was worse, the major had a copy of Lee's order of march, and had no time to dispose of it before capture. These documents were quickly forwarded to Pope, who hastened to evacuate Culpeper and put the Rappahannock between himself and Lee.

Lee's original plan now had to be revised. He would march his 50,000 men at dawn of 20 August, but not against Culpeper Court House. Instead, Longstreet marched to Kelly's Ford of the Rappahannock, while Jackson marched by way of Stevensburg and Brandy Station toward Rappahannock

Bridge, bivouacking for the night near Stevensburg. Stuart, with Beverly Robertson's cavalry brigade, had a spirited contest that day with George Bayard's cavalry, near Brandy Station. Forced from that point, Bayard took position between Brandy Station and Rappahannock Bridge, still guarding the Federal rear, from which position Stuart again routed him and drove him across the Rappahannock, under cover of Pope's batteries on the high northern bank. The Confederates captured 64 prisoners and lost 16 killed and wounded.

The morning of 21 August found Lee on the south bank of the Rappahannock, with Jackson on the left, extended from the Rappahannock Station railroad bridge to Beverly's Ford. Robertson's 5th Virginia Cavalry had made a dash there, scattering the Federal infantry nearby, disabling a battery, and spending most of the day on the north side of the river aided by Jackson's batteries on the south side. On the approach of a large Federal force, Thomas L. Rosser, under Stuart's orders, recrossed. Longstreet extended Lee's line from Rappahannock Bridge to Kelly's Ford. Pope's 55,000 men held the commanding ground on the north bank of the Rappahannock. Likewise, a lively artillery duel was maintained during the day between the confronting armies, but with little or no damage to either.

The open terrain here dictated caution; strategic movements could not be concealed. It was evident that Pope's army was not vulnerable to a frontal assault. Also, his left was difficult to approach. The fact that he received reinforcements steadily from the direction of Fredericksburg was of consequence too.

Accordingly, in conference with Jackson, Lee determined to turn Pope's right, a move that would place the Confederates in his rear, cutting him off from the old highway that led through the Piedmont country, through Warrenton toward Washington. Moreover, Lee could use the Bull Run mountains to screen his movements.

These ruins of the railroad bridge at Blackburn's Ford are typical of the damage inflicted during the efforts made by both sides to disrupt the enemy's lines of communications. LC

The railroad bridge near Union Mills remained intact, allowing Federal rolling stock to continue along this section of the Orange & Alexandria. LC

LEFT The Rebels had not destroyed this bridge, which spanned the Hazel River, a tributary of the Rappahannock. LC

BELOW Yet more of the handiwork of Union engineers is evident, in this case a bridge provided by men of McDowell's Corps just four days before the battle. LC

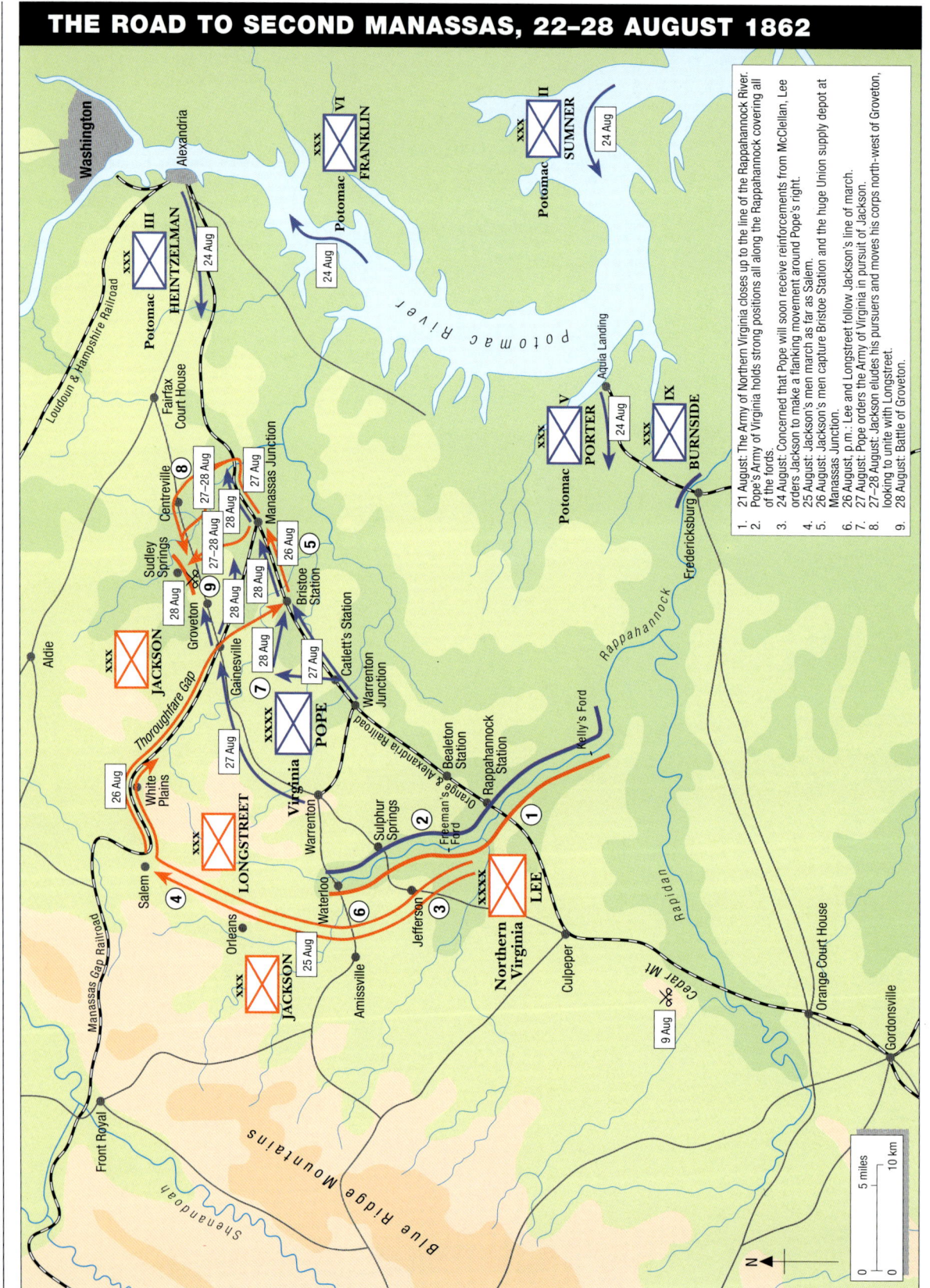

Supplying the Federal forces in the field required a network of wagons and railroads. Union operations in enemy country taxed both combat soldiers and logistical support personnel. USAMHI

Fresh beef for a famished Federal army sometimes came on the hoof – as evidenced by this photograph of a herd crossing a bridge on its way toward hungry troops. In comparison to his Southern adversary, the Northern soldier had ample sustenance during the campaign. USAMHI

The first step in this strategic envelopment was to mobilize the left wing of his army under Jackson, behind the protective screen of the mountain ranges, without Pope's knowledge. While Jackson and Stuart drew Pope's attention along the Rappahannock, north of the railroad, Lee moved Longstreet from his right, by concealed roads, and placed him in Jackson's rear. This left Jackson free to fall back after dark so he could march to a position further up the river, but still maintain contact with Longstreet's left.

This was accomplished during the night of 21/22 August. That day, preceded by cavalry, Jackson reached the neighborhood of Sulphur Springs, where the great highway, from Culpeper Court House toward Washington, crossed the Rappahannock and then passed through

Cedar Mountain rose amidst a pastoral Virginia setting, but this peaceful place would become a battlefield on 9 August. LC

Warrenton to Centreville. Simultaneously, Longstreet, through vigorous use of skirmishers and artillery, maintained Pope's attention, causing him to reinforce his position at Beverly's Ford, in the expectation that Longstreet would try to force a passage there and attack his center. Jackson's line of march was harassed by cavalry and infantry from a detached column that Pope was moving up the north bank of the river, to keep pace with whatever movement Lee might be making to his left.

At about noon an especially bold encounter ensued at Freeman's Ford as Jackson's rear was passing that point. His rearguard, under Isaac R. Trimble, deployed and awaited the Federal attack. Hood, with two of Longstreet's brigades, came up at about 4.00pm, when Trimble, aided by these reinforcements, launched a spirited attack on the Federal brigade, which had forded the river. Trimble drove back the Union troops in confusion. A third crossing, in pursuit of information, was made by Confederate cavalry, infantry, and artillery at Fant's Ford, but they soon retired, having gained little intelligence from this reconnaissance.

Elsewhere, when Jackson reached the river opposite Sulphur Springs, and found the ford unguarded, he at once began moving his troops to the other side. He sent over the 13th Georgia and two batteries, while Jubal Early crossed, on an old mill dam, about a mile further down the river. It began raining while these troops crossed, and an afternoon of showers was followed by a night of heavy downpour and darkness, preventing the crossing of more men. By morning the swollen river was unfordable and Jackson's advance guard under Early was isolated on the opposite shore.

Pope's main body continued to hold its position, near the railway, on 22 August, as he was unwilling to move farther from his expected reinforcements from Fredericksburg. Fearing an attack from Longstreet, whose whereabouts remained unknown to him, Pope did not move to his right to intercept Jackson's forces.

During the morning Lee dispatched Stuart with the main body of his cavalry to Waterloo Bridge, four miles above Warrenton Springs. There, Stuart, with 1,500 men and two guns, crossed the river and began a rapid march for Pope's rear, to break the railway leading to Washington and gather information, in a similar manner to his grand ride around

Federal artillery crosses a tributary of the Rappahannock near Cedar Mountain, during 9 August 1862. The gunners are on their way toward what soon would become a battleground. USAMHI

McClellan at Richmond earlier in the year. With a good road to march on, he reached Warrenton unopposed. After halting there for a short rest, he continued eastward via Auburn Mills to Catlett's Station on the Orange & Alexandria Railroad. He intended to destroy the bridge over Cedar Creek near that place. The downpour that had swelled the Rappahannock caught Stuart, and he reached his objective in the midst of rain and darkness. In the process, his troopers had captured a fleeing black man, who led Stuart to a camp where they seized Pope's headquarters wagons.

Stuart quickly captured the Federal commander's staff, his personal baggage, and official papers. Despite gaining these prizes, Stuart's efforts to destroy the wagon trains and the railroad bridge only partially succeeded. The rain and the darkness made it impossible for him to carry out his orders completely, so he began his return before daylight on 23 August with 300 prisoners. Recrossing the Rappahannock in the evening of the same day, he withdrew without further incident. He had taught Pope a lesson on the subject of rear guards, and caused some concern among Federal troops as to the safety of their lines of retreat. Additionally, Stuart had captured correspondence between Pope and Halleck, which provided Lee with a concise picture of the strength and the plans of his antagonist.

Meanwhile, the heavy evening rain of 22 August interrupted Jackson's movement and compelled Lee to temporarily abandon his intended flanking activities. Jackson repaired the bridge at the springs in order to extricate Early, who was still on the north bank of the Rappahannock.

Pope, knowing the river was impassable, gave up his scheme of crossing to attack Lee's rear. He was now determined to concentrate against the Confederates on the north side of the river. Early on the morning of 23 August he ordered Sigel toward Sulphur Springs, by way of Fayetteville, followed by Banks and Reno. McDowell, on Pope's left, received orders to burn the railroad bridge at Rappahannock Station, which to that point he had kept intact, and move toward Warrenton.

Artillerymen of Knapp's Pennsylvania Battery manned six 10-pdr Parrott rifles similar to this one at Cedar Mountain.

This would put him in a position to oppose any movement of Lee from Sulphur Springs toward Warrenton. John Reynolds' Division of 6,000 men, from Aquia Creek followed McDowell.

With Union forces on the move Early maintained a bullish facade while awaiting the reconstruction of the bridge in his rear. He held the road against the advance of Sigel's 25,000 men, who Pope had ordered forward to crush the Confederates on the north side of the river. Sigel believed that Lee's whole army was in front of him, however, and merely indulged in skirmishing and artillery fire until dark, after which he went into camp and advised Pope to withdraw his corps to a better position.

In the meantime, Ewell crossed the river to consult with Early during the night. They decided, in view of the large force before him, that it was not expedient to bring on a battle at that place. Orders were given at 3.00am for Early to withdraw, which he did soon after daylight, moving his men to Jackson's rear.

At about 10.00pm on 23 August, Pope himself, accompanied by McDowell's Corps and Reynolds's Division, reached Warrenton. At that time more than 50,000 men of the Army of Virginia had concentrated along the turnpike between Jackson at Sulphur Springs and Warrenton. By the next morning Pope was preparing to destroy Lee, whom he supposed was still north of the Rappahannock, as Sigel had reported. To gather more intelligence John Buford's cavalry was sent to Waterloo to reconnoiter and to destroy the bridge over the Rappahannock at that point. This would also permit him to slip behind Lee's supposed position. Sigel, Banks, and Reno were to move toward the same point, from opposite Sulphur Springs, while McDowell was placed along the roads leading to Sulphur Springs and to Waterloo to support the movement. As Sigel approached the river, A.P. Hill opened up his batteries and an artillery engagement ensued. Thus, Sigel cautiously continued his march up the river stung by Hill's batteries. It was well into the afternoon before Buford learned that there were no Confederates on the north side of the Rappahannock.

ABOVE **Union troops charging Jackson's left flank on 9 August 1862 met stiff resistance. LC**

LEFT **Days later, after the stinging combat had ended, Union men could remove their jackets and coats in the summer heat and humidity to relax, at least those who were fortunate enough to have survived Cedar Mountain. LC**

Sigel took most of 24 August to cover the six miles from Sulphur Springs to Waterloo, where he arrived late in the afternoon. Once on the scene he found the Confederates on the south side of the river, but holding and defending the bridge. The continuing thunder of Lee's guns had thoroughly engaged Sigel's concentration during the entire day. This was exactly as Lee had intended, as he wished to divert attention from the new flank movement that he had already begun.

Nor did Pope have any idea of what was transpiring. In the afternoon, after learning that there were no Confederates north of the Rappahannock, he communicated with Halleck that he would "early to-morrow … move back a considerable part of my force to the neighborhood of Rappahannock station … " Apparently concerned by his lack of information about Longstreet, he wanted to regroup his own forces while considering what to do next.

As a result of Stuart's 22–23 August raid on Catlett's Station, debris still littered the ground when Union troops returned to reoccupy the site. NA

Still desiring to strike a telling blow at Pope before McClellan's main body could reach him, Lee ordered divisions from Richmond under John C. Walker, Lafayette McLaws and D.H. Hill, which had been withheld as a safeguard in case McClellan attempted another assault on the capital. Lee and Jackson devised a plan of attack by which the latter would move rapidly to Pope's rear, cut his line of communication at Bristoe Station, destroy the Federal depot at Manassas Junction, then fall back to the north of the Warrenton Turnpike. There, he was to await the arrival of Lee with Longstreet's Wing. In turn, Longstreet would remain one more day on the banks of the Rappahannock to detain and confuse Pope.

During the night of 24 August, Longstreet's men took the place of Jackson opposite Sulphur Springs, allowing Jackson to begin his march early on the morning of 25 August. Leaving their baggage train behind and taking only ambulances and ordnance wagons with them, Jackson's men once more traveled light, leaving behind their knapsacks and carrying three days' cooked rations in their haversacks. Confident of being able to supply his men from the enemy's stores, Jackson was once again on the prowl.

Leaving Jeffersonton, Jackson headed north-west along the great highway leading to the Valley by way of Chester Gap. His sun-bronzed veterans were elated by the conviction that they were again bound for the scene of their victories of the preceding spring. But a short distance beyond Amissville, they changed course, turning from the north-west to the north-east. Jackson's column pressed steadily forward through the long August day, without halt, until they had covered 25 miles and reached the vicinity of Salem, on the Manassas Gap Railroad, just as the sun sank behind the ridge to their left.

At dawn on 26 August, Jackson's men were again puzzled to find themselves marching to the south-east, following the line of the Manassas Gap Railroad, through Thoroughfare Gap to Gainesville, where Stuart joined them with his cavalry and led the way from that hamlet directly to Bristoe Station. They reached there near dark, after a march of 24 miles, without having met opposition. Jackson and his 22,000 "foot cavalry" and Stuart with his intrepid troopers were now in Pope's rear.

They immediately proceeded to destroy everything in their path, while capturing trains moving toward Washington and breaking up detached Federal encampments along the railroad. Jackson then sent Trimble's Brigade of infantry and Stuart with a portion of his cavalry, through the darkness, four miles further to Manassas Junction, which they reached and captured after brief resistance at about midnight.

Weary from their rapid marches made on short rations, Jackson's fatigued and famished soldiers looked in disbelief at the mountains of supplies of every description they found piled high at Manassas.

This same day, Lee and Longstreet, leaving 6,000 men at Waterloo to guard the trains, followed Jackson marching as far as Orleans. Apprised of these various movements by his scouts and spies, but failing to comprehend their destination or purpose, Pope issued orders that scattered, rather than concentrated, his large army. He first ordered a concentration on Warrenton; Fitz John Porter with 10,000 men reached Bealeton, and Samuel F. Heintzelman with his 10,000 men reached Warrenton Junction on their way to obey this order. The corps from McClellan's army under Edwin V. Sumner, William B. Franklin, and Jacob D. Cox were that day marching toward Pope from Alexandria. Late in the night Pope again changed his orders, directing his troops to march on Gainesville, to intercept what he supposed would be Jackson's line of retreat from Manassas. Different portions of his command were now headed in that direction, but all were hindered by a confusion of orders and a resulting mixing of marching columns.

On 27 August, Lee rode with Longstreet through Salem and the Plains station. On the ride, an attack of a small body of Federal cavalry came near to capturing General Lee. Likewise, in the early morning Jackson marched the divisions of William B. Taliaferro (previously under Charles Winder, killed at Cedar Mountain) and of A.P. Hill to Manassas Junction, where they rested and joined in the feasting on the vast stores of quartermaster and commissary supplies that the Federals had gathered at this important depot. Ewell was left behind, at Bristoe, to protect Jackson's rear and oppose any advance from the line of the Rappahannock. There, in the afternoon, he fought a vigorous engagement with Porter, repulsing him before withdrawing across Broad Run. Late in the day Ewell's column continued to Manassas Junction. The storm clouds of the approaching battle were beginning to gather.

BRAWNER'S FARM AND THOROUGHFARE GAP, 28 AUGUST 1862

When Jackson began his withdrawal from Manassas on the evening of 27 August, which included the wholesale destruction of whatever his men could not carry off, he marched north toward Centreville and other sites along the Warrenton Pike. This would make it more difficult for Pope to cut him off from the approaching Longstreet. By the next morning, Jackson reported that he made immediate disposition of his command based upon the belief that the Union main body "was leaving the road and inclining toward Manassas Junction." Thus, in his own words, he advanced his command "through the woods, leaving Groveton on the left, until it reached a commanding position near Brawner's house [the residence of a local farmer named John Brawner]."

Jackson's guess about Pope's plans proved correct. He had indeed directed the Army of Virginia to converge upon Manassas Junction, where he believed the Confederates were in position. A brief fracas with some of Sigel's troops on the morning of 28 August confirmed Jackson's suspicions. During the fight, Captain George Gaither's troop of the 1st Virginia Cavalry managed to capture a courier, who carried the order of march for the Union forces dictated by Pope. Jackson knew what his enemy had in mind – the same could not be said of Pope.

In fact, Sigel had captured some Confederate prisoners as well, but the information they gave misleadingly indicated Jackson was still at Manassas. In reality the men of William Taliaferro's Division were concealed in the woods north of Groveton, with another division under

In the aftermath of Cedar Mountain, local citizens, such as the Robinson family, who owned this home, could return to their precarious lives. USAMHI

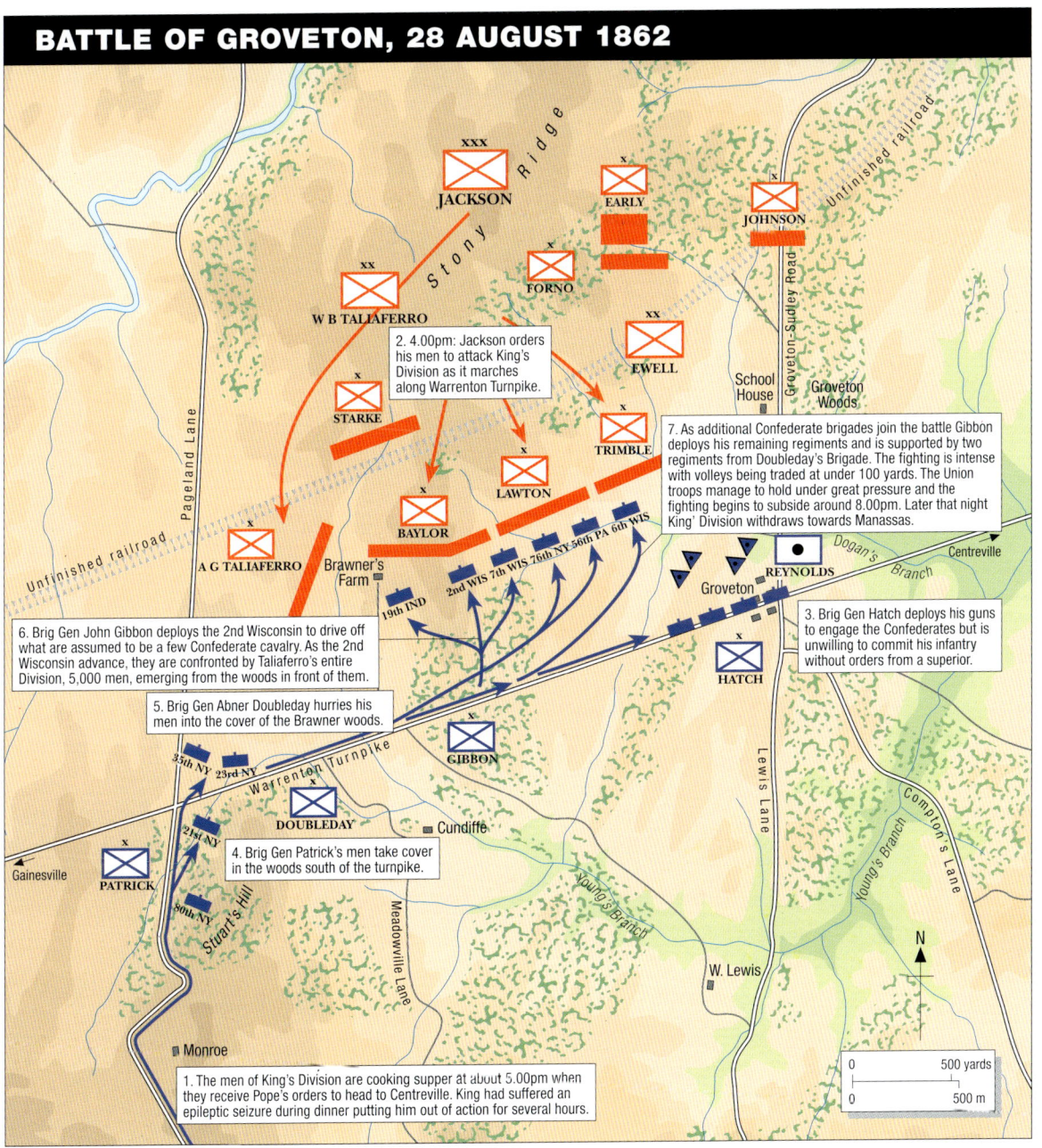

Richard S. Ewell heading toward Stone Bridge, and A.P. Hill's Light Division moving westward from Centreville towards the Groveton area.

Late in the afternoon with Jackson's men out of sight in the woods, a Federal column marched onto the scene. Brigadier General John F. Reynolds's Division was in the vanguard, and engaged in a brief clash with a Southern screening detachment. The action was brief and Reynolds continued on toward Manassas Junction, not realizing the Confederates were concealed nearby.

Following behind came Rufus King's Division at around 5.00pm. A little earlier, McDowell had been with King, but had departed in search of Pope to confer with his superior. King was thus the senior officer although he

LEFT **Given the number of troops who fell on 9 August the Confederate name for the battle, Slaughter Mountain, was appropriate. But it was the home of Reverend Slaughter, who lived on the mountain that was the source of the name.**

BELOW **The Confederates lost 1,418 troops killed or wounded at Cedar Mountain, including Brigadier General Charles S. Winder, who led Jackson's 1st Division. Winder breathed his last in this rustic residence. USAMHI**

was unwell, having recently suffered an epileptic seizure. Unfortunately, he would be debilitated by another attack later that evening.

Unaware of their commander's condition, the division proceeded along the turnpike, with the 1st Rhode Island Cavalry riding point for the lead brigade under John P. Hatch. The cavalrymen noticed nothing unusual, nor did the 14th Brooklyn, a zouave unit that Hatch sent out as flankers to guard against surprise attack. They, too, failed to detect the enemy waiting in numbers to spring an ambush.

Stonewall had placed three batteries in front of William E. Starke's brigade above the village of Groveton along Stony Ridge. Jackson told his division commanders Ewell and Taliaferro "Bring up your men, gentlemen!" In short order, the Virginia gunners of Captain Asher Garber's Staunton Artillery began to fire over the heads of Confederate skirmishers. The gates of Hell had opened; Manassas would once again be the arena for a bloody struggle between North and South.

Garber's artillerists had the Federals targeted after only three rounds. They were soon joined by the other two batteries, causing the Union troops to sprint for cover. Hatch ordered up one of his own batteries, Battery L, 1st New York Light Artillery, captained by John Reynolds. The six 3-in. ordnance rifles took position north-west of the scattering of half a dozen simple buildings that made up Groveton. Men of the 24th New York Infantry rapidly dismantled a fence obstructing the field of fire, allowing Reynolds to bring his pieces to bear.

The Yankees were outgunned though, as George Breck, a lieutenant in the outfit indicated. Breck wrote: "The shot and shell fell and burst in our midst every minute, exploding in the middle of the road between men and horses and caissons, throwing dirt and gravel all over us, and making it impossible for the cannoniers to man their pieces."

The Union buried 314 of their dead on the field, almost in the shadow of Cedar Mountain. In all 2,403 Union men were wounded, killed, or missing after the battle. LC

OVERLEAF **On 28 August at Brawner's Farm the untried 2nd, 6th, and 7th Wisconsin infantry regiments, and the 19th Indiana of BrigGen John Gibbon's "Black Hat Brigade" underwent their baptism of fire. Around 6.00pm they engaged what Gibbon believed to be a cavalry rearguard supported by artillery. Leading his men forward Gibbon soon realized that the Rebels were present in strength. His 2,100 Midwesterners faced Taliaferro's Division 6,200 strong. Before reinforcements could arrive, the Federal and Confederate forces had closed to within 75 yards of each other. The action continued until nightfall and Gibbon's units took 33 per cent casualties. The resolve displayed by Gibbon's men in this and later actions was soon to win them a new name as "The Iron Brigade" of the Union Army. (Mike Adams)**

RIGHT **The 10th Maine served in Brigadier General Samuel Crawford's Brigade, 1st Division, II Corps of the Army of Virginia. The regiment was at Cedar Mountain. Officers from this unit have returned a few days after the clash, perhaps to reflect on the fighting of 9 August. USAMHI**

BELOW **Men and horses fell at Cedar Mountain. The carnage of war was evident for sometime after the battle. USAMHI**

During the pounding, Hatch's infantrymen remained frozen in place. Marsena Patrick's unblooded command, which brought up the rear of the column, likewise halted and sought protection in the woods to the south of the roadway. Another of King's brigades led by Abner Doubleday left the pike, too, and headed into the woods that stood on Brawner's farm.

Only Southern-born John Gibbon, who had three brothers in the Confederate forces took the fight to the enemy. After Gibbon's 6th Wisconsin, which marched at the head of his column, came under attack, he formed his men into a battleline. He also deployed the artillery of Captain Joseph Campbell's Battery B, 4th US Artillery.

Confederate soldiers taken as prisoners of war during Cedar Mountain hang out their laundry to dry from their impromptu place of incarceration in Culpeper, Virginia. LC

Campbell's regulars unlimbered their 12-pdr Napoleons on high ground to the east of Brawner's farmstead.

In the meantime, without a corps or division commander to take charge, Gibbon rushed off to consult with Doubleday. The latter officer postulated that Jackson was in Centreville, and therefore the column only faced cavalry, who could be driven off with relative ease. With that Gibbon rode back to his men and launched his only veteran unit, the 2nd Wisconsin, against the Confederate artillery.

As the Federals advanced on the Southern guns, the 800 men of the veteran Stonewall Brigade emerged from the woods. The fighting was ferocious, with the two sides exchanging volleys at a scant 80 yds! Despite the devastating power of rifled musketry at this range, neither Union nor Confederate forces gave way. Confederate Brigadier General Taliaferro stated, "Out in the sunlight, in the dying daylight, and under the stars they stood, and although they could not advance, they would not retire."

Talaiferro further described the scene as "one of the most terrific engagements that can be conceived … " Confederate troops "held the farmhouse," he concluded, while "the enemy held the orchard. To the left our men stood in the open field without shelter of any kind." It appeared to Taliaferro like a painting depicting a moment of battle frozen in time. This surreal situation continued for some 20 minutes before the 19th Indiana came up to support the stalwart Wisconsin soldiers on their left. The commanding officer of the Hoosier troops, Colonel Solomon Meredith, captured the moment: "The enemy was secreted under cover of a fence and did not make their appearance until we had approached to within 75 yards. Immediately upon our halting the enemy fired. Three different times they came up at a charge, but the 19th stood firm." And each time the Confederates fell back to their fence line.

RIGHT **Some residences in the vicinity of Cedar Mountain were pressed into service as medical facilities for the several thousand casualties that were sustained during this brief, but sharp engagement. USAMHI**

BELOW, RIGHT **After Cedar Mountain, Clara Barton was one of the individuals who set to work to care for the wounded and dying. Decades later she became a prime mover in the founding of the American Red Cross. NA**

Meanwhile, on the right, Starke's Louisianians pressed the Federal troops. Jackson also sent nearly half of the Georgians from Lawton's Brigade to lengthen the Confederate line, but they met stiff opposition from the 7th Wisconsin, which Gibbon had added to his line. These blue-coated foot soldiers stood their ground, keeping the Southerners from moving forward, although the two forces remained but 100 yds apart.

The 6th Wisconsin, the last remaining regiment under Gibbon, also was sent to the front of Campbell's Battery. This regiment's commanding officer, Colonel Lysander Cutler, after learning that the 2nd Wisconsin was being slaughtered, and receiving the order to "join on the right of the 7th [Wisconsin] and engage the enemy," took his place in front of his command. Once in position, he called out, "Forward, guide center, march." In response, according to Major Rufus Dawes of the 6th, " … every man scrambled up the bank and over the fence, in the face of shot and shell … " Thus, by 6.45pm Gibbon's whole brigade was engaged in furious action.

Their adversaries clearly were not just a few Confederate cavalry troopers, but a strong force of infantry with substantial artillery support. There were six Southern brigades with 6,000 fighting men pitted against Gibbon's 2,100. Gibbon certainly needed urgent support, and made this known in a dispatch to divisional headquarters. When no response was forthcoming, Gibbon turned to the other brigade commanders. Again there was silence, except from Doubleday. To his credit, Doubleday did not stand by and watch the butchery. He sent two of his regiments, the

Confederate forces had wintered around Manassas, but had abandoned Fort Beauregard by the time this picture was taken in March 1862. USAMHI

76th New York and the 56th Pennsylvania into the whirlwind. Still the battle raged. Colonel Dawes again depicted what he saw: "Through the intense smoke, through which we were advancing, I could see a blood red sun sinking behind the hills … The two crowds, they could not be called lines, were within, it seemed to me, fifty yards of each other, and they were pouring musketry into each other as rapidly as man can shoot."

Captain James S. Blain of the 26th Georgia Infantry knew what it was like to be on the receiving end of these volleys. He indicated the Georgians had been "ordered in just after dark." They "marched steadily across an open field for about 400 yards, over which the balls were flying by the thousands." Brigadier General Lawton was determined to press on. He ordered a charge. Captain Blain admitted: "The Yankees did fearful execution; men fell from the ranks by the dozens."

Undaunted, by 7.15pm Jackson decided to increase the intensity of the offensive. He had reserves from Ewell's command on hand, and Hill was approaching. He thought it was time for a head-on onslaught. This action fell to the 21st Georgia and the 21st North Carolina, known as the "Twin Twenty-ones", of Brigadier General Isaac Trimble's Brigade. They were ordered to assault the right of the Federal line, while Alexander Lawton's Brigade was to press the attack to their right, closer to the Union center.

Captain James F. Beal, who commanded a company of the 21st North Carolina, provided a Southern perspective on this stage of the fighting. He revealed that the Confederate infantrymen halted at a fence, which they quickly tore "down and piled the rails in front. It offered good protection." He went on to assert: "The Federals were in a gully, or branch about 100 yards distant. We opened fire on them, but it soon became so dark that we could not see their position, but could only fire at the flashes from their guns, as I suppose they would fire at ours."

Sergeant Uberton Burnham of the 76th New York Infantry provided a view of the engagement from the Northern ranks: "Waving their colors defiantly, the rebels advanced from the woods to charge upon Gibbon's

Curious Virginia lads look on as Yankee cavalrymen water their mounts. Soldiers from both sides criss-crossed the state as the summer of 1862 campaign was waged. LC

brigade to our left. Gibbon's men did not run. Those western men are not easily scared. They stood still and fired as fast as they could. We gave the Rebs a crossfire, thinning their ranks and prostrating their color bearer. The Rebels finding they were getting the worse of it turned their backs and pointed for the woods."

When Jackson did not achieve his aim on the right, the Union left became his next target. The gallant Confederate artilleryman John Pelham rushed his guns to within 100 yds of the 19th Indiana. Following Pelham's bombardment, the last three regiments in W.B. Taliaferro's Division, commanded by his uncle Colonel A.G. Taliaferro, advanced. Gibbon was forced to withdraw the 19th, but the Indianians were able to slow Taliaferro's Third Brigade. The attack ceased, as darkness and exhaustion brought an end to the fighting.

A private from the 2nd Wisconsin, Nathaniel Rollins, summed up the trying events of that 28 August. "Rebel infantry," he said, had "poured from the woods by the thousand." He continued: "For an hour and fifteen minutes the most terrific fire imaginable was kept up; the hill top, the valley, and the wooded side of the hill beyond was a continuous sheet of flame. Darkness came on, the stars came out, and still the bullets filled the air." By 9.00pm, however, Gibbon and Doubleday agreed that it was time to make an orderly withdrawal.

Gibbon's men in particular had performed admirably. The steely determination displayed in this and subsequent actions would earn his men the reputation as the "Iron Brigade" of the Northern armies. Despite the fact that they had been set upon without warning, the Federals sustained fewer casualties than the Confederates, with an estimated 1,000 dead and wounded.

The former Confederate facilities at Fort Beauregard provided the Union men with all the comforts of home, including a privy. Routine camp life would give way to campaigning once Pope took charge. USAMHI

Nevertheless, the Confederates gave a good account of themselves that evening, and during the course of the fighting some 1,250 had fallen, including nearly 40 per cent of Stonewall's seasoned brigade. This was a dreadful blow in all respects, as was the loss of Ewell, who having been wounded during the encounter, subsequently lost his leg to amputation. This put him out of action for some time, depriving Lee of one of his more pugnacious and dependable officers. William Taliaferro likewise was wounded. Because of this, William E. Starke was temporarily assigned command of the division, while Ewell's Division was placed under a Harvard-educated attorney named Alexander R. Lawton.

Both wounded divisional commanders had demonstrated shortcomings during the action. Ewell had been slow in bringing his forces to the field and William Taliaferro had held back one of his brigades, and committed the others piecemeal.

Although Pope now knew the whereabouts of Jackson's wing, he seemed totally unconcerned as to the location and intentions of Longstreet's men. This oversight was to prove costly in the days to come.

In fact, Longstreet and Lee had halted at White Plains on the evening of 27 August. His column did not press forward with any great urgency despite Jackson's apparent vulnerability. Even on 28 August, Longstreet's forces did not break camp until 11.00am. to march toward Thoroughfare Gap. This was a rugged cut through the Bull Run Mountains that narrowed to as little as 100 yds in some places. Its north face was nearly perpendicular, with the south face less steep, but covered with tangles of ivy and boulders that provided excellent cover for anyone determined to hold the pass. Down the center ran a muddy stream from which rose walls of rock that measured several hundred feet in height.

Jackson had passed through the Gap on his march to Manassas, and it was an obvious route for the rest of the Army of Northern Virginia. Indeed, the Federals had received intelligence that Longstreet was marching on the Gap. As such, it seemed reasonable to expect this pass would be guarded by a strong Union force. On his own initiative, Major General McDowell ordered the 5,000 men of James B. Ricketts's 2nd Division to secure this vital pass, which was held only by the 1st New Jersey Cavalry.

McDowell's instincts were excellent, but Ricketts's command was no match for Longstreet's superior numbers. Even as he approached Thoroughfare Gap the New Jersey troopers were falling back, having been overwhelmed by the Southern advance.

Ricketts's response was to commit the 11th Pennsylvania Infantry, just as the Confederate 9th Georgia were setting up camp just east of the Gap. The Federal strike caught the Georgians by surprise, and the Pennsylvanians briefly gained the upper hand – that is until Brigadier General D.R. Jones sent forward a brigade from his division with another in support. Even then the Northerners did not yield and the arrival of the 13th Massachusetts helped bolster the line. Ricketts' men soon took up defensive positions, creating an impasse.

After dawdling for almost two days, Lee now became a dynamo. Colonel Evander Law's Brigade was sent scrambling over the rugged mountains on Ricketts' right, and C.M. Wilcox's Division was sent further north to Hopewell Gap in a bid to turn Ricketts's position. In addition, two regiments of Benning's Brigade had won a race with a detachment of 13th Massachusetts to seize the summit of Pond Mountain on the southern side of Thoroughfare Gap. Law's and Benning's men succeeded in flanking Ricketts's making his position untenable. He summarized the situation as follows: "The men moved forward gallantly but owing to the nature of the ground, the strongest positions being already held by the enemy, we were subjected to severe loss, without any prospect of gaining the gap." Even under these circumstances Ricketts's Division fought until darkness fell and then retired. At that point, nothing stood in Longstreet's path to Jackson.

Longstreet's move arguably constituted a major turning point for the Confederates. Not only did his breakthrough at Thoroughfare Gap allow him to combine with Jackson, but the fact that Pope seemed unaware of his presence had grave implications for the Army of Virginia.

Pope remained ignorant of Longstreet's approach as he took a late supper around 10.00pm on 28 August. While dining, news reached him of King's action at Groveton. He was delighted to learn that Jackson was still in the field, and was confident he could now bring the elusive Stonewall to bay. Pope dispatched orders for his commanders to concentrate their men at Groveton while King was to hold his ground to prevent Jackson escaping.

Although Pope intended King to maintain contact with Jackson, he learned that King had withdrawn to Manassas Junction at around 1.00am. A perturbed Pope issued new orders to his commanders around 5.00am on 29 August. These instructed McDowell to head toward Gainesville, taking King's men with him, while Sigel was to attack the enemy vigorously, pinning him in position. However, Pope's plan to surround Jackson was to disintegrate before him.

THE BATTLE OF MANASSAS

THE FIRST DAY, 29 AUGUST 1862

On the morning of Friday 29 August, one of Stuart's fellow cavalry officers, Captain W.W. Blackford, surveyed the aftermath of the drama that had unfolded almost on the doorstep of John Brawner's home. He recorded the Union position was "marked by the dark rows of bodies stretched out on the broomsedge field, lying just where they had fallen, with their heels on a well defined line." These men would not be the only casualties of fighting in the area. Even as Captain Blackford took stock of the previous evening's engagement, troops under Sigel and Reynolds were closing on Jackson's forces. Reynolds's Division was near Groveton, on the south side of the Warrenton Turnpike. North of the pike were Sigel's two divisions under Robert Schenck and Carl Schurz, with Robert Milroy's independent brigade further to the east, near the crossing of the Sudley Springs Road. At daylight Union troops opened the attack.

Jackson had positioned his command along a line running from Catharpin Creek, near Sudley Springs in the north to the heights above the turnpike near Groveton, facing east and south-east. Jackson's old division held the right; Ewell's Division under Alexander Dawton, Ewell having been wounded the evening before, held the center, with A.P. Hill's Division on the left. Their main line rested on the excavation of an unfinished railroad; a project started in the 1850s as the Independent Line of the Manassas Gap Railroad, but abandoned before tracks could

The land around Henry Hill had barely healed from the First Battle of Manassas, when the former foes began to make their way to this killing ground once more. USAMHI

LEFT **Ten days prior to the battle, Pope's engineers completed this bridge across the North Fork of the Rappahannock in order to keep his troops on the march. USAMHI**

BELOW **Union forces gathered around Manassas, making use of open fields near quiet homes as they prepared for the coming fight. LC**

be laid. These embankments ran in a north-easterly direction toward Sudley Mill and provided ready-made defense works for the Confederates. In front of the greater part of this old railroad were relatively thick woods, which were occupied by Southern skirmishers.

The Union forces advanced westwards, with Reynolds on the extreme left, as his Division was already the farthest west. On his right and still south of the pike, came Schenck, while on Schenck's right and just north of the pike was Milroy's Independent Brigade. Schurz's Division was north of Milroy on the far right of the Union line. The Federals advanced with spirit, their batteries shelling the woods, their skirmishers driving the enemy before them. Upon his arrival on the far left, Reynolds changed front to the north and advanced George Meade's Brigade across the pike, with the intention of turning the enemy's right. Meade's attack was inadequately supported by Schenck, however, who had detailed Julius Stahel's Brigade to assist Milroy, who was attacking the center of the Confederate line and was hard pressed. Reynolds eventually fell back some distance behind Schenck.

Meanwhile, Milroy's Brigade was pressing forward north of Warrenton Turnpike with skirmishers pushed forward beyond Groveton and Schurz's Division advancing on their right. Milroy sent two of his four regiments to support Schurz, but either through misunderstanding or perhaps as a result of getting lost, the 82nd Ohio and 5th West Virginia found themselves assaulting the center of Jackson's line. Although part of the 82nd Ohio actually managed to penetrate the Confederate line at the boundary of Lawton and Starke's divisions, a counter-attack by Trimble's Brigade soon threw them back. Further north, both Schurz's brigades, under Krzyzanowski and Schimmelfennig, were heavily engaged against Gregg's Brigade of South Carolinians. In a very aggressive defense Gregg succeeded in holding off Krzyzanowski and throwing back Schimmelfennig. After two hours of fighting, and having received no support from neighboring brigades, however, Gregg decided it was time to withdraw.

Schurz had no intention of allowing Gregg to withdraw unmolested, and around noon renewed the attack, driving the enemy through the woods. The 61st Ohio and 74th Pennsylvania of Alexander Schimmelfennig's Brigade even gained possession of a portion of the railroad embankment, holding it against repeated enemy counter-attacks, until about 2.00pm. Then the whole division was relieved by fresh troops, Hooker having been instructed by Pope to bring his, as yet unengaged, division forward. Schurz's men, exhausted and by now short of ammunition, withdrew to re-form on Dogan's Ridge.

During the morning the Union forces had acted with considerable determination, locating Jackson's line and in places even breaching it. The scene appeared set for Pope to deliver a telling blow once the rest of his army arrived on the field.

During late morning Heintzelman came up with the two divisions of Philip Kearny and Joseph Hooker, and Jesse Reno also arrived with his own and Isaac Stevens's divisions. By this time Sigel's troops, who had been marching and fighting since 5.00am, were exhausted. Expecting the co-operation of McDowell and Porter in the afternoon, Pope authorized a rest for Sigel's weary troops. As a consequence, there was a lull in the fighting until around 3.00pm, although heavy skirmishing and artillery exchanges continued.

Troopers commanded by Colonel Thorton Broadhead, who rode at the head of the 1st Michigan and 5th New York cavalry regiments, were responsible for cornering Stuart and nearly taking him prisoner. Weeks later, Broadhead was not so fortunate. After the second day of fighting at Bull Run, he was surrounded, but refused to surrender. When he would not give up, a Confederate soldier fired, striking Broadhead in the leg. The wound proved fatal. CPL

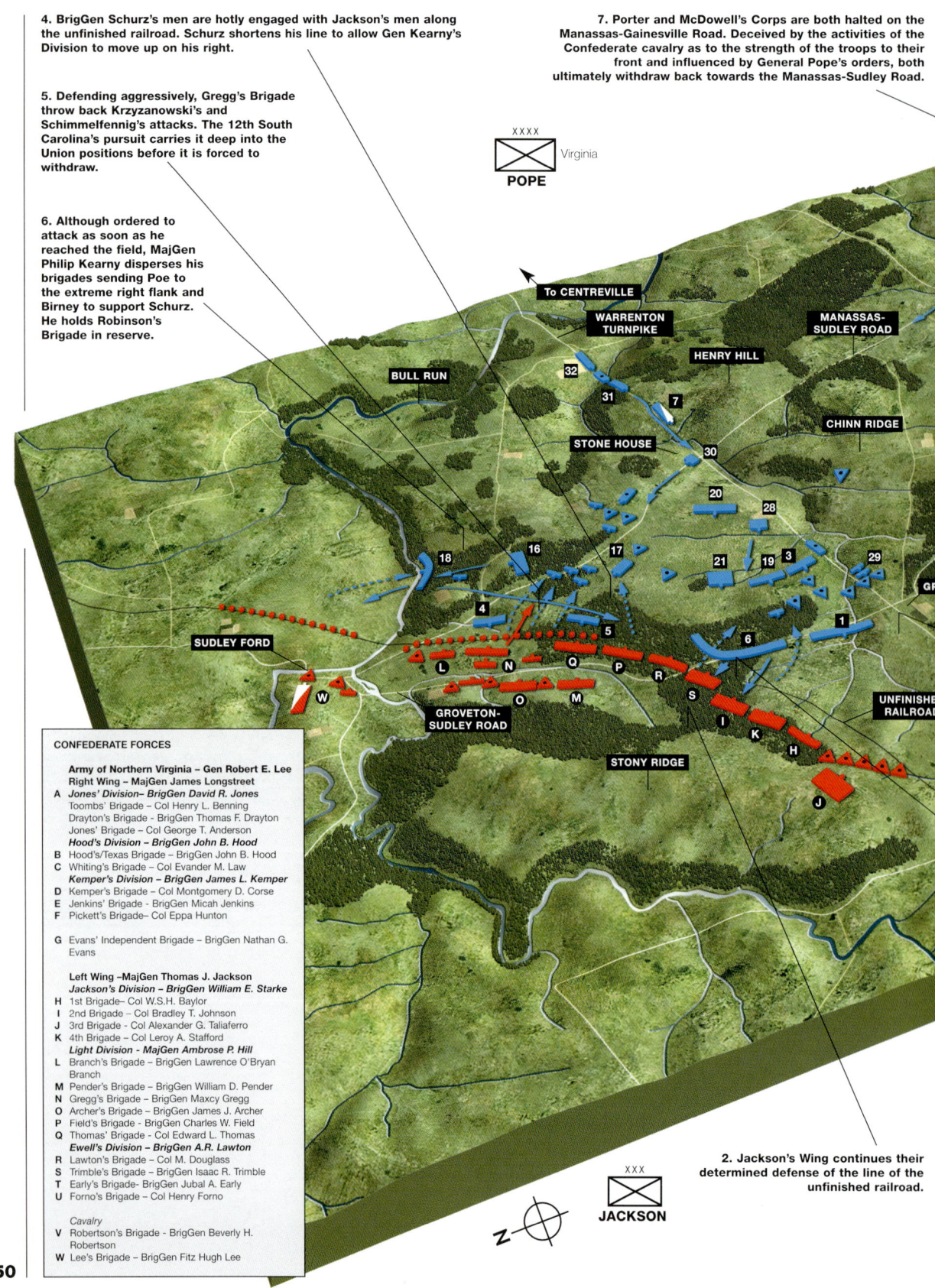

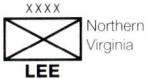

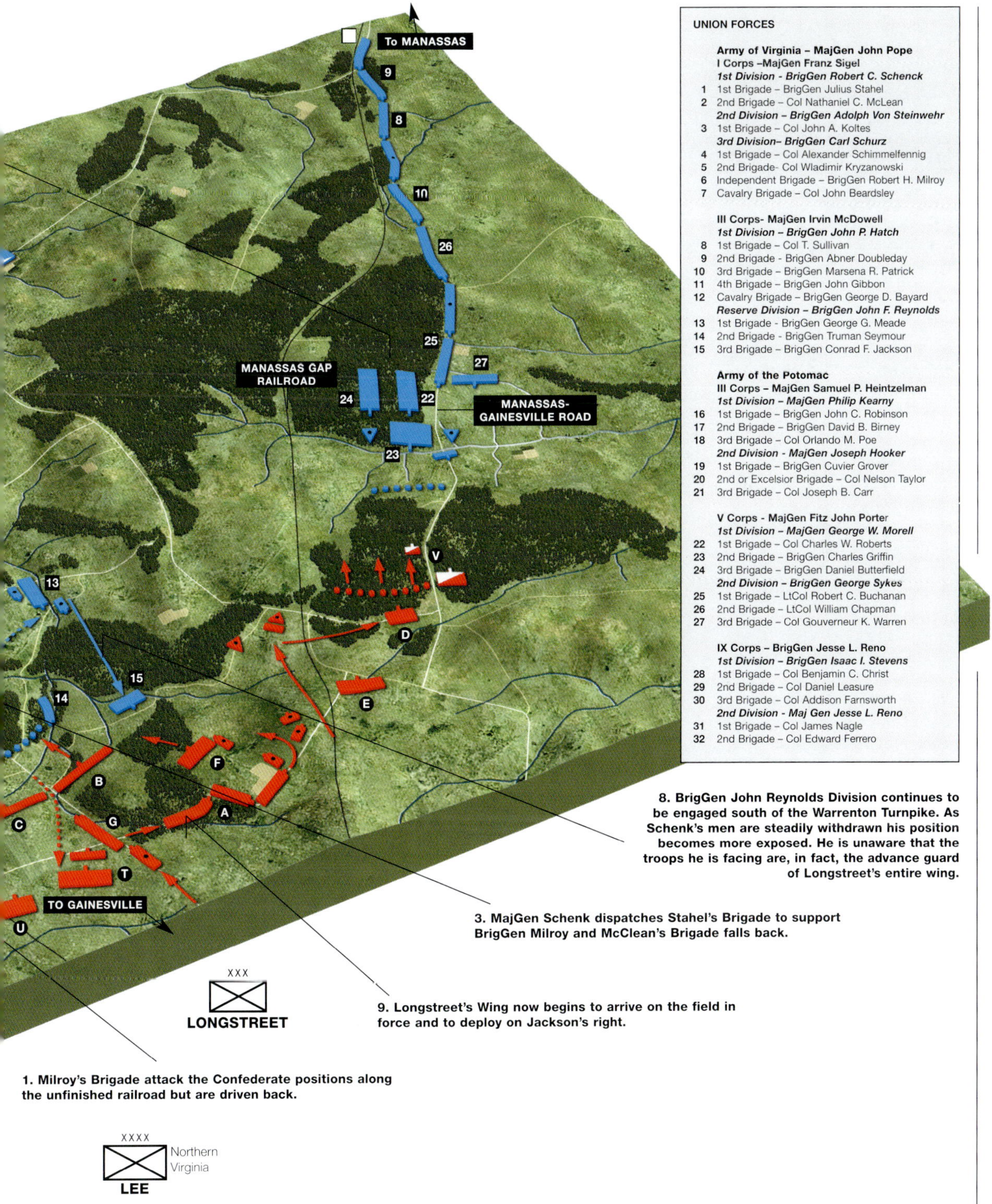
To MANASSAS
MANASSAS GAP RAILROAD
MANASSAS-GAINESVILLE ROAD
TO GAINESVILLE
UNION FORCES
Army of Virginia – MajGen John Pope
I Corps –MajGen Franz Sigel
1st Division - BrigGen Robert C. Schenck
1 1st Brigade – BrigGen Julius Stahel
2 2nd Brigade – Col Nathaniel C. McLean
2nd Division – BrigGen Adolph Von Steinwehr
3 1st Brigade – Col John A. Koltes
3rd Division– BrigGen Carl Schurz
4 1st Brigade – Col Alexander Schimmelfennig
5 2nd Brigade- Col Wladimir Kryzanowski
6 Independent Brigade – BrigGen Robert H. Milroy
7 Cavalry Brigade – Col John Beardsley
III Corps- MajGen Irvin McDowell
1st Division – BrigGen John P. Hatch
8 1st Brigade – Col T. Sullivan
9 2nd Brigade - BrigGen Abner Doubleday
10 3rd Brigade – BrigGen Marsena R. Patrick
11 4th Brigade – BrigGen John Gibbon
12 Cavalry Brigade – BrigGen George D. Bayard
Reserve Division – BrigGen John F. Reynolds
13 1st Brigade - BrigGen George G. Meade
14 2nd Brigade - BrigGen Truman Seymour
15 3rd Brigade – BrigGen Conrad F. Jackson
Army of the Potomac
III Corps – MajGen Samuel P. Heintzelman
1st Division – MajGen Philip Kearny
16 1st Brigade – BrigGen John C. Robinson
17 2nd Brigade – BrigGen David B. Birney
18 3rd Brigade – Col Orlando M. Poe
2nd Division - MajGen Joseph Hooker
19 1st Brigade – BrigGen Cuvier Grover
20 2nd or Excelsior Brigade – Col Nelson Taylor
21 3rd Brigade – Col Joseph B. Carr
V Corps - MajGen Fitz John Porter
1st Division – MajGen George W. Morell
22 1st Brigade – Col Charles W. Roberts
23 2nd Brigade – BrigGen Charles Griffin
24 3rd Brigade – BrigGen Daniel Butterfield
2nd Division – BrigGen George Sykes
25 1st Brigade – LtCol Robert C. Buchanan
26 2nd Brigade – LtCol William Chapman
27 3rd Brigade – Col Gouverneur K. Warren
IX Corps – BrigGen Jesse L. Reno
1st Division – BrigGen Isaac I. Stevens
28 1st Brigade – Col Benjamin C. Christ
29 2nd Brigade – Col Daniel Leasure
30 3rd Brigade – Col Addison Farnsworth
2nd Division - Maj Gen Jesse L. Reno
31 1st Brigade – Col James Nagle
32 2nd Brigade – Col Edward Ferrero
8. BrigGen John Reynolds Division continues to be engaged south of the Warrenton Turnpike. As Schenk's men are steadily withdrawn his position becomes more exposed. He is unaware that the troops he is facing are, in fact, the advance guard of Longstreet's entire wing.
3. MajGen Schenk dispatches Stahel's Brigade to support BrigGen Milroy and McClean's Brigade falls back.
XXX
LONGSTREET
9. Longstreet's Wing now begins to arrive on the field in force and to deploy on Jackson's right.
1. Milroy's Brigade attack the Confederate positions along the unfinished railroad but are driven back.
XXXX
Northern Virginia
LEE

SECOND MANASSAS – FIRST DAY

29 August 1862, 10.00am–12.00pm, viewed from the north-west showing the Union probes against Jackson's Wing, the arrival of Longstreet's Wing and Porter and McDowell's abortive advance along the Manassas-Gainesville Road.

ABOVE **Dashing Confederate cavalier J.E.B. Stuart narrowly missed being captured on the morning of 18 August, but enemy troopers did manage to seize his plumed hat, as well as some important intelligence about Lee's plans. USAMHI**

ABOVE, RIGHT **As a preliminary to the main clash of the Union and Confederate forces at Manassas, Confederate troops raided into Union territory, striking a section of the Orange & Alexandria Railroad near Catlett's Station, on 22 August. Pope, having made his headquarters there, left behind his general's dress uniform and his dispatch book. The latter prize provided useful intelligence about the movements of the Federal Army. LC**

Pope was now confident of achieving his long-sought victory over Jackson. He was unaware that Longstreet was by now through Thoroughfare Gap, and that even now men of Brigadier General John Bell Hood's Division were arriving on Jackson's right. Indeed, the only troops Pope was expecting from that direction were McDowell's and Porter's corps, which he believed were marching from Gainesville and closing on Jackson's flank and rear at that very moment. The reality was very different. Porter and McDowell had encountered a Confederate force of indeterminate size on the Manassas–Gainesville road. Porter had halted his corps and McDowell had turned his corps around and was now marching, by way of the Manassas–Sudley road, to link up with Pope's left east of Groveton. The troops they had encountered were only six regiments of Stuart's cavalry screen, but Stuart had the 5th Virginia drag brush along the road behind them, which succeeded in convincing Porter and McDowell that they faced a formidable Confederate force. The result was that far from threatening Jackson, it was Pope's left flank that was increasingly vulnerable.

Pope's first or original report on the action, which was dated 3 September 1862, demonstrates his expectations: " ... I sent orders to McDowell to advance rapidly on our left, and attack the enemy on his flank, extending his right to meet Reynolds' left, and to Fitz John Porter to keep his right well closed on McDowell's left and to attack the enemy in flank and rear while he was pushed in front." General Pope's memory proved faulty here because he sent no such order. Around 2.00pm he did, however, order Heintzelman to organize an attack by Hooker's and Kearny's divisions. Hooker picked Cuvier Grover's Brigade to spearhead his attack, which was to be directed against the enemy's center. The brigade consisted of the 1st, 11th, and 16th Massachusetts regiments, the 2nd New

Union soldiers put aside their weapons and pick up tools to repair the damage done by Stuart's raiders. NA

Hampshire, and the 26th Pennsylvania. After Milroy's experiences earlier in the day, Grover was convinced that the only chance of success lay in speed and impact. The resultant charge ranks as one of the most gallant and determined of the war. The men were ordered to advance slowly and steadily until they took the enemy's fire, then deliver a volley and carry the position with the bayonet without pausing to reload. The men obeyed the orders to the letter.

The 11th Massachusetts was the first to feel the sting of Rebel riflemen, but they continued the assault and pierced the Confederate line even as the 1st Massachusetts fell upon the 49th Georgia at the railroad embankment, taking the position after a brief but desperate resistance, in which bayonets and clubbed muskets were freely used. Beyond the embankment, Grover's men attacked the second line of Thomas's Brigade of Georgians and threw them back too. Grover had unexpectedly broken A.P. Hill's line. It seems almost certain that if this splendid assault had been properly supported, it would have succeeded in breaking the center of Jackson's line, but the support did not come. Indeed, Union troops under Brigadier General John B. Robinson had been so lackluster in their part of the attack that the Confederates were able to withdraw the 12th South Carolina to send against Grover. Numbers began to tell and the Southerners managed to turn Grover's left flank, throwing back his men in full retreat at the cost of 33 per cent casualties during the half hour of fighting.

What is more, Kearny's attack was to have been made simultaneously with Grover's assault, but further north against A.P. Hill's Division. Once again something went amiss. Kearny did not strike until after Grover had been driven back. When he did go into action, however, Kearny did so with great gallantry. He likewise received strong support from Stevens's Division, but all this would prove to little avail.

At first the blue-clad infantry made progress. Hill's troops had suffered greatly in all the skirmishing and fighting of the day, and ran short of ammunition. Kearny's violent, determined attack rolled up the Rebel line. It seemed as if their left was turned. In fact, under the

When Jackson's men became the unexpected guests of the Union supply depot at Manassas Junction on 26 August, they were rewarded for marching some 50 miles in two days. They found warehouses and freight cars stretching for two miles stacked with barrels of flour, biscuits, wagons, and all manner of items, including uniforms and shoes that were welcomed by Confederate soldiers, many of whom were nearly naked and went barefoot as a result of the arduous campaigning they had endured. Here Yankees survey the aftermath of this Rebel foraging party. NA

one-armed Kearny the division made it across the unfinished railroad embankment, and pushed the Southerners back to the Groveton–Sudley road (present day Route 622), the 1st South Carolina on the far left of the line falling back as Kearny's men pressed hard against the Confederate left.

Seeing his brigade begin to collapse Maxcy Gregg waved his sword furiously and shouted, "Let us die here, my men." Hill concluded that at this point victory hung in the balance, with his own troops barely able to stand this new charge. But Gregg told Hill that he would hold his position with the bayonet. Gregg was able to make good his pledge when the 37th North Carolina reinforced him at a point several hundred yards behind the railroad line, where he had managed to halt his retreating men to make a stand.

The tenacity of the soldiers was not in doubt, but the Federals were applying tremendous pressure. Fortunately for Hill, he was able to call in two brigades of Ewell's Division on his right, those of Lawton and Early. These troops hurled themselves forward and now the tide of fighting turned as the determined Confederates drove the Union infantry out of the position they had won with so much blood.

Two of Brigadier General Lawrence Branch's regiments vigorously clashed with Kearny's right, while two more of his regiments kept Hill's right from buckling long enough for 2,500 more troops under Early to arrive and stem the Union advance. The fresh fighting forces under Early not only held the line but also counter-attacked with sufficient force to halt the Yankees and drive them back.

Finally, between 5.00 and 6.00pm, McDowell arrived, bringing Rufus King's Division with him, commanded by John P. Hatch, as King was severely ill. James B. Ricketts's Division had not yet joined the fray. When Hatch came on the scene the Rebels were in the process of readjusting their line of battle after all the fighting of the day.

At that point, the seesaw struggle of that afternoon had come to a halt. The cost would prove high, Kearny having lost a quarter of his command. Despite that fact, he boasted of beating the Confederates. To some degree he was correct. Some of the Southern units, such as

LEFT **What the Confederate troops could not take, they destroyed, leaving the repair to the Federals who came in their wake. In this case the locomotive "Commodore" has been overturned. NA**

BELOW **Both sides attempted to deny the other use of vital railroad links. As such, Pope ordered equipment of the Orange & Alexandria burned when he thought it might fall into enemy hands; only wheels and metal parts remained. USAMHI**

To preclude additional raids on rolling stock, Federal troops were posted along sections of the track, such as at Pope's Run near Union Mills. NA

Gregg's Brigade, lost as much as half their number. Gregg sustained 613 officers and men killed and wounded, including all but two of the field officers in the brigade. Furthermore, ammunition had run dangerously low. Branch was aghast when he found out that after regrouping his command there were only 24 rounds remaining in his entire brigade.

Pope became convinced that the Southerners were in retreat and ready to be beaten. However, this outlook was made without knowledge as yet of Longstreet's presence, despite the fact that one of his subordinates, Irvin McDowell, realized that he faced Longstreet, but did not bother to inform Pope of this important intelligence.

In fact, during the morning of 30 August Lee had ordered Longstreet's newly arrived troops to move up on Jackson's right, where the Confederate line overlapped Pope's left, which was by this point exposed. The trap was ready to be sprung.

Longstreet recorded the situation in his official report, noting that early on 29 August his troops advanced toward Jackson. As they reached Gainesville they could hear the din of fighting so, "The march was quickened ... The excitement of battle seemed to give new life and strength to our jaded men, and the head of my column soon reached a position in rear of the enemy's left flank and within easy canon shot."

At that point Longstreet deployed some of Brigadier General John Bell Hood's batteries, and placed Hood's Division either side of the Warrenton Turnpike, supported by Brigadier General Nathan Evans' independent brigade. In turn three brigades of Brigadier General Cadmus Wilcox deployed to support Longstreet's left flank and another three under James Kemper, who had been promoted to brigadier

On the evening of 27 August Pope ordered Irvin McDowell and Franz Sigel to relocate their corps to Manassas, thereby leaving the road open for Longstreet to unite with Jackson. Among the troops who participated in this ill-advised move were the foot soldiers of Sigel's, 41st New York Infantry, who like their corps commander had been born in Germany. LC

LEFT As the impending battle drew near, the rain came. Federal troops clogged the way to Bull Run. First Lieutenant Alanson M. Randol of the 1st US Artillery described the confusion as he saw it on 24 August: " ... the roads and crossings of the various streams along our route were blocked with wagons, the teams of some floundering in the mud, vainly endeavoring to move on. ... " LC

general just a few months earlier, supported the right. Finally, Brigadier General D.R. Jones's division took up position on the Manassas Gap Railroad, "to the right and in echelon with the last three brigades," according to Longstreet's report. All this had been accomplished by around noon.

Hatch, however, knew nothing of this. Instead, he hurried along the pike toward Groveton, to press the Confederates as they tried to escape the field and, if possible, to convert this into a rout. He soon found out the state of affairs was far different from the picture in Pope's mind's eye. At about 6.30pm, at the head of three of his brigades, Hatch encountered the enemy advancing to meet him. It was a part of Hood's Division of Longstreet's Corps – Hood's Texas Brigade, and Colonel Evander Law's Brigade. The action was a sharp, costly one. In the midst of the savage brawl, Hatch supposedly sat astride his horse complacently, "while every man who approached him pitched and fell headlong before he could deliver his message." The action lasted some three-quarters of an hour, Hatch's weary men left in good order, abandoning one gun, which fell into the hands of the enemy. This gun Colonel Law indicated: "continued to fire, until my men were so near it as to have their faces burnt by its discharges."

Late in the afternoon on the extreme Union left, Reynolds undertook to renew the attack. Still in his exposed position south of Warrenton Turnpike, Reynolds was ordered to "threaten the enemy's flank and rear." At about 3.00pm he complied, although he had already voiced his concerns to Pope about the growing numbers of enemy in his path. Soon after setting out he encountered heavy Confederate artillery fire to his front, while it appeared that a considerable Southern infantry force was moving into the woods directly before him. With that, Reynolds sent Pope a courier to make known his concerns. The reply from his superior was rash and proved somewhat costly. Pope bombastically retorted, "You are excited young man; the people you see are General Porter's command taking position on the right of the

Despite Jackson's objection, Confederate Brigadier General William Booth Taliaferro assumed leadership of the Stonewall Division after Cedar Mountain. He would be wounded during the 28 August action at Groveton, NA

As sunset approached on 28 August, Brigadier General John Gibbon's Brigade braved the opening salvos of Jackson's wing at Brawner's farm. Two days later his newly blooded unit received orders to take up position along the Warrenton Turnpike east of Henry Hill, as part of the withdrawal of Union forces from the field. It was there that Major General Philip Kearny, who commanded one of Heintzelman's divisions, blurted out to his subordinate, "I suppose you appreciate the condition of affairs? It's another Bull Run, sir, it's another Bull Run!" NA

enemy." Despite Pope's complacent assurances Reynolds was forced to retire.

Pope also erred when, at about 4.00pm, he threw Colonel James Nagle's 1,500 men from Reno's Division against the woods east of the Groveton–Sudley road in another disjointed attack. Nagle's foot soldiers enthusiastically set to their task, and quickly overcame Confederate skirmishers at the outset of their advance. They pressed forward and drove off Alexander Lawton's Georgians from the railroad cut that they had occupied. Although they fell back, the Southerners did so in good order, and soon regrouped in the woods to the rear of their previous position. Jackson sent in reinforcements and with their arrival a counter-attack drove back Nagle's troops along with men of George Taylor's Excelsior Brigade, which had just come up in support of their Union comrades. Even as the Federal forces were being pressed hard, Colonel LeRoy Stafford added the weight of his brigade to the fray, and easily swept aside the Union 3rd West Virginia of Milroy's Brigade that had been sent forward to assist Nagle. At this point the center of Pope's line was in a shambles, but the commander himself had no grasp of the situation and indeed was convinced that Jackson had been bested and was even now preparing to retreat.

Thus ended the first day of the Second Battle of Manassas, which as Pope reflected in a dispatch dated 5.00am on 30 August "was fought on the identical battlefield of Bull Run, which greatly increased the enthusiasm of the men." It had been a desperate day of fighting. Pope estimated his losses at 6,000 or 8,000 men, but his estimate of the enemy's losses as twice his own was wildly out, particularly given that the Union troops were on the offense while the Confederates generally were in a superior defensive position on 29 August. On the Confederate side, however, Brigadier General Charles Field, and Colonel Henry Forno, both of A.P. Hill's Division, and Brigadier General Trimble, of "Bald Head" Ewell's Division were all severely wounded. On the Union side no general officer had been hit.

Perhaps it was this good fortune that contributed in part to Pope wrongly interpreting the action as a Union victory. While Pope's army had driven the enemy from a great deal of ground, which they held in the morning, Lee's men were far from defeated. The retirement of the enemy's line had, to a degree, been the Confederates "rolling" with Pope's punches, and were preparatory to taking the offensive the next day.

Pope completely misinterpreted the situation, as revealed in his 5.00am dispatch of 30 August, in which he gloated over his supposed triumph: "We fought a terrific battle here yesterday with the combined forces of the enemy, which lasted with continuous fury from daylight until dark, by which time the enemy was driven from the field, which we now occupy." He further related "that the enemy is retiring toward the mountains ..."

Jackson had certainly taken casualties, but in the woods west of the unfinished railroad his Wing remained battle worthy. Far from preparing to retire, Jackson's men were bracing themselves for the next day's battle. In addition they had now been joined by Longstreet. Pope was aware of this, but misinterpreted it disastrously. Pope was convinced that Longstreet was directly reinforcing Jackson's line as the latter's damaged formations prepared to retire. This chimed with the picture of the battle that Pope had convinced himself was reality. In fact, Longstreet was deploying his entire Wing on Jackson's right, perfectly placed to smash into Pope's vulnerable left flank and so to roll up his line. Pope's self-delusion was to have terrible consequences on the morrow.

THE SECOND DAY, 30 AUGUST 1862

The fighting of 29 August had proved inconclusive, although at times it appeared the Union might prevail, a point Pope would make later when facing criticism for his lack of success at Manassas. Some of the blame was also placed at McClellan's door for failing to forward reinforcements from the Army of the Potomac to Pope with alacrity. Ultimately though Fitz John Porter would be made the scapegoat for the Federal disaster that was about to unfold, but his court martial was still in the future. For the moment, as 30 August opened clear and bright, Pope was confident that he was about to pursue a defeated enemy.

This was far from the case as the two armies readied to renew the match. By this point, Richard Anderson's Division had finally rejoined Longstreet, thereby negating the superior numbers Pope had enjoyed during the first day of the battle. Lee's two reinforced wings remained in their positions of the previous day, except that he had massed 36 guns, under Colonel Stephen D. Lee, on the commanding watershed in the center of his lines, where they could fire down the center of the shallow valley followed by Young's Branch and threaded by the turnpike leading through the midst of the Federal force to the stone bridge over Bull Run.

Longstreet's Corps, deployed from the center of Lee's line southward, consisted of brigades under Cadmus M. Wilcox, John B. Hood, James L. Kemper, and David R. Jones. Robert H. Anderson's 6,000 men were in reserve on the turnpike to the rear. Lee now had approximately 50,000 troops at his command in his two spread wings, the great jaws of a trap into which Pope was preparing to move, unconscious of the fate that awaited his army.

Robert E. Lee reported that after Longstreet's arrival the enemy "began to concentrate opposite Jackson's left. Colonel [J.B.] Walton placed a part of his artillery upon a commanding position between the lines of Generals Jackson and Longstreet … and engaged the enemy vigorously for several hours. Soon afterward General Stuart reported the approach of a large force from the direction of Bristoe Station, threatening Longstreet's right. The brigades under General Wilcox were sent to reinforce General Jones [Longstreet's right], but no serious attack was made …" While the battle raged on Jackson's left, "Longstreet ordered Hood and Evans to advance, but before the order could be obeyed Hood was himself attacked …"

As all this was taking place, George Sykes's Division was situated on the plateau where the Henry House stood, the site of the first battle of Bull Run. Other Federal units were nearby, when Pope noticed that the Southern skirmishers of the day before had disappeared. Again this led him to conclude that the Confederate army had been defeated, by his assaults of the previous two days and was now in full retreat, seeking safety behind the Bull Run Mountains. Wanting to cut off their supposed escape, he ordered a prompt advance along the Warrenton Road to Gainesville, and then toward the Thoroughfare Gap. In fact, far from running the rebels were spoiling for a fight and actually feared that Pope might withdraw before they could fall upon him.

While he later became known for his role in popularizing baseball, during the fight at Groveton Brigadier General Abner Doubleday had a more crucial game to play. He brought his brigade into action to support Gibbon on the evening of 28 August. NA

Union cavalry brigade commander John Buford warned that Thoroughfare Gap was vulnerable, but Pope paid little heed to this information. He sent a small force to hold the vital avenue, thereby allowing Lee and Longstreet to reach Jackson. Buford and his horse soldiers would face Lee again at Gettysburg. NA

One of Stuart's brigade commanders had followed in his uncle Robert E. Lee's footsteps. On the morning of 29 August, Brigadier General Fitzhugh Lee's troopers served as skirmishers north of Bull Run Creek. NA

John Pelham, who came to be called "The Gallant Pelham", resigned from West Point in May 1861 to head South with the intention of offering his services to the Confederacy. He served as a captain of artillery during the early part of the war, before being promoted. He still was a battery commander on 29 August, when his guns pelted Colonel Orlando Poe's 3rd Brigade of Kearny's 1st Division. NA

But he did not withdraw. Instead he called his commanders together at 8.00am near the Stone House to make final plans for the assault that he thought would defeat Lee. With this goal in mind he had brought up Porter's Corps, which had been holding the line of Dawkin's Branch, and placed it in his center. Recalling Cold Harbor, Porter did not believe, as Pope did, that Lee and Jackson had given up and were retreating, so he formed his men into a triple line of battle, across the turnpike, and placed King's Division to support his right and Reynolds's on his left. Sigel's Corps and half of Reno's was to his rear. These troop dispersals ranged into the dense forest along the turnpike and to the east of the Sudley Road. Porter was ready to advance on Lee's center. Similarly, troops under James Ricketts and Isaac Stevens reported that Jackson had not budged and was in front of them in the woods. John Reynolds also concluded that the Southerners remained in strength before him.

In fairness, Pope was not totally oblivious to the situation. Having experienced the sharp teeth of Jackson's left, he massed the whole of Samuel Heintzelman's and half of each of the corps of Irvin McDowell and Jesse Reno, to pit them against this stronghold in support of Porter's attack on the center. McDowell and Heintzelman reconnoitered the area before advancing, but they failed to detect that Jackson was waiting for them.

So it was that on the morning of 30 August, Heintzelman moved against A.P. Hill with Ricketts's Division on the assumption that his force was in no danger. This false sense of security was about to be shattered; it was just what Lee had hoped for. Pope's renewal of the engagement allowed Longstreet to pound the Union left as a diversion, while Jackson would be able to ease around the Yankee's right flank and place his wing between Pope and Washington, DC. The trap was set, and all the Rebels had to do was wait for the prey to take the bait.

Ricketts's advance was the first signal that Pope was doing just that. In short order his men had to withdraw from the hot reception they met. Reynolds's skirmishers met similarly stiff resistance, in this case from S.D. Lee's 18 artillery pieces, as they advanced to probe the enemy center. Pope finally admitted Lee had not fled but was very much present. Undaunted, he decided to press the attack. Consequently at 1.00pm he ordered Porter's two divisions along with Hatch's to make frontal attacks. Unfortunately he failed to launch any diversions or give support to this assault, thereby all but dooming the advance to failure. Interestingly enough, he did not even make any provisions for what action to take should Hatch actually carry the field.

It was 3.00pm, however, before Porter's 10,000 troops were ready to advance. Pope was finally ready to throw his entire army into the breach. From left to right were the brigades of Henry Weeks, Charles Roberts, and Hatch, while US Army regulars under Sykes formed the reserve.

The signal was given and Porter's men rushed forward, wheeling on their left. Members of Hiram Berdan's Sharpshooters in their green uniforms and carrying Sharps rifles moved out at 2.30pm, negotiating fences that ran along the Groveton–Sudley road. Before long they began skirmishing with men of Starke's Brigade, who had taken up position at a place known as The Dump. For 30 minutes they exchanged fire with their Rebel opponents, supported by two New York regiments.

Men of the 24th and 30th New York were also on the move. Holding the Federal right they withstood heavy Confederate fire. One of them recorded the savage shouts and the pandemonium as they faced their determined foe. In the process they were "transformed from the time, from a lot of good-natured boys to the most blood-thirsty demonics." The New Yorkers made it to the opposite side of the railroad embankment where their Louisiana opponents blazed away at them, ultimately driving the Northerners back down the embankment.

Roberts and Weeks fared no better, although according to one Confederate they began their advance "in magnificent style, lines as straight as an arrow, all fringed with glittering bayonets and fluttering flags." Before long though there were piles of Union bodies strewn all over the quarter-mile that lay between them and the Confederates. When they finally reached the Virginians they faced a devastating volley and were "blown away" according to one of the Southern defenders.

The dead and dying on both sides were scattered everywhere. As Porter closed in across the open field, his left was exposed to the Rebel-masked batteries. Southern shot and shell swept through his lines. Porter's attack staggered, while Longstreet opened with three batteries upon his left rear. Even then the Union men refused to give way. Jackson's troops, who had marched more than 50 miles in the past day and a half and withstood the onslaught of the previous day, were taking casualties as well. With Jackson under pressure, Lee ordered Longstreet to close in upon the Federal left. The order was superfluous because his veteran soldiers had already reached the same conclusion. Without waiting for word from their commander, they leaped forward, swinging on their left. Lee rode out in front of them as Jackson's men on the left also counter-attacked, accelerating the rout of the Federal army. The Confederate batteries soon joined in the rushing charge and were abreast of their infantry comrades all along the lines. According to one eyewitness Longstreet's gunners poured "solid shot, shell and sections" of cut up railroad track into the oncoming Federals. The results were

Orlando Poe, seen here as a brigadier general, was still a colonel when on 29 August his four regiments crossed Bull Run below Sudley Ford, placing them in Jackson's rear. This chance occurrence unleashed a hornet's nest from the Southern side that eventually caused the brigade to turn back at the "double quick" amidst a "hail of grape and canister, which ripped the sod under our feet," as a member of the 2nd Michigan Infantry, John Reuhle, recollected. NA

During the second day of the battle Lee was on the field. His presence and the arrival of Longstreet's Wing provided Jackson with the necessary reinforcements to meet the superior numbers of Union troops successfully and drive them from the field. LC

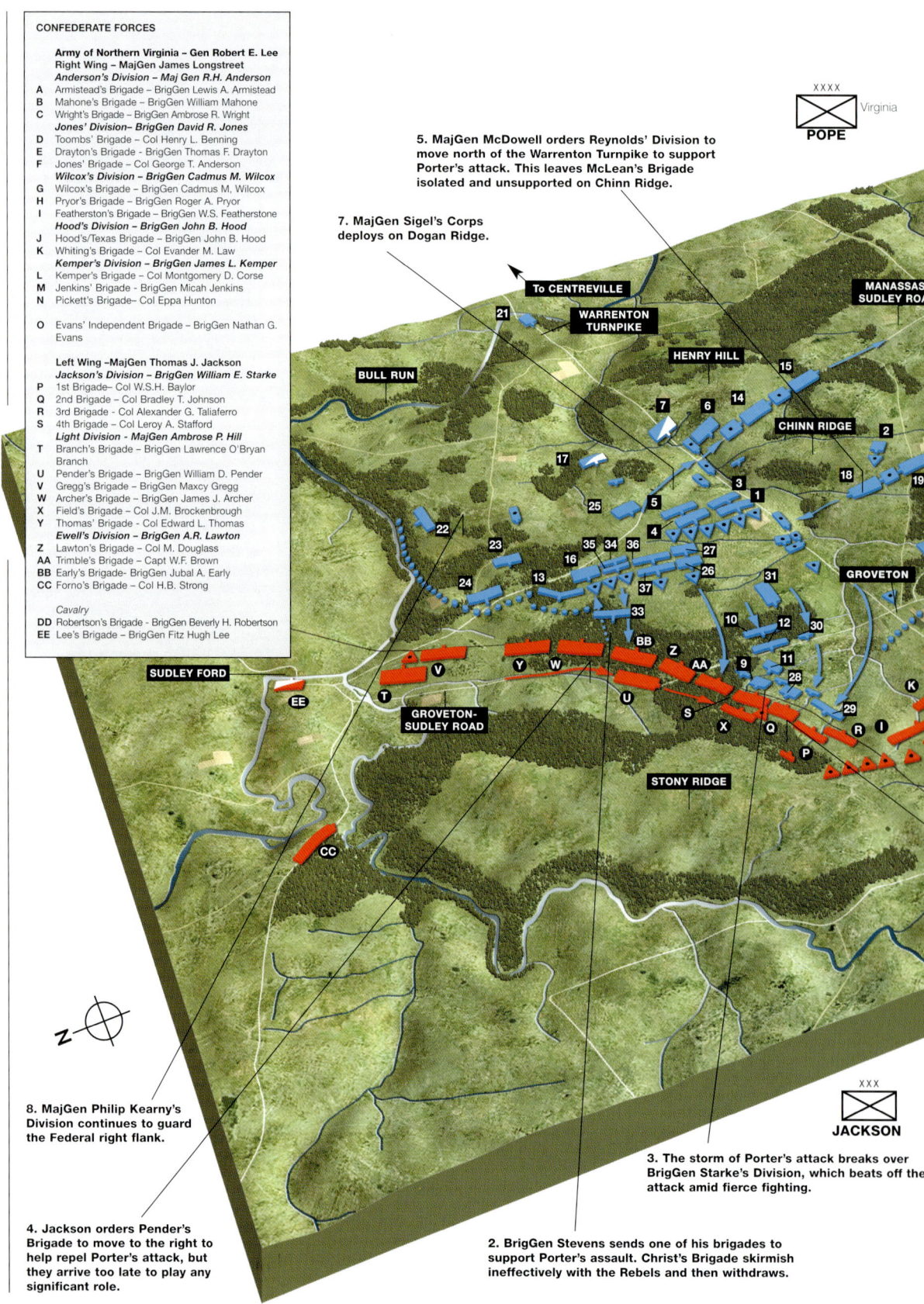

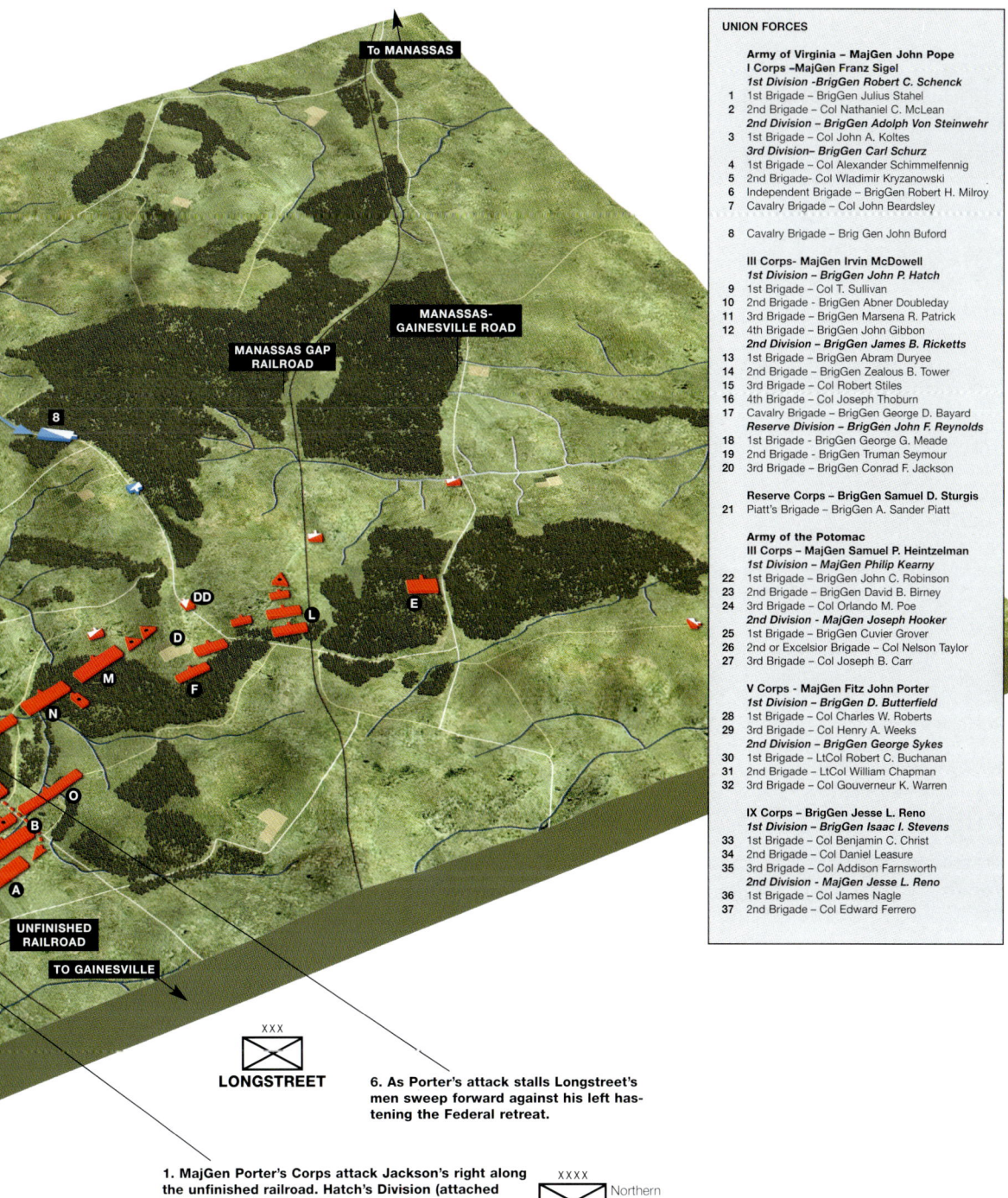

SECOND MANASSAS – SECOND DAY

30 August 1862, 3.00– 3.45pm, viewed from the north-west showing the unsuccessful attack of Porter's V Corps against Jackson's Wing behind the unfinished railroad.

1. MajGen Porter's Corps attack Jackson's right along the unfinished railroad. Hatch's Division (attached from McDowell's Corps) is on the right and Butterfield's Division on the left. They are beaten back by a storm of fire from Jackson's men.

6. As Porter's attack stalls Longstreet's men sweep forward against his left hastening the Federal retreat.

UNION FORCES

Army of Virginia – MajGen John Pope
I Corps –MajGen Franz Sigel
1st Division -BrigGen Robert C. Schenck
1 1st Brigade – BrigGen Julius Stahel
2 2nd Brigade – Col Nathaniel C. McLean
2nd Division – BrigGen Adolph Von Steinwehr
3 1st Brigade – Col John A. Koltes
3rd Division– BrigGen Carl Schurz
4 1st Brigade – Col Alexander Schimmelfennig
5 2nd Brigade- Col Wladimir Kryzanowski
6 Independent Brigade – BrigGen Robert H. Milroy
7 Cavalry Brigade – Col John Beardsley

8 Cavalry Brigade – Brig Gen John Buford

III Corps- MajGen Irvin McDowell
1st Division – BrigGen John P. Hatch
9 1st Brigade – Col T. Sullivan
10 2nd Brigade – BrigGen Abner Doubleday
11 3rd Brigade – BrigGen Marsena R. Patrick
12 4th Brigade – BrigGen John Gibbon
2nd Division – BrigGen James B. Ricketts
13 1st Brigade – BrigGen Abram Duryee
14 2nd Brigade – BrigGen Zealous B. Tower
15 3rd Brigade – Col Robert Stiles
16 4th Brigade – Col Joseph Thoburn
17 Cavalry Brigade – BrigGen George D. Bayard
Reserve Division – BrigGen John F. Reynolds
18 1st Brigade – BrigGen George G. Meade
19 2nd Brigade - BrigGen Truman Seymour
20 3rd Brigade – BrigGen Conrad F. Jackson

Reserve Corps – BrigGen Samuel D. Sturgis
21 Piatt's Brigade – BrigGen A. Sander Piatt

Army of the Potomac
III Corps – MajGen Samuel P. Heintzelman
1st Division – MajGen Philip Kearny
22 1st Brigade – BrigGen John C. Robinson
23 2nd Brigade – BrigGen David B. Birney
24 3rd Brigade – Col Orlando M. Poe
2nd Division - MajGen Joseph Hooker
25 1st Brigade – BrigGen Cuvier Grover
26 2nd or Excelsior Brigade – Col Nelson Taylor
27 3rd Brigade – Col Joseph B. Carr

V Corps – MajGen Fitz John Porter
1st Division – BrigGen D. Butterfield
28 1st Brigade – Col Charles W. Roberts
29 3rd Brigade – Col Henry A. Weeks
2nd Division – BrigGen George Sykes
30 1st Brigade – LtCol Robert C. Buchanan
31 2nd Brigade – LtCol William Chapman
32 3rd Brigade – Col Gouverneur K. Warren

IX Corps – BrigGen Jesse L. Reno
1st Division – BrigGen Isaac I. Stevens
33 1st Brigade – Col Benjamin C. Christ
34 2nd Brigade – Col Daniel Leasure
35 3rd Brigade – Col Addison Farnsworth
2nd Division - MajGen Jesse L. Reno
36 1st Brigade – Col James Nagle
37 2nd Brigade – Col Edward Ferrero

Major General Fitz John Porter led V Corps of the Army of the Potomac. A veteran of both the Mexican War and the Utah Expedition under Albert Sidney Johnston, this West Pointer became a scapegoat for the Union failure at Second Manassas. Pope would have Porter relieved "for disobedience, disloyalty, and misconduct in the face of the enemy" as a reaction to the fact that he supposedly had not advanced aggressively on 29 August. Pope also faulted Porter for not succeeding in the final Union strike against the Confederates on the following day. NA

devastating, and casualties mounted as Porter threw in more troops, who at one point came on in such numbers and so bunched up that one Southern defender claimed it was "impossible to miss them." The Rebels poured on a torrential fire and as a Confederate riflemen reported, "What a slaughter of men that was."

This was more than the Yankees could bear. Although Jackson's forces were nearly at breaking point, and in the case of Stafford and Johnson's brigades, were all but out of ammunition, Porter cancelled the attack of his second line. The final blow came when Charles Field's Virginia Brigade arrived to support the beleaguered Confederate line. His unit's appearance caused Porter's troops to flee in a "disorderly rout" in masses, followed by the men of Jackson's old division from his right, who leaped across their defenses and chased them in hot pursuit. Pope's fierce attacks on Jackson's left had, in the meantime, also been repulsed. Jeb Stuart, on the right, along the old Alexandria Road, heard the famed Rebel Yell in pursuit. He rushed his brigades and batteries far in advance against the Federal left. Union General Gouverneur Warren attempted to stem the tide just east of Groveton, but at tremendous expense. Five of Hood's regiments attacked the 5th and 10th New York regiments of Warren's line. The New Yorkers deployed their skirmishers as Hood's veterans "yelling all the while" fell upon their outgunned prey. Alfred Davenport, a member of the 5th, recounted the chaos of this moment. First the recruits began to give way, then the entire regiment "broke and ran for their lives … There was no hope but in flight." As Davenport joined his fleeing comrades he "saw men dropping on all sides, canteens struck and flying to pieces, haversacks cut off, rifles knocked to pieces, it was a perfect hail of bullets."

When it was over the 5th New Yorkers in their brightly colored red and blue Zouave uniforms were in the words of one observer strewn on the ground like a "posy garden". Within ten desperate minutes of being

LEFT **At approximately 2.30pm on 30 August, Porter launched his attack against Jackson. Skirmishers led the way, followed within a half-hour by the main body of 10,000 infantrymen intent on carrying the day. Heavy casualties followed, as the Confederate riflemen and cannoneers pummeled the advancing Yankees. One of Porter's staff officers, a 20-year-old lieutenant named Stephen M. Weld, recorded that after being fired upon by a Rebel battery, the troops advanced through a wood, "and went across the plains into the woods," where they faced strong enemy fire "from the railroad gap in which they were posted." Soon they were caught in a crossfire "of grape, canister, and musketry which mowed men down like sheep." LC**

ABOVE, RIGHT **Brigade commander Colonel George T. Anderson deployed his fellow Georgians with daring as his regiments were thrown against Chinn Ridge. He would be wounded during the fierce fighting there. He was later promoted to brigadier general. NA**

set upon by Hood's killing machine, the 5th New York, as historian Will Green points out, had lost more men killed "than any other regiment would lose in a single battle during the entire Civil War."

In the meantime, survivors from Porter's ill-fated attack fell back into Groveton Woods, even as Sigel's Corps and units under Milroy tried to hold fast and prevent a complete collapse on this part of the field.

Meanwhile, on the Union left, Schenck hung on to Bald Hill, but the determined Confederates swarmed upon his flank and forced him from the summit. Hood swept the line of the turnpike to the west of the Stone House. Pope's reserves, on Henry Hill, the focus of the fighting at Manassas the year before, resisted the onslaught for a time. But Jackson's left closed upon the retreating Federals toward the Stone Bridge until darkness put an end to his advance. Sigel and McDowell had fought a delaying action on Chinn Ridge but their regiments had been committed piecemeal and they were ultimately overwhelmed and forced to retire. This did, however, give Pope's demoralized brigades an opportunity to follow the crowd of fugitives that, long before the sun went down, crowded over that bridge, seeking safety behind the earthworks at Centreville and William B. Franklin's Corps, then advancing from Alexandria.

The two days at Manassas cost Pope perhaps as many as 13,824 of his men, killed, wounded, and missing. He had also lost 30 pieces of artillery and many thousands of military stores and small arms worth millions of dollars in value. This great victory at Manassas cost Lee 1,305 killed and 7,048 wounded, mostly in Jackson's command, including many fine officers.

In the wake of these losses, Pope's Army of Virginia arrived at Centreville on the evening of 30 August. Although there were many stragglers, unit cohesion remained relatively intact. General Lee's army had also suffered in these battles and, considering its very inability to

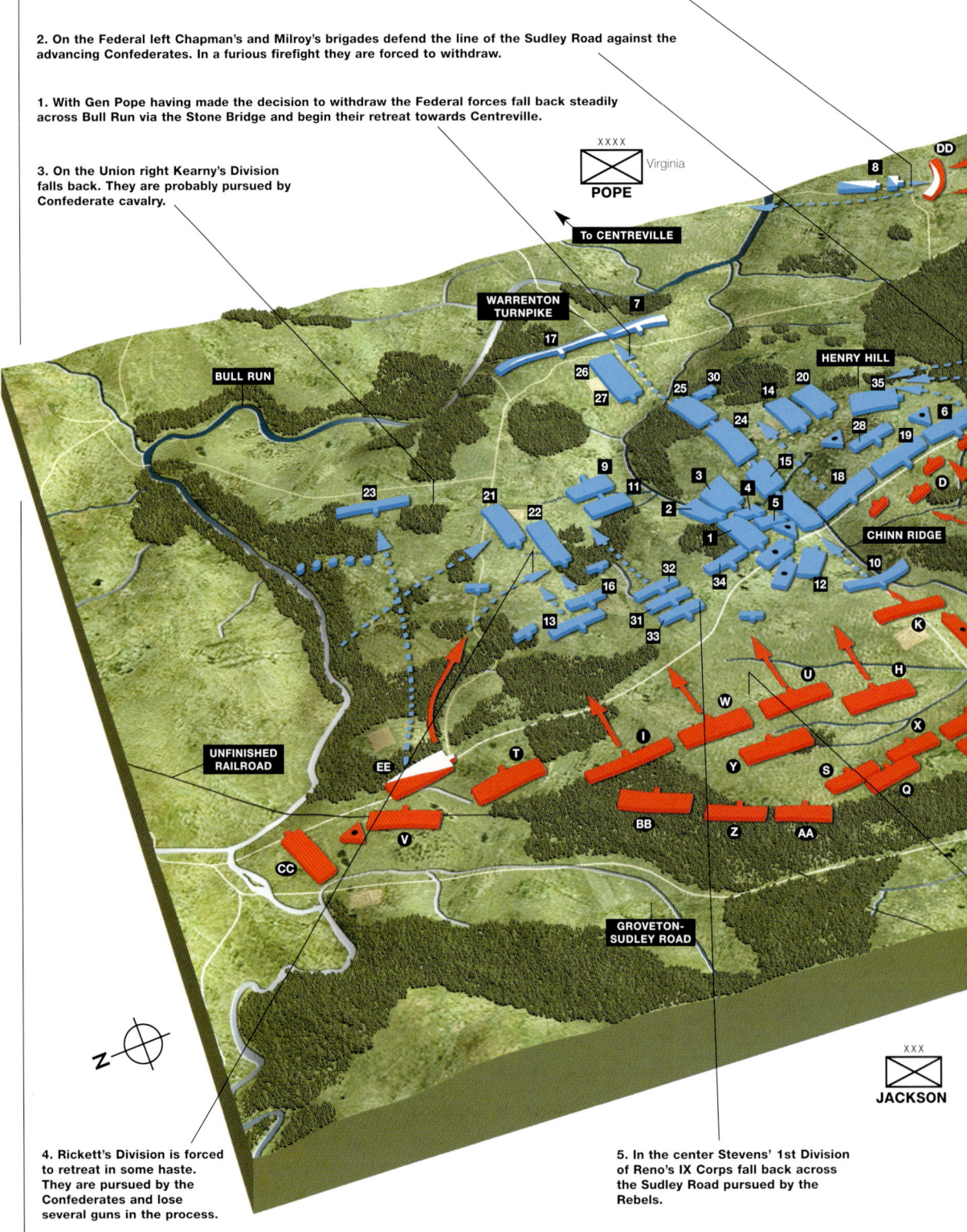

SECOND MANASSAS – SECOND DAY

30 August 1862, 6.00– 6.45pm, viewed from the north-west showing the advance of the Army of Northern Virginia and Union forces beginning to retreat towards the Stone Bridge across Bull Run.

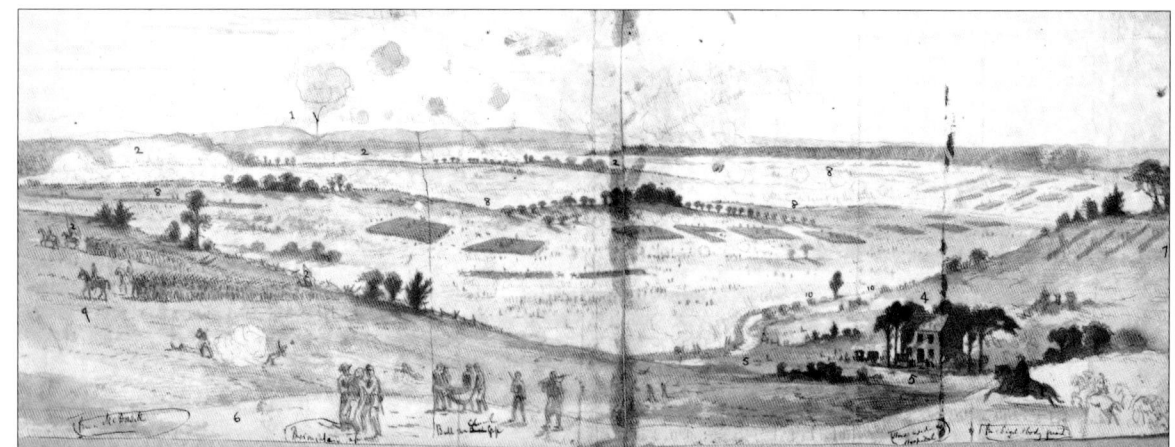

ABOVE **Newspaper artist Edwin Forbes sketched the activities of Saturday 30 August as they unfolded at around 3.30pm. From his position looking toward Groveton and north to Henry Hill from Baldface Hill he depicted: Thoroughfare Gap (1); Longstreet's line as it commenced its attack against the Union left (2); the railroad embankment that had afforded the Southerners their defense works (3); the Stone House that became a hospital (4) along with the Warrenton Turnpike to its front (5); Baldface Hill (6) and Henry Hill (7) are shown in the foreground and to the right respectively; in the distance the Federal line carries on the fight (8) as McDowell's corps move to the left flank to repel the assault (9). Finally Federal supply wagons move along Sudley Springs Road (10). LC**

ABOVE, RIGHT **The cannon that raked Porter's ranks were ably manned. Here Confederate field pieces of Stephen D. Lee's artillery battalion unleash their lethal firepower. LC**

quickly replace its losses, the Federals were, apart from their morale, in a better position than the enemy to take the offensive. Not that Pope's retreat was unwise, despite the fact that he all but apologized for it in his report. On the contrary, some critics maintained he should have placed his force behind Bull Run on the morning of 30 August. But that was a moot point.

His reputation had been heavily tarnished by the defeat at Manassas. Now his Union host was turning back to Washington, only two dozen miles away. Some alarmists feared this defeat would be followed by the capture of the capital, but this faction exaggerated the threat. General Pope summed up the situation more accurately, although with a favorable slant in his communiqué to Halleck after nightfall had ended the battle. He optimistically stated: "We have had a terrific battle again to-day." He went on to depict the engagement as a furious one that lasted "for hours without cessation, and the losses on both sides very heavy. The enemy is badly whipped, and we shall do well enough. Do not be uneasy. We will hold our own here."

ABOVE **Union forces clung to Chinn Ridge during the afternoon of 30 August, thereby allowing Pope to establish a second defensive line at Henry Hill. At around 5.00pm Longstreet's men poured on the fire, converging on both sides of the Federal line. The pressure eventually broke the Union resolve. Pope's foot soldiers began to scatter, creating a state of "perfect bedlam", according to one of the men from the 88th Pennsylvania Infantry who witnessed the scene. LC**

Colonel David A. Weisiger, commanding officer of the 12th Virginia Infantry, also received a wound at Second Manassas, but recovered. He too went on to become a brigadier general. USAMHI

BELOW **Northern troops were not the only ones to flee from Bull Run. Fearful of the consequences, these African American civilians cross the Rappahannock to follow the Federal soldiers. LC**

AFTERMATH

Unfortunately for Pope the nation was in no mood for reacting calmly and resolutely after his army had been sent packing. People saw only an uninterrupted retreat from the Rapidan to Centreville. They had watched the campaign open with his bombastic proclamation that his army was to see only the backs of its enemies, and lines of supplies and bases of communication were to be discarded. The Northern population now witnessed a retreating army before a victorious enemy after a bloody struggle. Its supplies had been captured and its communications more than once seriously threatened. They took no account whatever of the counterbalancing circumstances; they saw only what they termed results; and they were unjust to General Pope. Moreover, the strong partisanship that existed in the Army of the Potomac for McClellan rendered many, if not most, of the Peninsula officers harsh judges of their new general.

But the ordeal was not yet over. The day after the battle was rainy, rendering the fords near the turnpike impassable. Lee wanted to follow up his victory and consequently had his men on the road again in the after-noon. Jackson once more took the lead, with Longstreet not far behind.

The Southerners crossed Bull Run high up, at Sudley Ford. They then forged ahead to Little River turnpike, a fine road which ran from Aldie Gap through Fairfax Court House to Alexandria. Turning southeast they marched for Fairfax Court House, a scant seven miles east of Centreville, where they looked to strike the line of communication of the Federal army and further harass the retreat of the defeated Northern forces. The enemy surely must be demoralized and now they could strike hard again to great effect.

With this attitude, Jackson, as he did on the way to Manassas Junction, threw caution to the wind as his foot cavalry raced toward Chantilly on the afternoon of 1 September. Jackson's march had been detected by the detachments that Sumner had sent out in compliance with an order of Pope's dated 3.00am, 1 September. Stonewall left his bivouac at Sudley Ford early that morning, marched down the turnpike, and, late in the afternoon, after reaching Ox Hill, came in contact with the troops of the IX Corps under Stevens (Jesse Reno being ill) who had been ordered by General Pope across the fields between the Warrenton and the Little River turnpikes to hold the latter road, and stop the advance of the enemy toward Fairfax Court House. The Federal troops were falling back toward Germantown and Fairfax Court House. Jackson's approach on the Little River Pike had to be checked or the retreat would be jeopardized.

Stevens, though he moved with great speed and vigor, could not get to the Little River Pike in advance of the enemy. His troops encountered

ABOVE **The independently wealthy, one-armed general Philip Kearny had started his military career in the 1830s as a young dragoon officer. He was known for his bravery in combat, and was regularly at the front of the fray. Kearny's heroic manner cost him his life at the Battle of Chantilly, or Ox Hill as the Confederates referred to it, on 1 September 1862. NA**

Confederate skirmishers behind the old railroad embankment a quarter of a mile or so south of the pike. Stevens at once determined to attack with all possible energy, and the charge of his own division, numbering some 2,000 troops, proved victorious. He checked Jackson's further advance.

Stevens himself saw his men brought to a momentary halt by the terrible fire to which they were subjected in crossing the open ground in front of the enemy's positions. He seized the colors of the 79th New York Highlanders, which he had formerly commanded, and led it forward in person. This brave act cost Stevens his life.

Kearny's Division promptly supported IX Corps. The fighting was very sharp for an hour or more. During the melee Kearny, who recklessly exposed himself as usua,l was also was killed.

Neither side gained an advantage. During part of the time it rained heavily, and it grew dark before the action closed. Both sides suffered considerably. For instance, the Confederates in Lawrence Branch's Brigade of Hill's Division were thrown into great disorder by flanking fire. Its commander concluded that the engagement ranked among the severest ever faced by the unit. Gregg's Brigade, which lost so many men at Manassas, again took heavy casualties. Trimble's Brigade also endured a brutal ordeal.

On the Northern side, Stevens's death denied the Union a resolute, clear-headed, able officer. When Kearny fell, he was mourned by both Northerners and Southerners as a man made for the profession of arms. In the field he was skilful, resolute, brave, and alert.

Personnel losses and the indecisive character of the engagement, which after all was only a repulse of the enemy, adversely impacted the morale of the Union Army. The Confederates outflanked the Federal right. Longstreet was up in the course of the night. On 2 September, at noon, the army being weary and the Lincoln administration under political pressure, orders came for the Union forces to hasten on to the defenses of Washington. The campaign of the army under Pope had ended ingloriously for the man who had boasted he would achieve a ringing victory for the Union. His army was soon to be disbanded.

Now the road was open for Lee to bring the war north. Lee sent forces to Harpers Ferry to snipe at the Union outposts there, but this was only a sideshow. While Lee realized an assault on Washington would be foolhardy, shifting the war away from northern Virginia and Richmond would have both strategic and psychological value. Desirous of maintaining momentum and retaining the initiative, Lee turned his victorious troops toward Maryland, a border state with mixed sympathies. An invasion there, if followed by another Confederate victory, might bring Marylanders into the Confederate cause, thereby surrounding Washington and cutting it off from direct contact with the Northern states.

More immediately, however, Lee knew he could draw his enemy a way from Confederate territory. Because Lee still sought a classic Napoleonic-style major victory, which would weaken Union resolve and perhaps lead to a negotiated peace, he pressed on into Maryland, taking the war to the North. His superiors in Richmond supported this plan to take the Army of Northern Virginia onto the offensive in Northern territory.

ABOVE **One-time Washington Territory Governor Isaac Stevens was another Union general officer who was struck down at Chantilly, Virginia. LC**

PAGES 78-79 **By the afternoon of 30 August, BrigGen William Starke's Louisiana Brigade of Jackson's Division had begun to run very low on ammunition. Then around 3.00pm the men of John Hatch's Federal Brigade advanced on the Louisiana troops who were defending a section of the unfinished railroad near the "Deep Cut". Despite heavy fire Hatch's men pressed forward. A number of the Southern infantrymen eventually ran out of cartridges and rather than stand idly by they began throwing stones at the advancing Yankees. The Confederate line was never in serious danger; Porter's attack had already spent itself and the Louisianans were speedily reinforced by C.W. Field's Brigade of Virginians. However, the symbolism of the event was too powerful to ignore and the episode became one of the most famous of the war. (Mike Adams)**

THE ROAD TO CHANTILLY – LEE'S FLANKING MOVEMENT

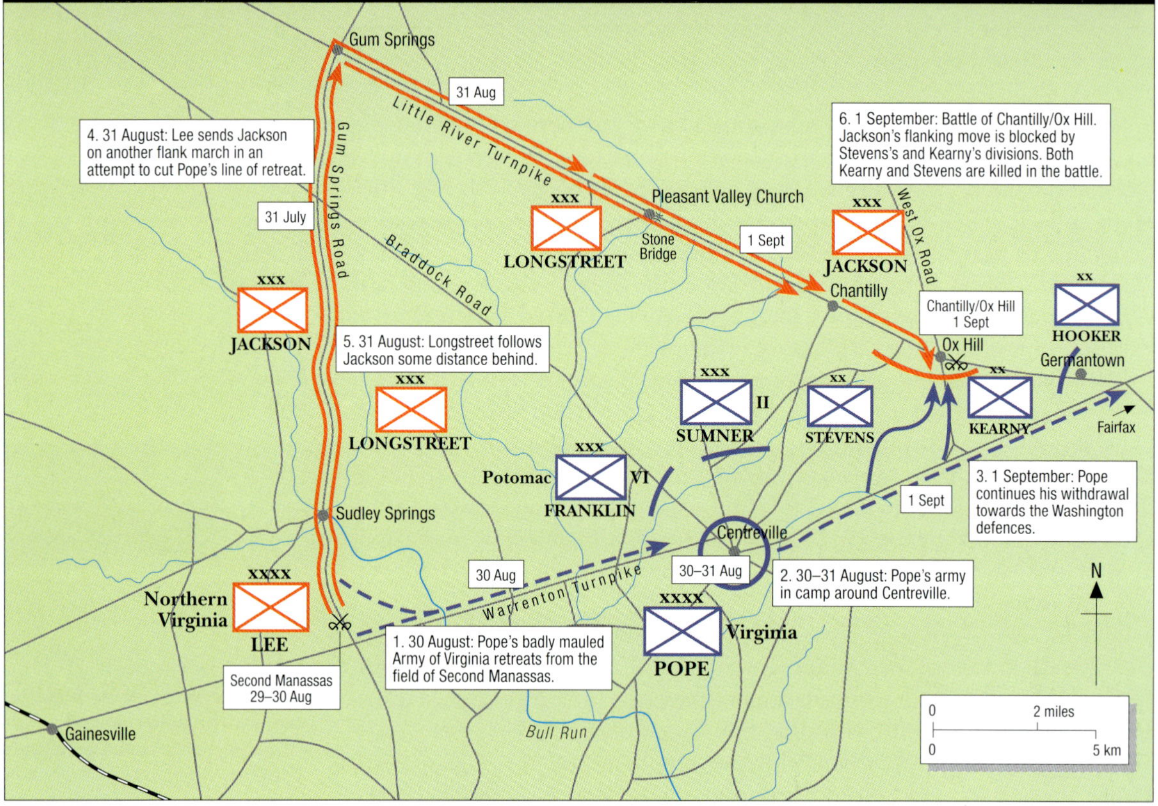

In less than three weeks Lee and McClellan would clash along the banks of a small Maryland creek near the town of Sharpsburg. The fighting at Second Manassas would pale in comparison to the rivers of blood that would flow at Antietam Creek. By this time, the South had complete confidence in Lee, who after Second Manassas had emerged as the pre-eminent military leader of the Confederacy. From that point forward Lee remained in command, and for nearly three more years he was instrumental in keeping the Confederate States alive at the head of his loyal army.

Pope made his headquarters to the rear of the Stone House on 30 August. This structure has been restored to its appearance at the time of the war and forms part of the national park that interprets this battle.

THE BATTLEFIELD TODAY

In 1922, Confederate veterans and some of their decendents had the foresight to purchase 128 acres around Henry Hill. Some 16 years later the land was turned over to the United States government. By 1940, the site was dedicated as the Manassas National Battlefield Park.

Subsequently, considerable additional land was acquired, and today the National Park Service, US Department of Interior administers a 5,000-acre reserve, which because of its proximity to Washington, DC, makes it one of the most accessible of all Civil War battlegrounds. Driving from the center of the national capital, take Interstate 66 southwest for approximately 20 miles. At the junction of US 66 and US 29 there are two choices. Either continue on Interstate 66 to Virginia Route 234 (Sudley Road), using exit 47, which heads north for three-quarters of a mile to the park's Visitors Center, or take the fork of US 29, which runs south-west along the historic Warrenton Turnpike. This is the course trod by many of the combatants during the engagement. The turnpike goes past the reconstruction of the stone bridge that crossed Bull Run where the retreating Union forces withdrew on their way back to Washington. Approximately one mile west of **Stone Bridge**, on the

This monument was erected to the fallen men of the 84th New York Infantry (14th Brooklyn Militia) by their comrades after the war.

right, appears **Stone House**, the handsome two-storey former home of Henry P. Matthews and his family, which served as a hospital during both battles, and the locale of Pope's headquarters on 30 August (just to the rear of the home). The building is refurnished in period style, and is open during a portion of the summer season.

Just past the two-story residence runs Sudley Road Make a left turn on this road and proceed south for approximately a half-mile to the **Visitor Center** (turn in on the left).

The park likewise can be reached with relative ease from Dulles International Airport. Upon leaving the airport proceed to US 28 south past Chantilly to the intersection of Interstate 66. At that juncture, follow either of the two alternatives given for the route from Washington.

In all cases begin your tour at the Visitor Center. Not only is this the place where the required nominal fee (applicable to ages 17 through 61) is to be paid, but also the facility offers many useful features that will make the experience more memorable. Museum exhibits, a media presentation, and a brief battle map orientation gives background. A free color handout also concisely covers both battles. The brochure is particularly valuable in that it depicts an easy to follow, 12-mile self-guided driving tour. The book store also provides a wide range of excellent material, including audio sources and some inexpensive pamphlets that are handy references for walking tours.

Combining this latter means of exploring the site with a vehicle is an excellent way to absorb details, but be sure to wear comfortable clothing and walking shoes. Furthermore, during hot weather make sure you have drinking water. Tick repellent is also strongly suggested during certain times of the year; these insects can cause more than just an

Henry Hill, the site of the Visitors Center, offers an excellent starting point for tours of the battlefield. In the background stands the monument erected by Union veterans to commemorate the Battle of First Bull Run, a stone column that numbered among the earliest memorials to the Civil War.

irritating bite. Consult with Park Service personnel to determine if it is the season when such a precaution is advisable.

During the summer, park staff members conduct tours, as they also do on weekends for the remainder of the year, weather permitting. In addition, group tours may be arranged in advance, subject to availability. For information on this facility as well as other matters related to the site, contact the Superintendent, Manassas National Battlefield Park, 12521 Lee Highway, Manassas, VA 22109-2001, or call (703) 361 1339. Internet access is found at www.nps.gov/mana

Visitor Center hours are from 8.30am to 5.30pm daily, except Christmas. The park itself opens at sunrise and closes at sunset.

Besides the Visitor Center, Stone Bridge, and Stone House, Henry Hill also is highly recommended. The imposing statue of Thomas Jackson overlooks this vantage point where he gained his nickname during the first clash at Manassas. An easy walking path meanders over the terrain on which Porter's, Reno's, and Sigel's corps stood against Longstreet before being forced from the field on 30 August, during Second Bull Run. Information about First Bull Run also is found on this high ground. In fact, if possible, visitors should allow extra time to follow the events of both First and Second Manassas during their stay.

Other points of interest include the Unfinished Railroad, Deep Cut, the New York Monuments, Battery Heights, and Chinn Ridge. Taken together, these vestiges of the encounter help bring the battle to life.

In addition to the battlefield, the nearby Manassas Museum, 9101 Prince William St., Manassas, VA 20110, Tel.(703) 368 1873, places the military aspects of the area in local historical context. Exhibits, programs, such as Civil War re-enactors in late July and late August, and the museum store all enhance the interpretation. Visitors should also find the Conference and Visitors Bureau website at www.visitpwc.com of interest, when planning a trip to the area.

There are ample accommodations in the vicinity, many of which are more reasonably priced than lodging found closer to Washington. Restaurants and shopping are nearby as well, which while convenient have threatened to encroach on the historic scene. A picnic area north of US 29 and Sudley Road offers a good place to lunch and take in the setting.

While key reminders of Manassas remain in a setting reminiscent of 1862, the same good fortune did not befall Ox Hill (Chantilly). Except for a few acres around the two monuments erected prior to World War One, in memory of Generals Kearny and Stevens, modern structures, street lights, and other incursions have rendered the scene almost unrecognizable from its 19th-century appearance. Nevertheless, for those who are intent on completing the story of the Bull Run Campaign, proceed east from the Manassas National Battlefield on US 29 toward Centreville until it crosses Virginia 28. Take this road north until reaching US 50, then turn right and continue on for just under 5 miles to West Ox Road. Turn right and drive another 700 yds onto a residential street, where a right turn should be made. Proceed another 350 yds until coming to a small rise where the two monuments stand.

ORDERS OF BATTLE

Units present are followed by the commander's rank and name, and their estimated strength at the start of the first day of battle.

ABBREVIATIONS
Abbreviations of rank: **LtGen** – Lieutenant General, **MajGen** – Major General, **BrigGen** – Brigadier General, **Col** – Colonel, **LtCol** – Lieutenant Colonel, **Maj** – Major, **Capt** – Captain, **1stLt** – First Lieutenant

Abbreviations for types of artillery pieces are: **B** – Blakely rifle, **DBG** – Dahlgren Boat Gun, **N** – Napoleon gun, **NBH** – Navy Boat Howitzer, **W** – Wiard rifle, **6G** – 6-pdr field gun, **10H** – 10-pdr howitzer, **10PR** – 10-pdr Parrott rifle, **12H** – 12-pdr howitzer, **12R** – 12-pdr rifle, **20R** – 20-pdr rifle, **24H** – 24-pdr howitzer, **3R** – 3in. rifle.

The number before the abbreviation indicates the quantity of the pieces in that unit.

\+ – type or number of gun estimated
(k) – mortally wounded or killed
(w) – wounded
* – name of commanding officer unknown

NB: Commanding officers listed are those at the outset of the battle; some subsequently were replaced as a result of wounds, death, or other reasons, during the course of the battle.

ARMY OF VIRGINIA, 29–30 AUGUST 1862
MajGen John Pope
(77,000)

Note: This figure includes those units of the Army of the Potomac assigned to Pope's command. Only certain elements of the Army of the Potomac were assigned to Pope, the majority of units remaining under McClellan's command

I CORPS
MajGen Franz Sigel
(12,500)

1ST DIVISION
BrigGen Robert C. Schenck
(3,800)

1st Brigade
BrigGen Julius Stahel
8th New York – Col Carl B. Hedterich
41st New York – LtCol Ernest W. Holmstedt
45th New York – LtCol Edward C. Wratislaw
27th Pennsylvania – Col Adolphus Bushbeck
New York Light Artillery 2nd Battery – Capt Louis Schirmer (6/10PR)

2nd Brigade
Col Nathaniel C. McLean
25th Ohio – Col William P. Richardson
55th Ohio – Col John C. Lee
73rd Ohio – Col Orland Smith
75th Ohio – Maj Robert Reilly
1st Ohio Light Artillery Battery K – 1stLt George B. Haskins (4/12H; 2/6G)

2ND DIVISION
BrigGen Adolph Von Steinwehr
(2,500)

1st Brigade
Col John A. Koltes (k)
29th New York – Col Clemens Soest (w)
68th New York – LtCol John H. Kleefisch (w)
73rd Pennsylvania – LtCol Gustave A. Muhleck

3RD DIVISION
BrigGen Carl Schurz
(2,800)

1st Brigade
BrigGen Henry Bohlen (k)
61st Ohio – Col Newton Schlech
74th Pennsylvania – Maj Franz Blessing
8th West Virginia – Capt Hedgman Black
Pennsylvania Light Artillery Battery F – Capt Robert B. Hampton (4/10PR)

2nd Brigade
Col Wladimir Kryzanowski
54th New York – LtCol Charles Ashby
58th New York – Maj William Henkel (w)
75th Pennsylvania – LtCol Francis Mahler (w)
2nd New York Light Artillery Battery L – Capt Jacob Roemer (6/3R)

Unattached
3rd West Virginia Cavalry Company I – Capt Jonathan Sthal
1st Ohio Light Artillery Battery I – Capt Hubert Dilger (4/12H; 2/6G)

Independent Brigade
BrigGen Robert H. Milroy
82nd Ohio – Col James Cantwell (k)
2nd West Virginia – Col George R. Latham
3rd West Virginia – Col David T. Hewes
5th West Virginia – Col John L. Zeigler
1st West Virginia Cavalry Companies C, E, and I – Maj John C. Krepps
Ohio Light Artillery 12th Battery – Capt Aaron C. Johnson (6/W)

CAVALRY BRIGADE
Col John Beardsley
1st Battalion Connecticut – Capt L.N. Middlebrook
1st Maryland – LtCol C. Wetschky
4th New York – LtCol Ferries Nazer
9th New York – Maj Charles McL. Knox
6th Ohio – Col William R. Lloyd

Reserve Artillery
Capt Franz Buell (k)
1st New York Light Artillery Battery I – Capt Michael Wiedrich (4/10PR, 2/12H)
New York Light Artillery 13th Battery – Capt Julius Dieckmann (6/10PR)
West Virginia Light Artillery Battery C – Capt Wallace Hill (6/12N)

II CORPS
MajGen Nathaniel P. Banks

Note: Not engaged in any of the main fighting with the exception of the cavalry, therefore, strengths not included except in the case of the cavalry

1ST DIVISION
BrigGen Alpheus S. Williams

1st Brigade
BrigGen Samuel W. Crawford
5th Connecticut – Capt James A. Betts
10th Maine – Col George L. Beal
28th New York – Capt William H.H. Mapes
46th Pennsylvania – LtCol James L. Selfridge

2nd Brigade
(Combined with the others)

3rd Brigade
BrigGen George H. Gordon
27th Indiana – Col Silas Colgrove
2nd Massachusetts – Col George L. Andrews.
3rd Wisconsin – Col Thomas H. Ruger

2ND DIVISION
BrigGen George S. Greene

1st Brigade
Col Charles Candy
5th Ohio – Col John H. Patrick
7th Ohio – Col William R. Creighton
29th Ohio – Capt Wilbur Stevens
66th Ohio – LtCol Eugene Powell
28th Pennsylvania – Gabriel De Korponay

2nd Brigade
Col Matthew Schlaudecker
3rd Maryland – Col David Dewitt
102nd New York – Col Thomas B. Van Buren
109th Pennsylvania – Col Henry J. Stainrook
111th Pennsylvania – Maj Thomas M. Walker
8th U. S. Infantry Battalion – Capt T. Anderson
12th U. S. Infantry Battalion – Capt T. Anderson

3rd Brigade
Col James A. Tait
3rd Delaware – William O. Redden
1st District of Columbia – LtCol Lemuek Towers
60th New York – Col William B. Goodrich
78th New York – LtCol Jonathan Austin
Purnell Legion (Maryland) – Col William J. Leonard

Artillery
Capt Clement L. Best
Maine Light Artillery 4th Battery (D) – Capt O'Neill W. Robinson (4/20R). Not on field
Maine Light Artillery 6th Battery (F) – Capt F. McGilvery (4/20R)
New York Light Artillery 10th Battery – Capt John T. Bruen (4/N). Not on field
1st New York Light Artillery Battery M – Capt George W. Cothram (6/10PR). Not on field
Pennsylvania Light Artillery Battery E – Capt Joseph M. Knap (6/10PR). Not on field
4th U.S. Artillery Battery F – 1stLt Edward D. Muhlenberg (6/3R)

Cavalry Brigade
BrigGen John Buford
(1,500)
1st Michigan – Col Thornton F. Brodhead (w)
5th New York – Col Othniel De Forest
1st Vermont – Col Charles H. Tompkins
1st West Virginia – LtCol Nathaniel P. Richmond

III CORPS
MajGen Irvin McDowell
(20,000)

1ST DIVISION
BrigGen Rufus King
(9,000)

1st Brigade
Brig Gen John P. Hatch (w)
14th New York State Militia (84th New York) – LtCol Edward B. Fowler (w)
22nd New York – Col Walter Phelps, Jr.
24th New York – Col Timothy Sullivan
30th New York – Col Edward Frisby (k)
2nd U.S. Sharpshooters – LtCol Henry A.V. Post

2nd Brigade
BrigGen Abner Doubleday
76th New York – Col William P. Wainwright
95th New York – LtCol James B. Post
56th Pennsylvania – LtCol Sullivan Hoffmann (w)

3rd Brigade
BrigGen Marsena R. Patrick
20th New York State Militia (80th New York) – Col George W. Pratt (k)
21st New York – Col William F. Rogers
23rd New York – LtCol Nirmon M. Crane
35th New York – Col Newton B. Lord

4th Brigade
BrigGen John Gibbon
19th Indiana – Col Solomon Meredith
2nd Wisconsin – Col Edgar O'Connor (k)
6th Wisconsin – Col Lysander Cutler (w)
7th Wisconsin – Col William W. Robinson (w)

Artillery
Capt Joseph B. Campbell
New Hampshire Light Artillery 1st Battery – Capt George A. Gerrish (6/N)
1st New York Light Artillery Battery L – Capt John A. Reynolds (6/3R)
1st Rhode Island Light Artillery Battery D – Capt J. Albert Monroe (6/12H)
4th U.S. Artillery Battery B – Capt Joseph B. Campbell (6/N)

2ND DIVISION
BrigGen James B. Ricketts
(9,000)

1st Brigade
BrigGen Abram Duryee
97th New York – LtCol John P. Spotford
104th New York – Maj Lewis C. Skinner
105th New York – Col Howard Carroll
107th Pennsylvania – Col Thomas F. McCoy

2nd Brigade
BrigGen Zealous B. Tower (w)
26th New York – Col William H. Christian
94th New York – Col Arian R. Root
88th Pennsylvania – LtCol Joseph A. McLean (k)
90th Pennsylvania – Col Peter Lyle

3rd Brigade
Col Robert Stiles
12th Massachusetts – Col Fletcher Webster (k)
3th Massachusetts – Col Samuel H. Leonard
9th Militia (83rd New York) – Col John W. Stiles
11th Pennsylvania – Col Richard Coulter

4th Brigade
Col Joseph Thoburn
7th Indiana – LtCol John F. Cheek
84th Pennsylvania – Col Samuel M. Bowman
110th Pennsylvania – Col William D. Lewis, Jr.
1st West Virginia – LtCol Henry P. Hubbard

Artillery
Maine Light Artillery 2nd Battery (B) – Capt J. Hall (4/20R)+
Maine Light Artillery 5th Battery (E) – Capt G.F. Leppien (4/20R)+
1st Pennsylvania Light Artillery Battery F – Capt Ezra Matthews (6/3R)
Pennsylvania Light Artillery Battery C – Capt James Thompson 4/10PR)

Cavalry Brigade
BrigGen George D. Bayard
1st Maine – Col Samuel H. Allen
1st New Jersey – LtCol Joseph Karge (w)
2nd New York – Col J. Mansfield Davies
1st Pennsylvania – Col Owen Jones
1st Rhode Island – Col A.N. Duffie

RESERVE DIVISION
BrigGen John F. Reynolds(4,700)
(Temporarily attached to III Corps)

1st Brigade
BrigGen George G. Meade
3rd Pennsylvania Reserves – Col Horatio D. Sickles
4th Pennsylvania Reserves – Col Albert L. Magilton
7th Pennsylvania Reserves – LtCol Robert M. Henderson
8th Pennsylvania – Capt William Lemon
13th Pennsylvania Reserves (lst Rifles six companies) – Col Hugh H. McNeil

2nd Brigade
BrigGen Truman Seymour
1st Pennsylvania Reserves – Col R. Biddle Roberts
2nd Pennsylvania Reserves – Col William McCandless (w)
5th Pennsylvania Reserves – Col Joseph W. Fisher
6th Pennsylvania Reserves – Col William Sinclair

3rd Brigade
BrigGen Conrad F. Jackson
9th Pennsylvania Reserves – LtCol Robert Anderson
10th Pennsylvania Reserves – Col James T. Kirk (w)
11th Pennsylvania Reserves – LtCol Samuel H. Jackson
12th Pennsylvania Reserves Col Martin D. Hardin (w)

Artillery
Capt Dunbar P. Ranson
1st Pennsylvania Light Artillery Battery A – Capt John G. Simpson (4/N)
1st Pennsylvania Light Artillery Battery B – Capt James H. Cooper (6/10PR)
1st Pennsylvania Light Artillery Battery G – Capt Mark Kerns (w) (4/10PR)
5th U.S. Artillery Battery C – Capt Dunbar R. Ransom (6/N)

Unattached
16th Indiana Battery – Capt Charles A. Naylor (6/N)
Maine Light Artillery 3rd Battery (C Pontoniers) – Capt James G. Sweet (4/20R)+
4th U.S. Artillery Battery E – Capt Joseph C. Clark, Jr. (6/10PR). Not on field during the battle

RESERVE CORPS
BrigGen Samuel D. Sturgis (800)

Piatt's Brigade
BrigGen A. Sander Piatt
(Temporarily attached to V Corps 27–31 August)
63rd Indiana Companies A, B, C, and D – LtCol John S. Williams
86th New York – Col Benjah P. Bailey

MISCELLANEOUS
1st New York Battery C (1 Section)– 1stLt S.R. James (2/N). Not on field
2nd New York Heavy Artillery – Col Gustave Waagner
11th New York Battery – Capt A.A. von Puttkammer (6/N)

ARMY OF THE POTOMAC

III CORPS
MajGen Samuel P. Heintzelman
(10,000)
5th New York Cavalry – 3 troops as escort

1ST DIVISION
MajGen Philip Kearny
(4,500)

1st Brigade
BrigGen John C. Robinson
20th Indiana – Col William L. Brown (k)
63rd Pennsylvania – Col Alexander Hays (w)
105th Pennsylvania – LtCol Calvin Craig (w)

2nd Brigade
BrigGen David B. Birney
3rd Maine – Maj Edwin Burt
4th Maine – Col Elijah Walker
1st New York – Maj Edwin Burt
38th New York – Col J.H. Hobart Ward
40th New York – Col Thomas W. Egan
101st New York – LtCol Nelson A. Gesner
57th Pennsylvania – Maj William Birney

3rd Brigade
Col Orlando M. Poe
2nd Michigan – LtCol Louis Dillman
3rd Michigan – Col S.G. Champlin (w)
5th Michigan – Capt William Wakenshaw
37th New York – Col Samuel B. Hayman
99th Pennsylvania – Col Asher S. Leidy

Artillery
1st Rhode Island Battery E – Capt George E. Randolph (4/10PR; 2/N)
1st U.S. Battery K – Capt William M. Graham (6/N)

2nd Division
MajGen Joseph Hooker
(5,500)

1st Brigade
BrigGen Cuvier Grover
1st Massachusetts – Col Robert Cowdin
11th Massachusetts – Col William Blaisdell
16th Massachusetts – Maj Gardner Banks
2nd New Hampshire – Col Gilman Marston
26th Pennsylvania – Maj Robert L. Bodine

2nd or Excelsior Brigade
Col Nelson Taylor
70th New York – Capt Charles L. Young
71st New York – LtCol Henry L. Potter (w)
72nd New York – Capt Harman J. Bliss
73rd New York – Capt Alfred A. Donalds (w)
74th New York – Maj Edward L. Price

3rd Brigade
Col Joseph B. Carr
5th New Jersey – LtCol William J. Sewell
6th New Jersey – Col Gershom Mott (w)
7th New Jersey – Col Joseph W. Revere
8th New Jersey – LtCol William Ward (w)
2nd New York – Capt Sidney W. Park
115th Pennsylvania – LtCol Robert Thompson

Artillery
Maine Light Artillery 6th Battery – Capt Freeman McGilvery (4/20R)

V CORPS
MajGen Fitz John Porter
(10,100)

1ST DIVISION
MajGen George W. Morell
(6,000)

1st Brigade
Col Charles W. Roberts
2nd Maine – Maj Daniel F. Sargent
18th Massachusetts – Capt Stephen Thomas
22nd Massachusetts – Maj Mason W. Burt
1st Michigan – Col Horace S. Roberts (k)
13th New York – Col Elisha G. Marshall
25th New York – Col Charles A. Johnson

2nd Brigade
BrigGen Charles Griffin
(Not in action)
9th Massachusetts – Col Patrick R. Guiney
32nd Massachusetts – Col Francis J. Parker
4th Michigan – Col Jonathan W. Childs
14th New York – Col James McQuade
62nd Pennsylvania – Col Jacob W. Sweitzer

3rd Brigade
BrigGen Daniel Butterfield – Commanded 1st and 3rd Brigades during 30 August
Michigan Sharpshooters Brady's Company – Capt Brady
16th Michigan – Capt Thomas J. Barry (w)
12th New York – Col Henry A. Weeks (w)
17th New York – Col Henry S. Lansing
44th New York – Col James C. Rice
83rd Pennsylvania – LtCol Hugh S. Campbell (w)

Sharpshooters
1st U.S. Sharpshooters – Col Hiram Berdan

Artillery
3rd Massachusetts Light Artillery Battery C – Capt Augustus P. Martin (6/N)
1st Rhode Island Light Artillery Battery C – Capt Richard Waterman (2/10PR; 4/N)+
5th U.S. Artillery Battery D – 1stLt Charles Hazlett (6/10PR)

2ND DIVISION
BrigGen George Sykes
(4,100)

1st Brigade
LtCol Robert C. Buchanan

3rd U.S. Infantry – Capt John D. Wilkins
4th U.S. Infantry – Capt Joseph B. Collins (w)
12th Infantry 1st Battalion – Capt Matthew M. Blunt
14th Infantry 1st Battalion – Capt John D. O'Connell (w)
14th Infantry 2nd Battalion – Capt David B. McKibbin

2nd Brigade
LtCol William Chapman
1st U.S. Infantry Company G – Capt Matthew R. Marston
2nd U.S. Infantry – Maj Charles S. Lovell
6th U.S. Infantry – Capt Levi C. Bootes
10th U.S. Infantry – Maj Charles S. Lovell
11th U.S. Infantry – Maj De Lancy Floyd-Jones
17th U.S. Infantry – Maj George L. Andrews

3rd Brigade
Col Gouverneur K. Warren
5th New York – Capt Cleveland Winslow
10th New York – Col John E. Bendix

Artillery
Capt Stephen H. Weed
1st U.S. Artillery Batteries E & G – 1stLt Alanson M. Randol (4/N)
5th U.S. Artillery Battery I – Capt Stephen H. Weed (6/3R)
5th U.S. Artillery Battery K – Capt John R. Smead (k) (4/N)

VI CORPS
(Note. VI Corps, 1st Division, 1st Brigade was engaged only on 27 August at Bull Run Bridge)

1ST DIVISION

1st Brigade – (800)
BrigGen George W. Taylor (w)
1st New Jersey – Maj William Henry, Jr.
2nd New Jersey – Col Samuel L. Buck
3rd New Jersey – Col Henry W. Brown
4th New Jersey – Capt Napoleon B. Aaronson

IX CORPS
BrigGen Jesse L. Reno
(8,000)

1ST DIVISION
BrigGen Isaac I. Stevens
(4,000)

1st Brigade
Col Benjamin C. Christ
8th Michigan – LtCol Frank Graves
50th Pennsylvania – LtCol Thomas S. Brenholtz (w)

2nd Brigade
Col Daniel Leasure (w)
46th New York (5 Companies) – Col Rudolph Rosa (w)
100th Pennsylvania – LtCol David A. Leckey

3rd Brigade
Col Addison Farnsworth (w)
28th Massachusetts– Maj George W. Cartright (w)

79th New York – Maj William St. George Elliot (w)

Artillery
Massachusetts Light Artillery 8th Battery – Capt Asa M. Cook (6/N) Not on field
2nd U.S. Artillery Battery E – 1stLt Samuel N. Benjamin (4/20R)

2ND DIVISION
Maj Gen Jesse L. Reno
(4,000)

1st Brigade
Col James Nagle
2nd Maryland – LtCol J. Eugene Duryea
6th New Hampshire – Col Simon G. Griffin
48th Pennsylvania – LtCol Joshua K. Sigfried

2nd Brigade
Col Edward Ferrero
21st Massachusetts – Col William S. Clark
51st New York – LtCol Robert B. Potter
51st Pennsylvania – Col John F. Hartranft
Pennsylvania Light Artillery Battery D – Capt George W. Durell (4/10PR; 2/6G)

KANAWHA DIVISION (DETACHMENT)
Col W. Parker Scammon
(1,800)
(Note. The Kanawha Division was en route from West Virginia to the Army of Virginia and the Provisional Brigade.)

First Provisional Brigade
Col E. Parker Scammon
11th Ohio – Maj Lyman J. Jackson
12th Ohio – Col Carr B. White

Unattached
30th Ohio – LtCol Theodore Jones
36th Ohio – Col George Crook

NB: There was no cavalry in the Army of the Potomac elements

ARMY OF NORTHERN VIRGINIA, 29–30 AUGUST 1862
Gen Robert E. Lee
(55,000)

LONGSTREET'S CORPS (RIGHT WING)
MajGen James Longstreet
(27,800)

ANDERSON'S DIVISION
MajGen R.H. Anderson
(7,000)

Artillery
Maj John S. Saunders
Norfolk (Virginia) Battery – Capt Frank Huger (1/3R; 2/6G; 10PR)
Lynchburg (Virginia) Battery – Capt M.N. Moorman (2/10PR; 2/12H)
Ashland (Virginia) Battery– Capt Pichegru Woolfolk (2/6G; 2/12H)+

Armistead's Brigade
BrigGen Lewis A. Armistead
9th Virginia – Col David Goodman
14th Virginia – Col James Hodges
38th Virginia – Col Edward C. Edmonds
53rd Virginia – LtCol John Grammer
57th Virginia – Col David Dyer
5th Virginia Battalion – *

Mahone's Brigade
BrigGen William Mahone (w)
6th Virginia – Col George T. Rogers
12th Virginia – Col David Weisiger
16th Virginia – Col Charles A. Crump (k)
41st Virginia – Col William A. Parham
49th Virginia – *

Wright's Brigade
BrigGen Ambrose R. Wright
44th Alabama – LtCol Charles A. Derby (w)
3rd Georgia – Col John R. Sturgis
22nd Georgia – *
44th Georgia – *
48th Georgia – *

JONES' DIVISION
BrigGen David R. Jones
(5,200)

Toombs's Brigade
Col Henry L. Benning
2nd Georgia – LtCol William R. Holmes
15th Georgia – Col William T. Millican
7th Georgia – Maj John H. Pickett (w)
20th Georgia – Maj J.D. Waddell

Drayton's Brigade
BrigGen Thomas F. Drayton
50th Georgia – Col William R. Manning
51st Georgia – Col William M. Slaughter
15th South Carolina – *
Phillips's Georgia Legion – Col William Phillips
Goochland (Leake's) (Virginia) Battery – Capt William Turner (1/3R; 3/12H)

Jones's Brigade
Col George T. Anderson
1st Georgia (Regulars) – Maj John D. Walker
7th Georgia – Col William T. Wilson (w)
8th Georgia – LtCol John R. Towers
9th Georgia – Col Benjamin Beck
11th Georgia – LtCol William Luffman

WILCOX'S DIVISION
BrigGen Cadmus M. Wilcox
(4,000)

Wilcox's Brigade
BrigGen Cadmus M. Wilcox
8th Alabama – Maj Hilary A. Herbert
9th Alabama – Maj J.H.J. Williams
10th Alabama – Maj John H. Caldwell
11th Alabama – Capt J.C.C. Sanders
Thomas (Virginia) Battery – Capt Edwin J. Anderson (2/10PR, 2/12H)+

Pryor's Brigade
BrigGen Roger A. Pryor
14th Alabama – LtCol James R. Broom
5th Florida – *
8th Florida – *
3rd Virginia – Col Joseph Mayo, Jr.
Donaldsonville (Louisiana) Battery – Capt Victor Maurin (2/3R; 2 10PR; 2/6G)

Featherston's Brigade
BrigGen W.S. Featherston
12th Mississippi – *
16th Mississippi – Col Canot Posey
9th Mississippi – *
2nd Mississippi Battalion – *
Monroe's (Dixie) (Virginia) Battery – Capt W.B. Chapman (2/3R; 2/N)

HOOD'S DIVISION
BrigGen John B. Hood
(3,800)

Hood's/Texas Brigade
BrigGen John B. Hood
18th Georgia – Col William T. Wofford
Hampton's (South Carolina) Legion – LtCol Martin W. Gary
1st Texas – LtCol P.A. Work
4th Texas – LtCol B.F. Carter
5th Texas – Col J.B. Robertson (w)

Whiting's Brigade
Col Evander M. Law
4th Alabama – LtCol O.K. McLemore
2nd Mississippi – Col P.F. Liddell
11th Mississippi – Col P.F. Liddell
6th North Carolina – Maj Robert F. Webb

Artillery
Maj Bushrod W. Frobel
German (South Carolina) Artillery – Capt W.K. Bachman (4/N)
Palmetto (South Carolina) Artillery – Capt Hugh R. Garden (1/N; 1/12H; 2/6G)
Rowan (North Carolina) Artillery – Capt James Reilly (2/3R; 2 10PR; 2/24H)

KEMPER'S DIVISION
BrigGen James L. Kemper
(4,000)

Kemper's Brigade
Col Montgomery D. Corse (w)
1st Virginia – LtCol F.G. Skinner (w)
7th Virginia – Col W.T. Patton (w)
11th Virginia – Maj Adam Clement
17th Virginia – LtCol Morton Mayre (w)
24th Virginia – Col William R. Terry
Loudoun (Virginia) Artillery – Capt A.L. Rogers (2/10PR; 2/12H)+

Jenkins's Brigade
BrigGen Micah Jenkins (w)
1st South Carolina (Volunteers) – Col Thomas J. Glover (k)
2nd South Carolina Rifles – Col Vinro Moore (k)
5th South Carolina – *
6th South Carolina – *
4th South Carolina Battalion – *
Palmetto (South Carolina) Sharpshooters – Col Joseph Walker
Fauquier (Virginia) Battery – Capt R.L. Stribling (1/3R; 3/N)

Pickett's Brigade
Col Eppa Hunton
8th Virginia – LtCol Norborne Berkeley
18th Virginia – Maj George C. Cabell
19th Virginia – Col James B. Strange
28th Virginia – Col Robert C. Allen
56th Virginia – Col William D. Stuart

Evans's Independent Brigade
BrigGen Nathan G. Evans
17th South Carolina – Col John H. Means (k)
18th South Carolina – Col J.M. Gadberry (k)
22nd South Carolina – Col S.D. Goodlett (w)
23rd South Carolina – Col H.L. Benbow (w)
Holcombe (South Carolina) Legion – Col P.F. Stevens
Macbeth (South Carolina) Artillery – Capt R. Boyce (4/N)

Right Wing Artillery
Washington (Louisiana) Artillery – Maj John B. Walton
1st Company – Capt Charles W. Squires (3/3R)
2nd Company – Capt J.B. Richardson (attached to Toombs) (2/12H; 2/6G)
3rd Company – Capt M.B. Miller (4/N)
4th Company – Capt B.F. Eshleman (attached to Hunton) (2/N; 2/6G)

Lee's Battalion
Col Stephen D. Lee
Bath (Taylor's) (Virginia) Battery – Capt J.L. Eubank (1/3R; 1/12H; 2/6G)
Bedford (Virginia) Artillery – Capt T.C. Jordan (2/3R; 1/12H; 1/6G)
Richmond (Parker's) (Virginia) Battery – Capt W.W. Parker (2/3R; 2/12H)
Rhett's (South Carolina) Battery – 1stLt William Elliot (2/20R; 2/10PR)
Portsmouth (Grimes's) (Virginia) Battery – 1stLt Thomas J. Oakham (4/NBH)

JACKSON'S CORPS (LEFT WING)
MajGen Thomas J. Jackson
(24,200)

JACKSON'S DIVISION
BrigGen William B. Taliaferro (w)
(5000)

1st Brigade
Col W.S.H. Baylor (k)
2nd Virginia – LtCol Lawson Botts (k)
4th Virginia – LtCol R.D. Gardner
5th Virginia – Maj H.J. Williams
27th Virginia – Col A.J. Grigsby
33rd Virginia – Col John E. Neff (k)

2nd Brigade
Col Bradley T. Johnson
21st Virginia – Capt William A. Witcher
42nd Virginia – Capt John E. Penn
48th Virginia – 1stLt Virginius Dabney (w)
1st Virginia (Irish) Battalion – Maj John Seddon

3rd Brigade
Col Alexander G. Taliaferro
47th Alabama – Col James W. Jackson
48th Alabama – Col J.L. Sheffield
10th Virginia – LtCol S.T. Walker
23rd Virginia – Col Alexander G. Taliaferro
7th Virginia – *

4th Brigade
BrigGen William E. Starke
1st Louisiana – LtCol Nolan
2nd Louisiana – Col J.M. Williams
9th Louisiana – Col Leroy A. Stafford
10th Louisiana – LtCol William Spencer (k)
15th Louisiana – Col Edmund Pendleton
Coppen's (Louisiana) Battalion – Maj Gaston Coppen

Artillery
Maj L.M. Shumaker
2nd Baltimore (Maryland) Battery – Capt J.B. Brockenbrough (also known as Maryland Horse) (1/3R; 1/12H; 2/B)
Alleghany (Virginia) Battery – Capt Joseph Carpenter (2/3R; 2/12H)
Richmond Hampden (Virginia) Battery – Capt William H. Caskie 1/10PR; 3/6G)
Winchester (Virginia) Battery – Capt W.E. Cutshaw (2/3R; 2/12H)
First Rockbridge (Virginia) Battery – Capt William T. Pogue (2/10PR; 2/12H)
Lynchburg (Lee's) (Virginia) Battery – Capt Charles J. Raine (3/3R; 1/12H)
Page– Shanandoah (Virginia) Battery – Capt W.H. Rice (also known as the 8th Star Battery) (1/3R; 1/10PR; 1/N; 1/6G)
Danville (Schumaker's) (Virginia) Battery – Capt George W. Wooding (1/3R; 2/10PR; 1/N)

HILL'S LIGHT DIVISION
MajGen Ambrose P. Hill
(12,000)

Branch's Brigade
BrigGen Lawrence O'Bryan Branch
7th North Carolina – Capt Edward G. Haywood (w)
18th North Carolina – LtCol T.J. Purdie
28th North Carolina – Col James H. Lane
33rd North Carolina – Col Robert F. Hoke
37th North Carolina – Col William M. Barbour

Pender's Brigade
BrigGen William D. Pender
16th North Carolina – Capt L.W. Stowe
22nd North Carolina – Maj C.C. Cole (w)
34th North Carolina – Col Richard H. Riddick (k)
38th North Carolina – Capt John Ashford (w)

Gregg's Brigade
BrigGen Maxcy Gregg
1st South Carolina – Maj Edward McCrady (w)
1st South Carolina Rifles (Orr's Rifles)– Col J.Foster Marshall (k)
12th South Carolina – Col Dixon Barnes
13th South Carolina – Col O.E. Edwards (w)
14th South Carolina – Col Samuel McGowan (w)

Archer's Brigade
BrigGen James J. Archer
5th Alabama Battalion – Capt Thomas Bush (k)
19th Georgia – Capt F.M. Johnston
1st Tennessee (Provisional Army) – Col Peter A. Turney
7th Tennessee – Maj S.G. Shepard
14th Tennessee – Col W.A. Forbes (k)

Field's Brigade
BrigGen Charles W. Field (w)
40th Virginia – Col J.M. Brockenbrough
47th Virginia – Col Robert M. Mayo (w)
55th Virginia – Col Frank Mallory
22nd Virginia Battalion – *

Thomas's Brigade
Col Edward L. Thomas
14th Georgia – Col R.W. Folsom
35th Georgia – *
45th Georgia – Maj W.L. Grice
49th Georgia – LtCol S.M. Manning
Richmond (Purcell's) (Virginia) Battery – Capt William J. Pegram (4/N)

Artillery
LtCol Robert L. Walker
Branch (Lantham's) (North Carolina) Battery – Capt John R. Potts (2/12N; 2/6G)
Pee Dee (South Carolina) Battery – Capt D.G. McIntosh (1/3R; 1/N; 2/10PR)
Fredericksburg (Virginia) Battery – Capt Carter M. Braxton (2/3R; 4/6G)
Richmond (Crenshaw's) (Virginia) Battery – Capt W.G. Crenshaw (1/12H; 1/N; 2/G)
Richmond (Letcher's) (Virginia) Battery – Capt Greenlee Davidson (1/3R; 2/N; 1/6G)
Middlesex (Fleet's) (Virginia) Battery – Capt W.B. Hardy (2/3R; 2/12N)+

EWELL'S DIVISION
MajGen Richard S. Ewell (w)
(7,200)

Lawton's Brigade
BrigGen A.R. Lawton
13th Georgia – Col C.M. Douglass
26th Georgia – Col Edmund Atkinson
31st Georgia – *
38th Georgia – *
60th Georgia – Maj T.J. Berry
61st Georgia – *

Trimble's Brigade
BrigGen Isaac R. Trimble (w)
15th Alabama – Maj A.A. Lowther
12th Georgia – Capt W.F. Brown
21st Georgia – Capt Thomas C. Glover
21st North Carolina – LtCol Sanders Fulton (k)
1st North Carolina Battalion – *

Early's Brigade
BrigGen Jubal A. Early
13th Virginia – Col James A. Walker
25th Virginia – Col George H. Smith (w)
31st Virginia – Col John F. Hoffman
44th Virginia – *
49th Virginia – Co. William Smith
52nd Virginia – *
58th Virginia – Col Samuel H. Letcher

Forno's Brigade
Col Henry Forno (w)
5th Louisiana – Maj B. Menger
6th Louisiana – Col H.B. Strong
7th Louisiana – *
8th Louisiana – Maj T.D. Lewis
14th Louisiana – Col Zebulon York

Artillery
Staunton (Balthis')(Virginia) Battery – 1stLt A.W. Garber (2/6G)
Chesapeake (4th Maryland) Battery – Capt William D. Brown (1/3R; 2 10PR)
Louisiana Guard Artillery – Capt Louis E. D'Aquin (1/10PR; 2/3R)
1st Maryland Battery – Capt William F. Dement (4/6G)
Bedford (Virginia) Battery – Capt John R. Johnson (2/3R; 1/12H; 1/6G)
Henrico (Courtney's) (Virginia) Battery – Capt James W. Latimer (2/3R; 2/N)

CAVALRY
MajGen J.E.B. Stuart
(3,000)

Hampton's Brigade – (Not present on the field)
BrigGen Wade Hampton
Cobb (Georgia) Legion – Col Thomas R.R. Cobb
1st North Carolina – *
2nd South Carolina – *
10th Virginia – *
Jeff Davis Legion – *

Robertson's Brigade
BrigGen Beverly H. Robertson
2nd Virginia – Col Thomas T. Munford
6th Virginia – Col Thomas S. Flournoy
7th Virginia – Col William E. Jones
12th Virginia – Col A.W. Harman
17th Virginia Battalion – Maj W. Patrick (w)

Lee's Brigade
BrigGen Fitz Hugh Lee
1st Virginia – Col L.T. Brien
3rd Virginia – *
4th Virginia – Col W.C. Wickham
5th Virginia – Col Thomas L. Rosser
9th Virginia – Col W.H.F. Lee

Artillery
Maj John Pelham
Ashby Horse Battery – Capt Robert P. Chew (1/B; 3/12R)
Stuart Horse Battery – 1st (Virginia) – Capt John Pelham (4/B)

FURTHER READING

Ambrose, Stephen E. *Halleck: Lincoln's Chief of Staff* (Baton Rouge, 1962).
Boatner, Mark M. III. *The Civil War Dictionary* (New York, 1959).
Cozzen, Peter. *General John Pope: A Life for the Nation* (Urbana, 2000).
Davis, William C. (Ed.) *The Image of War Vol. II The Guns of '62* (Gettysburg, 1982).
Douglas, Henry Kyd. *I Rode With Stonewall* (Chapel Hill, 1940).
Editors of Time-Life Books. *Lee Takes Command From Seven Days to Second Bull Run* (Alexandria, 1984).
Editors of Time-Life Books. *Voices of the Civil War* (Alexandria, 1995).
Evans, Clement A. *Outline of Confederate Military History Vol III* (Atlanta, 1899).
Fishel, Edwin C. *The Secret War for the Union: The Untold Story of Military Intelligence in the Civil War* (Boston, 1996).
Gordon, George H. *History of the Campaign of the Army of Virginia, Under John Pope ... from Cedar Mountain to Alexandria*, 1862 (Boston, 1880).
Greene, A. Wilson. *The Second Battle of Manassas* (Conshohocken, PA, 1995).
Griffith, Alfred H. *The Heart of Abraham Lincoln, Man of Kindness and Mercy* (Madison, 1948).
Hennessy, John J. *Return to Bull Run: The Campaign and Battle of Second Manassas* (Norman, 1999).
Hennessy, John J. *Second Manassas Battlefield Map Study*. 2nd ed. (Lynchburg, 1985).
Jensen, Leslie D. *Johnny Reb: The Uniform of the Confederate Army, 1861–1865* (London, 1996).
Johnson, Robert U., and Buel, Clarence C. *Battles and Leaders of the Civil War. Vol II* (New York, 1887).
Krick, Robert K. *Stonewall Jackson at Cedar Mountain* (Chapel Hill, 1990).
Lyon, James S. *War Sketches: from Cedar Mountain to Bull Run* (Buffalo, 1882).
Martin, David G. *The Second Bull Run Campaign July–August 1862* (Conshohocken, PA, 1997).
Polley, J.B. *A Soldier's Letters to Charming Nellie* (New York, 1908).
Ropes, John Codman. *The Army Under Pope* (New York, 1881).
Selby, John. *Stonewall Jackson as Military Commander* (New York, 1999).
Sheppard, E.W. *The Campaign in Virginia and Maryland June 26th to September 20th, 1862: Cedar Run, Manassas, and Sharpsburg* (New York, 1911).
Stackpole, Edward J. *From Cedar Mountain to Antietam* (Harrisburg, 1959).
Sutherland, Daniel E. *The Emergence of Total War* (Fort Worth, 1996).
Townsend, George Alfred. *Campaigns of a Non-Combatant* (Alexandria, 1982).
Weigley, Russell F. *Way of War: A History of United States Military Strategy and Policy* (New York, 1973).

INDEX

Figures in **bold** refer to illustrations.

African Americans 108, 113, **169**
  see also slavery
Alexander, Capt Edward Porter 57, 60, 68
Anaconda Plan 40
Anderson, Col George Thomas (1824–1901) **165**
Antietam (Sharpsburg), battle of 110, 174
Army of Northern Virginia (Confederate) 100, 133
  see also Southern army
  at 2nd Manassas
    first day 147, 149, 153, 154, 156–157, 158–159
      cavalry screen 152
      dispositions 147, 149
      Hood's advance 157
      Hooker's assault 153
      Kearny's assault 153–154, 156
      Longstreet deploys 156–157
      Reynolds' attack 157
      Union assaults 149
    second day 159, 161, **161**, 164, **170–171**
      Porter's attack 161, 164, **168**
      Ricketts' attack 160
      Union collapse 165
    and the Army of Virginia's advance 119
    artillery 116, 137, **168**
    at Brawner's Farm 134–135, 137, 142, 145
      advance to 134
      attacks 141, 143, 144
      casualties 145, 156, 165
      cavalry 116
    at Cedar Mountain 117, 119
    at Chantilly 172–173
    condition 165, 168
    Ewell's Division 135
      Gregg's Brigade 173
      Lawton's Brigade 142, 143
      Trimble's Brigade 143, 173
    exploits success 172–173
    foraging **154**
    at Freeman's Ford 128
    Hill's Division 135, 153
      Branch's Brigade 154, 173
      Gregg's Brigade 149, 154, 156
    Jackson's Corps 115–116, 119, 121, 128
      at Brawner's Farm 134–135, 145
    Longstreet's Corps 110, 119, 121, 132, 145, 156–157, 158–159, 161, 164, 173
      Anderson's Division 159
      Hood's Division 157, 164
    at Manassas Junction 133
    order of battle 182–185
    raids Pope's rear 132–133
    at the Rappahannock 121, 124, 128, 129, 130, 131, 132
    Taliaferro's Division 134, 144
    at Thoroughfare Gap 145–146
Army of the Potomac (Union) 101, 107, 108, 111, 117, 172
  see also Army of Virginia; Northern Army
  at 2nd Manassas
    first day 149
      Hooker's assault 152–153
      Kearny's assault 153–154, 156
      Nagle's attack 158
    second day 160
      Porter's attack 160–161, 164–165, **164–165**
  III (Heintzelman's) Corps 160, 181
    1st (Kearny's) Division 149, 153–154, 156, 173
    2nd (Hooker's) Division 149
      Grover's Brigade 152–153
  V (Porter's) Corps 160–161, 164–165, **164–165**
    5th New York **111**, 115, 164–165
    Berdan's Sharpshooters 160
  IX (Reno's) Corps 149, 160, 172–173, 182
    2nd (Reno's) Division, Nagle's Brigade 158
    casualties 153, 154, 164–165
    at Chantilly 172–173
    order of battle 181–182
Army of Virginia (Union) 104, 107, 108, 113, 117, 173
  see also Army of the Potomac; Northern Army
  I (Sigel's) Corps **157**, 178–179
    1st (Schenck's) Division 149, 165
    3rd (Schurz's) Division 149
  II Corps **140**, 179
    at 2nd Manassas 111, **148, 156, 157**
    first day
      advance on Jackson's forces 147
      dispositions 149
      Hatch's action 157
      and Jackson's forces 149
      McDowell's arrival 154
      Reynolds' attack 157–158
    second day 159–160
      collapse 165, **169**
      Ricketts' attack 160
  III (McDowell's) Corps **110**, 154, 160, **168**, 179–180
    1st (King's) Division 135, 137, 157
      2nd US Sharpshooters **112**, 115
      2nd Wisconsin **114**, 115, **138–139**, 142
      6th Wisconsin **138–139**, 142
      7th Wisconsin **138–139**, 142
      Iron Brigade **138–139**, 144
    2nd (Ricketts') Division 146, 160
    Reserve (Reynolds') Division 135, 149, 157–158
    advance to the Rapidan 119
    and Beverley's Ford 128
    at Brawner's Farm 141, 142–143, 144
      advance to 134, 135, 137
      Confederate artillery fire 137, 140
      Confederate attacks 143–144
      deploys artillery 140–141
      withdrawal 144
    casualties **137**, 144, 158, 165

at Cedar Mountain 117, 119, **130, 131, 137, 140**
at Centreville 165
condition 165, 168
at Freeman's Ford 128
order of battle 178–180
at the Rappahannock 124, 128, **129,** 129–130, 131, **148**
at Thoroughfare Gap 146
at Verdiersville 120
artillery 29–30

Banks, Gen Nathaniel Prentiss (1816–94) 101–102, 106–107, **107,** 119
Barry, Maj William F. 80
Barton, Clara (1821–1912) **142**
Bartow, Col Francis 61, 62, **62,** 73, 97
Beauregard, Fort **143, 145**
Beauregard, Gen Pierre Gustave Toutant (1818–93) 14, 18, **18,** 37, 48, 52, 52–53, 90
  arrives at Henry Hill 72–73
  background 18–19
  character 73
  command control 63–66
  division of command 72
  orders 42, 69
  plans 49, 53, 91
  preparation for battle 41
  promotion to General 92
  strategic advantages 49
Bee, BrigGen Barnard Elliott (1824–61) 61–62, **62,** 72
Beverley's Ford 124, 128
Blackburn's Ford 45–48, **46–47,** 52, **121, 124**
Blenker, Col Louis (1812–63) **88–89**
Brandy Station 127
Brawner's Farm, battle of **100,** 134–135, **135,** 137, 140–145, 147
bridges **120, 121, 124, 125**
Broadhead, Col Thornton **149**
Brown, John (1800–59) 12
Buford, BrigGen John (1862–63) 130, **159**
Bull Run, 1st battle of (1st Manassas) **64–65,** 101, **103,** 107, 111, 115, 116
  casualties 48, 77, 90
  chronology 5–6
  dispositions **50–51,** 53, **54–55, 86–87**
  lessons of 10

northern Virginia theatre of operations **38**
officers 23
organisation 25, 30, 33
Burnside, Col Ambrose Everett (1842–81) **60,** 60–61

Cameron, Col James 81
Catlett's Station **132, 152**
cavalry 30, 33, 34, 36
Cedar Mountain, battle of 107, 111, 117, **118,** 119, **122–123, 128, 130, 131, 134, 136, 137, 140, 142**
Centreville 165
Chancellorville, battle of 111
Chantilly, battle of 172–173, **174,** 177
Chappel, Alonzo: painting by **88–89**
Chase, Samuel Portland (1808–73) 107
Chinn Ridge 84
chronology 5–7
Civil War, origins of 11–15
civilians 66, 77, 87, 89
Confederate States
  birth of 13–15
  forces of 100, 110, 115–116
    see also Army of Northern Virginia; Southern army
  uniforms **113,** 116
  and Pope 104–105
Confiscation Act (1862) 113
Corcoran, Col Michael (1827–63) 81, **81**
Cutler, Col Lysander (1806–66) 142

Davis, Jefferson, President of the Confederate States (1808–89) 13–14, 15, 16, 17, **17,** 92, 109
  visits battlefield 90
discipline 26, 34, 36, 42
Doubleday, BrigGen Abner 142–143, **159**
Duryée, Abram **111**

Early, BrigGen Jubal Anderson (1816–94) 84, **84,** 128, 129, 130, 154
Elzey, Col Arnold (1816–71) 83–84, **84**
Emancipation Proclamation, the 113
Europe 113
Evans, Col Nathan George 'Shanks' (1824–68) 55–56, **56,** 57, 60, 61
Ewell, BrigGen Richard Stoddert (1817–72) 68, **68,** 119, **119,** 130, 133, 145

Fairfax 44
Fitz Hugh, Maj Norman R. 120, 121
Franklin, BrigGen William Buel (1823–1903) **80**
Freeman's Fort 128
Frémont, Gen John Charles (1813–80) 100, 103, 104, 111
Fry, Capt James Barnett (1827–94) 46, 48

Gainsville 133
Gibbon, BrigGen John (1827–96) **138–139,** 140–141, 142, **158**
Glover, BrigGen Cuvier (1828–85) 152–153
Greenhow, Rose O'Neal (1817–1864) 41
Gregg, BrigGen Maxcy (1814–62) 149, 154
Griffin, Capt Charles (1825–67) 76, **77,** 80
Groveton, battle of *see* Brawner's Farm, battle of

Halleck, Gen Henry W. (1815–72) 100, 104, **104,** 105–106
Hampton, Col Wade (1818–1902) 66, **68,** 69
Harpers Ferry 12, 37, 39
Hatch, BrigGen John Porter (1822–1901) 137, 154, 157
Heintzelman, MajGen Samuel Peter (1805–80) 43–44, 62–63, **63,** 80, **116**
Henry, Judith: rave of **93**
Henry Hill **10,** 64, 66, 83, **147, 168,** 176, **176**
  battle for 69–82, **76,** 87, 97
  dispositions 64, **70–71,** 72, **74–75, 82–83, 86–87**
Henry House 66, **67,** 76, **78,** 94, **95**
Hill, MajGen Ambrose Powell (1825–65) 117, 119, **119,** 130, 154
Hood, MajGen John Bell (1831–79) **120**
Hooker, MajGen Joseph (1814–79) **117**
Hunter, BrigGen David (1802–86) **60,** 61

Imboden, Capt John Daniel (1823–95) 37, 39, 72, 76, 77, 79
individualism 26
infantry 23–30
intelligence 33–34, 41

Jackson, Gen Thomas Jonathan 'Stonewall' (1824–63) 37, **37, 69, 72, 100, 109,** 111, 116, 119, 120, 129
  at 1st Bull Run **103**
  background 110–111
  at Brawner's Farm 134, 137, 142, 143, 144
  at Cedar Mountain 107, 111, 117, 119
  flaws **103**
  at Henry Hill 72, 75, 79, 80, 82
  named 'Stonewall' 72
  raids Pope's rear 132–133
  in Shenandoah Valley 100, 106–107, 111
  statue of 94, **95**
Jahn, E.: paintings of **78**
Johnston, Gen Joseph Eggleston (1807–91) 20, **20,** 39, 41, 48, 68–69, 101, 102, 109
  arrives at Henry Hill 72, 73
  assumes command 52–53
  background 19–20
  character 73
  disagrees with Beauregard's plans 49
  division of command 73
  on victory 92

Kearny, Maj Gen Philip (1814–62) **172,** 173
Kernstown, battle of 111
King, BrigGen Rufus (1814–76) 135, 137

Lawton, BrigGen Alexander Robert (1818–96) 145
Lee, BrigGen Fitzhugh (1835–1905) **160**
Lee, Gen Robert Edward (1807–70) 12, 16–17, **17, 101,** 102
  at 2nd Manassas
    first day 156
    plans 112–113, 119–120, 121, 124, 132
    and Pope 105
    at the Rappahannock 124, 127, 129
    second day 159, 161, **161**
    Southern confidence in 174
    stakes 112–113
    strategy 109
    at Thoroughfare Gap 146
  and Army of Virginia's advance 119
  background 108–109
  and Cedar Mountain 119
  exploits success 172, **174**
  invades Maryland 173–174
  and Jackson 111
  and Longstreet 109–110
Lincoln, Abraham, 16th President of the United States (1809–65) 13, **13,** 14, 16, 39, 90, 101, 102, 108, 109, 113
  and Pope 103, 104, 105
Long Bridge, Potomac River **34**
Longstreet, Gen James (1821–1904) **45,** 46, **108,** 109–110, 120, 127, 128
  at 2nd Manassas 110, 156, 161

McClellan, Gen George Brinton (1826–85) 92, 101–102, **104,** 107, 113, 117, 159
McDowell, MajGen Irvin (1818–85) 21, **21,** 101, 102, **105,** 107–108, 135, 146, 165
  at 2nd Manassas 152, 154, 156
Mahone, BrigGen William (1826–95) **113**
Manassas, 2nd battle of (2nd Bull Run)
  battlefield **168**
  casualties 165
    at Brawner's Farm 144–145, 147
    at Cedar Mountain **137, 142**
    first day 153, 154, 156, 158
    officers 158
    second day 164–165
  chronology 6–7
  dispositions 113, **150–151, 162–163, 166–167, 168**
    at Brawner's Farm 135
    at Cedar Mountain **118**
    first day 147, 149, 156–157
    second day 159, 160
  strategic situation 117
  theatre of operations **98, 126, 174**
  western theatre, the 100
Manassas Gap Railroad 132–133, 147, 149
Manassas Junction 133
Manassas National Battlefield Park 94, 175–176
marksmanship 61, 77
Maryland 173–174
Matthews Hill **58–59,** 60–61, 63, 64–65, 66, 69, 94
memorials **100, 176**
Mexican War (1846–49) 103, 107, 109, 110
Miles, Col Dixon S. 90, 92
Mississippi River, Union operations along 103–104
Mitchell's Ford 53
monuments **93,** 94, 97
morale 81–82
motivation 25

New Market, battle of 108
newspapers **19, 26**
Northern army (Union) 23, 29, 53, 69, 91
  see also Army of the Potomac; Army of Virginia
  1st (Tyler's) Division 45–48, 52, 55
    Sherman Brigade 63–64, 80–81
  2nd (Hunter's) Division 56, 62
    Burnside Brigade 60–61
  2nd New York Regiment **30**
  3rd (Heintzelman's) Division 56, 62–63, 82
    Franklin's Brigade 80
    Howard's Brigade 84
  5th (Miles's) Division 52, 90
  artillery, at Henry Hill 75–80, 78
  cavalry 30, 32
  inexperience 41
  order of battle 32–33
  routs 84, 85, **86–87,** 89
Northern States *see* Union, the

O'Connor, Col Edgar 115
Ox Hill, battle of *see* Chantilly, battle of

Patterson, MajGen Robert (1792–1881) 20, 21, **21,** 37, 39, 41, 91
  made scapegoat 92
Pea Ridge, battle of 108
Pelham, Capt John **160**
Poe, Col Orlando (1832–95) **161**
Pope, Gen John (1822–92) **105,** 113, 146
  background 103–105
  criticism of 159, 168, 172
  headquarters wagons captured 129
  and Lee's order to march 121
  at Manassas
    first day 149, 152, 156, 157–158
    interpretation of situation 158
    second day 159–160
  and McDowell 152
  optimistic report 168
  orders forces to concentrate 133
  plans 129–130, 146
  at the Rappahannock 128, 129, 131
  task 113
  and Thoroughfare Gap 145, 146

treatment of Southerners 104–105
at Warrenton 130
Port Hudson 107
Porter, Gen Fitz John (1822–1901) 107, 133, 152, 160, **164**
made scapegoat 159
Portici House (Confederate HQ) 73, **103**
Presidential Election of 1860 12–13
prisoners of war **141**
public opinion 39

railways 41, 49, 91, **124, 155, 156**
Rapidan, river 119
Rappahannock, river 121, 124, 127, 128, **129,** 129–130, 131, 132, **169**
Raymond, Henry J. (editor New York Times) 53
recruits 25–26, **33**
Red River Campaign 107
Reynolds, BrigGen John Fulton (1820–63) 149, 157
Reynolds, Capt John 137
Richardson, Col Israel Bush (1815–62) 46, **48**
Richmond, Virginia 101, 102
Ricketts, BrigGen James Brewerton (1817–87) 76, **77,** 80, 146
roads 44
Robinson's House 66, 69, 94
Russell, William Howard (Times correspondent) 34, 36, **89,** 92

Scott, Gen Winfield (1786–1866) 17–18, 18, **18,** 39, 40, 106, 107, 109
Seven Days Campaign 100
Sharpsburg (Antietam), battle of 110, 174
Shenandoah Valley 100, 106–107, 108, 111, 115–116
Sherman, Col William Tecumseh (1820–91) 42, **42,** 63–64, 81, 92
official report 80–81
at the Stone Bridge 57
withdraws 87
Sherman's Ford **63,** 63–64
Sigel, MajGen Franz (1824–1902) **106,** 108, 130, 131, 134, 165
Slaughter Mountain **136**
slavery 11–13, 108, 113
see also African Americans
Smith, BrigGen Edmund Kirby (1824–93) 83, **83**
Smith, Lt W.H.B. 46

Southern army (Confederate) 33, 46, 47, 82
see also Army of Northern Virginia
cavalry 33
I (Beauregard's) Corps
2nd (Ewell's) Brigade 68
4th (Longstreet's) Brigade 45, 46, 48
6th (Early's) Brigade 83, 84
Hampton's Legion 69, 72, 90
II (Johnston's) Corps
1st (Jackson's) Brigade 69, 72–73, 80
1st Virginia Cavalry 67, 77, 97
2nd (Bartow's) Brigade 61, 62
3rd (Bee's) Brigade 61, 62, 64, 72
4th (Kirby Smith's) Brigade 83–84
inexperience 34
order of battle 24–25
Southern States see Confederate States
Starke, BrigGen William E. (d.1862) 145
Stevens, BrigGen Isaac Ingalls (1818–62) 172–173, **173**
Stone Bridge 52, 53, 55, 56–57, **57,** 94, **120,** 176
Stone House **106, 168, 173,** 176
Stuart, James Ewell Brown 'Jeb' (1833–64) 37, 39, **39,** 41, 73, **75,** 84, 116, 124
at 2nd Manassas 152, 164
captures Pope's headquarters wagons 129
evades capture 120, **152**
marches on Pope's rear 128–129
raids **132, 152,** 153
Sudley Springs 52, 56, 87
Sulphur Springs 130, 132
Sumner, BrigGen Edwin Vose (1797–1863) 116
Sumter, Fort 13–14

Taliaferro, BrigGen William Booth (1822–98) 141, 145, **158**
Thoroughfare Gap 110, 145–146, **168**
'three-month' men 36, 41, 52
training 26, 34
Trimble, BrigGen Isaac B. 128
Tyler, BrigGen Daniel (1799–1882) 44–45, **45,** 46, 92
McDowell's rebuke 48
at the Stone Brisge 56–57, 62

uniforms 26–28, **27, 28, 29, 31, 35, 36,** 99–100
cause confusion 46, 64, 79–80, 80–81
Northern infantry 27, 35, **40, 43**
Southern **22,** 31, 43, **67, 79**
Union, the
advantages of 14–15
forces of 112, 113, 114–115
see also Army of the Potomac; Army of Virginia; Northern army (Union)
artillery **129, 130**
cavalry 116, **144**
Regular Army 114, **114**
in the Shenandoah Valley 100, 106–107, 108
supplies **127**
uniforms **110, 112, 114,** 115
and public opinion 172
secession from 11, 13, 14, **14,** 15, 16
United States: 'manifest destiny' of 11
United States Army 23

Verdiersville 120
Virginia **38**
Vizetelli, Frank: sketches of **44, 65, 78, 85**
volunteers
recruitment 23, 25
'three-month' men 36, 41, 52

Wallace, Col William Henry (1827–1905) **115**
war correspondents 21, 34, 36, 53, 89, 92
war memorials **93,** 94, 97
wargaming 98–100
Warren, Gen Gouverneur Kemble (1830–82) 164
Warrenton 128–129, 130, 133
Warrenton Turnpike 53, 63, 64, 66, 87
Washington DC 101, 168, 173
Waterloo 130, 131
weapons **22,** 29–30
Weisiger, Col David Adams (d.1899) **169**
Wells, LtCol George Duncan 46
Wheat, Maj Chatham Robertdeau (1826–62) 61
Wilcox, BrigGen Orlando Bolivar (1823–1907) 80
Wilson's Creek, battle of 108

Yorktown, siege of 101